The Whalers

The Whalers

The Rise, Fall, and Enduring Mystique of New England's (Second) Greatest NHL Franchise

Pat Pickens

Foreword by Gerry Cheevers

Essex, Connecticut

An imprint of Globe Pequot, the trade division of
The Rowman & Littlefield Publishing Group, Inc.
4501 Forbes Blvd., Ste. 200
Lanham, MD 20706
www.rowman.com

Distributed by NATIONAL BOOK NETWORK

First Paperback edition 2023

British Library Cataloguing in Publication Information available

Library of Congress Cataloging-in-Publication Data

The previous edition was catalogued by the Library of Congress as follows:

Names: Pickens, Pat, 1985- author.
Title: The Whalers : the rise, fall, and enduring mystique of New England's (second) greatest NHL franchise / Pat Pickens ; foreword by Gerry Cheevers.
Other titles: Rise, fall, and enduring mystique of New England's (2nd) greatest National Hockey League franchise
Description: Guilford, Connecticut : Lyons Press, [2021] | "Distributed by NATIONAL BOOK NETWORK"—T.p. verso. | Summary: "Details the Whalers' origin in Boston in 1972, the team's WHA championship in 1973, its stunning NHL playoff-series win against the top-seeded Quebec Nordiques in 1986, and its relocation south in 1997 as the Carolina Hurricanes"—Provided by publisher.
Identifiers: LCCN 2021010933 (print) | LCCN 2021010934 (ebook)
Subjects: LCSH: Hartford Whalers (Hockey team) —History. | Carolina Hurricanes (Hockey team) —History. | Hockey teams—United States—History. | National Hockey League—History.
Classification: LCC GV848.H37 P53 2021 (print) | LCC GV848.H37 (ebook) | DDC 796.962/640973—dc23
LC record available at https://lccn.loc.gov/2021010933
LC ebook record available at https://lccn.loc.gov/2021010934

ISBN: 978-1-4930-4402-3 (cloth : alk. paper)
ISBN: 978-1-4930-7309-2 (pbk. : alk. paper)
ISBN: 978-1-4930-4403-0 (ebook)

∞™ The paper used in this publication meets the minimum requirements of American National Standard for Information Sciences—Permanence of Paper for Printed Library Materials, ANSI/NISO Z39.48-1992.

Contents

Foreword

My previous experience with the Hartford Whalers came playing against them and coaching against them, largely as a member of the Boston Bruins.

We used to go into Hartford, play the game, and get out of town, because we bussed in from Boston. So I had no idea how powerful a team they were to their city and how strong a team they were.

Then when I went to Hartford to cover the team, and once I got to know the players, it was easy to see why they were such a hit there. The Whalers had really strong individuals like Ron Francis, Kevin Dineen, Joel Quenneville, John Anderson, Ray Ferraro, Dave Tippett, Mike Liut, Ulf Samuelsson, and Dean Evason, and they had pretty good personalities too. Little did I know at the time how many of these players would go on to successful coaching careers. I really thought they had the talent—especially in 1986, when they had an unbelievable seven-game series with Montreal.

I think playing in an area like Hartford, which is a very small market for a major-league team, is what made them a closely knit team. I was impressed with how the players were a part of the city, more than any other big-league city at the time. They stayed in town all summer, when other teams broke up for the offseason, and became a major part of the community.

The Bruins are a big part of Boston, but fans there have four teams to cheer for. In Hartford the Whalers were the only major-league act in town, and it was their team. *The Whalers* by Pat Pickens captures the rich history of a remarkable franchise that continues to live on in the hearts of hockey fans everywhere.

—Gerry Cheevers

Prologue

June 20, 2006 was a gorgeous day for a parade in Hartford, Connecticut.

It was a signature early-summer day in the state capital, with sun and comfortable temps in the low-80s that enhanced the cheery atmosphere. Only two years removed from a National Championship sweep in college basketball by the University of Connecticut, the Nutmeg State could've honored its first professional championship delivered by the Hartford Whalers.

Hartford fans could have watched the Whalers beat the Edmonton Oilers, their former World Hockey Association rivals, 3–1 in Game 7 of the Stanley Cup finals to capture the Stanley Cup. The run to the Cup, coupled with a Stanley Cup finals trip four years earlier, would have put hockey back into the forefront in Connecticut—a state that had been dominated by Huskies basketball for more than a decade.

Some of the biggest names would have been riding in convertibles and sitting on floats. You can almost picture the Howes, the first family of Hartford hockey, with Gordie Howe and his sons and former teammates Mark and Marty sitting next to him. The Howes have a banner in the rafters at XL Center, commemorating their contribution in helping the Whalers gain exposure and credibility first during the club's World Hockey Association days and then when they entered the National Hockey League in 1979.

There is team owner Peter Karmanos, a balding, mustachioed man in his convertible limousine wearing a navy suit and white shirt. What's left of his graying hair sashays in the breeze as he sits alongside former governor John Rowland, with whom he negotiated a new arena in the eastern section of Hartford.

Karmanos boasted when he bought the team that he and his group knew how to win in hockey, and the championship would've vindicated that. He certainly would've sat next to the team's general manager and minority owner Jim Rutherford. Rutherford, the former goalie turned

Stanley Cup–winning executive, helped build a championship-winning team in Hartford.

Emile Francis, who was almost 80 at that point, is also in the car with the owners. The diminutive former general manager was around for so many great Whalers moments that took place at the Civic Center. Francis helped build the team that claimed the franchise's first NHL playoff-series win, clinched at the Hartford Civic Center in 1986 when the upstart Whalers stunned the top-seeded Quebec Nordiques in the Adams Division semifinals. He oversaw the longest period of sustained excellence in the franchise's history, as the Whalers reached the postseason five straight seasons under his watch between 1986 and 1990.

Yet unlike Francis, who delivered the Whalers close to hockey's promised land, Rutherford would've been able to get the Whalers over the hump by bringing the Cup to Connecticut.

The championship parade would have been the first since 1986, when Hartford threw a parade for the Whalers' first playoff-series win. It also would have given closure to the litany of playoff misfortunes in the past—like when Hartford was bounced in the first round six straight seasons from 1987 to 1992 or missed the postseason six straight seasons between 1993 and 1998.

Those were the dark days in Whalers history, when ownership was in turmoil and on-ice success was rare. There were rumblings the Whalers would move, probably to a southern US city in the Sun Belt region as the country's and NHL's demographics changed remarkably.

But in 2006, Hartford could have erased all that. The franchise that was 0-3 in Game 7s until the turn of the century could have won two seven-game series en route to the championship.

The parade would have veered past the team's former home, the Hartford Civic Center. Thousands of fans clad in the team's trademark navy blue and green would have crowded the streets in celebration as "Brass Bonanza" blared from the speakers that lined the city's streets.

"I never thought this day would come," one season-ticket holder might have said.

Celebrating a championship would've shown how far both the once-dormant franchise and city had come. For years, the Whalers sat stuck between the home regions of the Boston Bruins and New York Rangers—two of the NHL's "Original Six," with some of the most passionate fans in the United States.

As the parade reached its final destination, the Connecticut State Capitol Building, Governor Jodi Rell might have addressed the crowd and called June 20, 2006 "Whalers Day" in the state. Coach Peter Laviolette could have been issued a key to the city and captain Rod Brind'Amour might have thanked the fans for their wonderful support in Connecticut.

The scene might have given hope to the legions of small towns and markets who had seen their teams bolt for greener pastures in the tumultuous 1990s sporting landscape.

If it sounds too good to be true, it's because it is.

The Whalers franchise celebrated a championship in 2006, but it didn't happen in Hartford. Roughly 600 miles southwest in Raleigh, North Carolina, the Carolina Hurricanes and their hockey-tonk fans flooded the parking lot outside the RBC Center to drink in the region's first professional title.

Those fans watched the Hurricanes clinch the Cup against the Oilers, then witnessed Brind'Amour exuberantly hoist the trophy over his head. The championship turned Karmanos into a prophet, because he delivered success to the franchise just 12 years after buying in, albeit in the heart of Tobacco Road instead of Connecticut.

The championship affirmed the NHL's Sun Belt movement, and the championship celebration was unlike anything hockey had seen. A John Deere–brand Zamboni rolled through the parking lot, the team's Storm Squad cheerleaders fired up the onlooking fans as mascot Stormy the Pig rode in a Pontiac convertible, inspiring a new generation of fans to hockey.

It was a scene far different from anything Whalers fans ever knew. Those who supported them watched the perfect storm of bungled deals, ownership squabbles, and disappointment—on and off the ice—before the club moved to Raleigh, North Carolina in 1997.

The Hartford Wolf Pack, an American Hockey League affiliate of the New York Rangers, play in front of paltry crowds at XL Center most nights, and professional hockey is still hanging on by a thread in Hartford.

The Whalers are still a very big part of that hockey life. Kids who weren't alive when the club existed flaunt hats and T-shirts with that green W and blue whale tail. A booster club exists, and many prominent Whalers alumni fill coaching, scouting, broadcasting, and front-office positions around the National Hockey League.

Despite that popularity, the rebuilding of the Whalers brand since their departure, and constant speculation, there are no serious talks about the NHL returning to Hartford any time soon. In fact, Hartford sits far down on the list of prospective expansion markets—even as the league announced plans to expand to 32 teams in 2019.

Many believe a major-league team in Connecticut is outrageous. The state sits between sports-crazed New York and Boston. In what dream-land could a team survive there? Plus Hartford is a small city, and even if you include densely populated New Haven County, the market would be among the NHL's smallest.

But even though the Whalers are long gone, their legacy lives on. This is their story.

Chapter I

The Mythical Brand

The Hartford Whalers' cultural significance is confounding, particularly given their extremely limited on-ice success.

Longtime *Boston Globe* hockey writer Kevin Paul Dupont dubbed Hartford "the forever .500 Whalers," and in truth, .500 would've been an upgrade. The Whalers finished with more wins than losses in only three of 18 NHL seasons, and qualified for the playoffs just eight times before leaving to become the Carolina Hurricanes in 1997.

But the Whalers live on in a mythical way. They still have fans, and their merchandise is more popular than ever. The Whalers ranked 11th in the NHL in merchandise sales in 2011 and boast the best-selling merch of any defunct hockey team by far. Tourists can even purchase Whalers hats, shirts, and other memorabilia at Bradley International Airport in Hartford.

"I'm a fan of the Hartford Whalers because they're a non-existent hockey team, and they still sell the shirts at Bradley Airport," John Hodgman, a former correspondent for *The Daily Show* and Yale University graduate, told The Connecticut Forum in 2013. "It's like a fictional hockey team."

The Whalers were never the "in" team during their NHL tenure but have somehow achieved cool status since they left. Adam Sandler wore a Hartford Whalers shirt in the movie *Grown Ups*, which came out in 2010, and paparazzi caught actress Megan Fox sporting a Whalers T-shirt also in 2010.

Travel to any NHL game, in any arena on any night, and you'll likely see at least one fan clad in Whalers clothing. High schoolers and college-age kids, two notoriously important groups in determining what is cool, have bought up hats, T-shirts, and jerseys—despite the fact many weren't born when the Whalers played their final NHL game at the Civic Center on April 13, 1997.

Connecticut residents can even get Whalers license plates with the original logo, with proceeds benefiting Connecticut Children's Medical Center, one of the team's oldest charities.

"[Former Whalers GM] Emile Francis said we're like the Green Bay Packers of the NHL," said Howard Baldwin, a team founder and former managing general partner, in 2013. "It's one of those cult logos that people love."

If it seems like Baldwin loves the logo, it's because he helped develop it. He hired Peter Good, a Chester, Connecticut–based artist, UConn graduate, and Hartford native who grew up playing pond hockey at the capital's Colt Park.

Good was solely in charge of creating a brand-new logo when the Whalers joined the NHL in 1979. The New England Whalers of the World Hockey Association had a white, yellow, and green color scheme with a harpoon across a W as their main logo. But Good made a big and bold change, one that was way ahead of its time.

"It looked different from any other NHL logo," Good said. "That turned out to be one of the virtues of it."

Good presented a slew of designs to Baldwin, fellow founder Bill Barnes, and then–general manager Jack Kelley. He presented a circle logo with a whale jumping through it. He floated designs with a whale swimming under water and other designs featuring tridents and harpoons, but Baldwin liked a design with a harpoon and an "H" and "W" married.

Good liked it too and went back to his shop to tinker. He ditched the harpoon, since it didn't jive with the team's whale mascot, Pucky, and came up with the final design: a royal-blue tail with a green W and a white H in the negative space.

It's still a hit more than 40 years later.

"I refer to it as a marriage of convenience with the whale's tail with the H in the negative space," Good said. "That's the interesting thing. It engages the mind, but a lot of people don't get it right away. I still have people come up to me and tell me they saw the H."

Good was also responsible for the team's color scheme, and although he initially dabbled with an orange accent, the combination of Kelly green, royal blue, and white became as iconic as their logo.

"The green was a connection to the New England Whalers," Good said of his color choices. "Blue and green is a good combo."

Good received just $2,000 for his design and still technically holds the rights to it since he did not sign any paperwork that made it property of the Whalers. He still sells Whalers-logo merch on his website.

Kelley wasn't fond of the logo because of its uniqueness from the rest of the NHL. Indeed, a cursory look at hockey logos of the day reveals fierce and dramatic designs. Brian Burke altered the logo and color scheme when he became general manager in 1992, changing from royal blue and Kelly green to navy and forest green and adding a gray outline.

But kitschiness is part of the Whalers' lasting appeal. Each NHL team has its own identity. Cities like Montreal, Toronto, and Boston might be known for legendary "Original Six" programs. Teams like the Edmonton Oilers or New York Islanders may be known for their dynastic teams. Hartford didn't have either, but it had green jerseys, a mind-engaging logo, and "Brass Bonanza."

Mention the Whalers and the team's now-iconic theme song will usually come up within seconds. It is perhaps the only thing as unique and lasting as their logo.

The song was originally recorded as "Evening Beat" by Belgian composer Jacques Ysaÿe during the 1970s. Ysaÿe, who composed it under the pseudonym Jack Say, was the grandson of world-class violinist Eugène Ysaÿe, but the family name is most associated today with the theme song for a now-defunct hockey team.

George Ducharme, Baldwin's assistant who also created the first team store at the adjacent Civic Center Mall, had been looking for music to fire up Whalers fans and stumbled upon it in bizarre fashion.

"The first few games I went to when we had the arena it was very quiet," Ducharme said in 2020. "There were too many people in the building who came to see the building, and there was a hockey game going on, and they didn't know what they were looking at.

"After a few games I went to Howard and said 'what if I found a piece of music that would get people out of their seats. Something loud and brassy.' And he looked at me and said 'what the fuck are you talking about?' and he walked away.

"The marketing department, the first year in Hartford, decided to put [highlights] on an LP, and there's a lot of dialogue and they needed some music to bridge the dialogue, and they came up with several pieces of music. They gave every staff member the LP, and I took it and put it on the coffee table because I lived it. I didn't need to listen to that thing.

"Now we have a bunch of grandchildren, and on Sunday they came over to see grandma, and they see the LP and say 'what's this' and I said 'it's the first season in Hartford,' and I walk out of the room to be with the adults. Then the next thing I knew I hear 'Brass Bonanza' and I'm screaming in the living room and asking the children 'what radio station are you listening to,' and they said 'we're not listening to the radio, we're listening to your record.'

"I said 'that's it,' and I could see people skating and I was so excited I was jumping up and the kids were looking at me like I was crazy."

Ducharme presented the song to Baldwin, who fell in love with it just as quickly, and "Brass Bonanza" became their official theme song in 1977. It played as the Whalers took the ice before home games and after they scored goals at Springfield Coliseum and Hartford Civic Center until 1992, when Burke again tried to toughen the organizational perception and pulled the song.

"It's a pretty catchy tune," former Whalers coach Pierre McGuire told NHL.com in 2008. "It was a good thing for the community too. [The song] brought a lot of energy to the building, and people got into it and the players got into it."

The song is still synonymous with Whalers hockey, even though it wasn't written for them and they haven't existed since 1997. But since the Whalers left, "Brass Bonanza" has become something of a New England sports anthem. It blared at Fenway Park as the Boston Red Sox turned around a 3–0 playoff series deficit against the New York Yankees in 2004.

The UConn and Quinnipiac University pep bands have it in their regular repertoire. Model/actress Carmen Electra even once shook her stuff to it on *The Late, Late Show with Craig Kilborn*.

Like most things in sports, what was old becomes new once again, and the song and the original uniform have outlived their replacements.

"'Brass Bonanza' and green [jerseys] are where it's at," said Jeff Jacobs, a sports columnist for Hearst Connecticut Media Group. "Nobody is pining for the navy and white jerseys."

Burke hated the song because he thought it wasn't tough enough for hockey, but many visiting players harbored disdain for it too. Hearing the song usually meant the Whalers were beating their teams, and the song represented an added frustration that NHL teams still employ.

"It's kind of like the cannon blast in Columbus," said Brad Shaw, a former Whalers defenseman who has been an assistant coach with the St. Louis Blues and Columbus Blue Jackets, referencing the gun eruption that occurs after every Blue Jackets goal at Nationwide Arena. "You enter as a visiting team, and it's kind of kitschy and cliche but when you can have something that they have to listen to every time they score a goal, I think it adds impact to the goal.

"When I was with St. Louis, we would go to Chicago, and they would play that stupid song ["Chelsea Dagger" by the Fratellis] for thirty seconds after the goal, and it'd be like 'can we drop the puck already?'"

Each player also has his own individual story about the song.

"I hated that song," said Barry Melrose, who played against the Whalers first as a member of the WHA's Cincinnati Stingers then with the Toronto Maple Leafs in the NHL. "When I played, Hartford had a guy named Al Hangsleben, and we fought every time we played them. So every time I heard that song, I knew I was going to have to fight Al Hangsleben that night."

The Whalers tend to show up in all sorts of pop-culture ways. They were a wedding theme for a couple in Massachusetts in 2013 when groom Sean Dwyer sported a green tuxedo with the Whalers crest on his back, and bride Kate Murphy donned the Whalers logo on the train of her dress.

"This is my second marriage; I've already had my dream wedding," Murphy told Fox Connecticut. "This is your dream wedding."

"She knew I was a diehard Whalers fan," Dwyer told Yahoo! in 2013. "It was her idea."

The Whalers even inspired The Zambonis, an indie rock band founded in Bridgeport, Connecticut. The Zambonis tour the country performing hockey songs and dub themselves "the only band whose two biggest influences are The Beatles and Wayne Gretzky."

"My dream was to work for the Whalers," said Dave Schneider, the band's frontman and founder. "We were sort of reached out to that last year and asked 'are you interested in writing a song,' and we said 'yes, but we're not going to challenge Brass Bonanza.'

"I think [the Whalers leaving] was more traumatic than my parents's divorce."

Aside from his team, Schneider also lost his most cherished Whalers jersey, a game-used Zarley Zalapski sweater that went missing after one of the band's shows. He still regularly sports Whalers jerseys at concerts and even made a Whalers-themed guitar that he uses too.

"I love the logo," Schneider said. "It was my favorite team, and that guitar, I made that guitar by hand, [and it took] two-and-a-half years."

Aside from merchandise sales, the team still gets modest support in Connecticut, mostly from the Whalers Booster Club. The Booster Club is made up of central Connecticut–based Whalers fans, mostly former season-ticket holders, and its member numbers are growing, from roughly 40 in the mid-2010s to more than 200 as of early 2020.

The Booster Club makes at least one annual pilgrimage to an NHL game each season, usually to support a former member of the Whalers. On March 24, 2018, 50 members flocked to Barclays Center in Brooklyn for a New York Islanders vs. Chicago Blackhawks game, to support then-Blackhawks coaches, and ex-Whalers players, Joel Quenneville, Kevin Dineen, and Ulf Samuelsson. After the game, they met up with the ex-Whalers and posed for a photo with them.

The Booster Club maintains an active presence in Hartford. Members annually march in the city's St. Patrick's Day parade. They hold regular meetings and annually donate a $1,000 scholarship to a graduating high school senior entering a university with a hockey program who demonstrates high academic standards and outstanding hockey ability.

They also facilitate events in the region, including the annual Whalers Alumni Weekend at Hartford's minor-league baseball park since 2017. Fans mingle, get autographs, and hear stories from the former Whalers—who are all too eager to relive their days in Hartford. Many familiar faces are regulars, including ex-players Jordy Douglas, Andre Lacroix, Dave and Wayne Babych, Marty Howe, and longtime broadcaster Chuck Kaiton. In 2019, Sean Burke, the final goalie to don the Whalers sweater, was in Connecticut for a wedding but still stopped by to take it all in. Ex-forward Mike Rogers was back in 2019 after missing the event in 2018—to attend his daughter's wedding—and joked that he had tried to make both work.

Ex-players and staff also really love Hartford and love coming back to Connecticut. Dave Babych, Joel Quenneville, Kevin Dineen, and Ron Francis met their Connecticut-born spouses while playing for the Whalers. Others made lifelong friendships with members of the communities where they lived.

"I lived in South Windsor on Cliffwood Drive, and I still go back," said Douglas, a Whalers forward from 1978 to 1982. "I visit friends and have cookouts."

"My kids grew up in Avon," said Lacroix, who played for the Whalers from 1977 to 1980. "I lived in this area for a long time. That's why this area means a lot to me. The Booster Club meant a lot to me, and to all of us."

That Booster Club is the most prominent for a defunct NHL team, and their goal is to keep the Whalers' memory alive. They've largely been successful too, despite little evidence that the team will return, by keeping a positive and upbeat attitude and welcoming anyone interested in learning more about the history of the Whalers.

The Whalers logo, color scheme, and kitsch of their history—who really has ever heard of professional sports in Hartford?—have raised their profile and mythology. Even though the Whalers are uniquely Hartford's team, the Carolina Hurricanes recently started co-opting that history.

There is a shared history between the markets, even though it went largely ignored for the Hurricanes' first two decades in Carolina. Kevin Dineen scored the Hurricanes' first goal after also scoring the final goal in Hartford, and Ron Francis was captain for both teams and was the general manager in Carolina.

Fans bought in too, and you can spot at least a few fans with Hartford jerseys at almost any Carolina home game—including at least one fan who wore a green Whalers jersey on the ice after the Hurricanes won the Stanley Cup in 2006.

The team began leaning into the Whalers' popularity after owner Tom Dundon purchased the majority stake from Peter Karmanos for $420 million in 2018. He first sold shirts in their team store, then offered a remix of "Brass Bonanza" as an option for Carolina's goal song before the 2018–19 season.

"I think there was some hesitation to acknowledge or embrace [the Whalers history] in some ways," said Mike Forman, the Hurricanes vice president of marketing and brand strategy. "Before [Dundon] even had purchased the team we'd had conversations about the Whalers because he knew and we did too what type of brand the Whalers still have, even though it'd been 20 or 21 years since they relocated.

"It was something that we hadn't tapped into, from a brand perspective; it was this giant waiting in the corner for us to tap into the history at some point and commemorate and celebrate that part of our history with that brand, which is still powerful. When Tom came on board he said 'we'd be foolish not to do that.'"

Dundon, Forman, and his staff took the idea to wear Whalers jerseys on-ice to Adidas, the league's jersey manufacturers, and the NHL, which loved the opportunity to prey on the insane popularity surrounding Hartford's brand renaissance.

"The league loved it," Forman said. "At the time, our club had been somewhat irrelevant for a while. This kind of broke through the noise that the Hurricanes were part of the national conversation for the first time in many years."

The Hurricanes then reintroduced Whalers green jerseys and "Brass Bonanza" when they honored their heritage with Whalers Night against the Boston Bruins on December 23, 2018.

"The Hurricanes hadn't been in the playoffs in a long while, and we were treating this game as our Super Bowl," said Dan LaTorraca, the

Hurricanes' senior director of marketing. "This was something that was fully in our control, that we knew would be happening that we wanted to capitalize on the right way."

Play-by-play commentator John Forslund, who called Whalers and Hurricanes games from 1994 to 2020, was among the many who had anxieties about bringing out the green uniforms.

"I saw it at the beginning as a marketing thing, and I wasn't too keen on it to be honest," Forslund said in 2019. "We were kind of apprehensive about this, but then when it happened it was a total celebration."

Carolina's presentation assuaged a lot of fears, mostly because of how the Hurricanes tipped their hats at Hartford's history. They consulted with then–general manager Ron Francis about which jerseys they should sport—the version they wore from 1985 to 1989 which had Pucky the Whale on the shoulder. They invited back Mike Rogers, one of the team's heroes in the early NHL, to drop the puck, and "Brass Bonanza" blared from the speakers for each of Hartford . . . er Carolina's five goals that night.

"It was a thrill to walk into that dressing room," Rogers said in 2019. "It just brought back a rush of memories. I was treated fantastic, and it's nice to see the new ownership group recognizing what the Whalers were."

Forslund sported a retro sweater on-air—a replica of the one he received as a present from Burke during his lone Christmas with the Whalers in 1992. Fox Sports Carolinas dedicated much of its broadcast to team history, with ex-Whalers turned hockey luminaries sharing stories from Hartford. Forslund even interviewed Skip Cunningham, the team equipment manager for every game from 1972 to 2020.

The Whalers uniform returned to New England 10½ weeks later, March 5. Many Whalers fans, clad in their own Hartford merch, made the trek to Boston to watch the Hurricanes don the green jerseys for their game against the Bruins at TD Garden.

The Booster Club held a watch party in Hartford as the Hurricanes TV broadcast again reminisced about the 25-year history of the New England/Hartford Whalers. For Forslund, the outcome, a 4–3 Bruins overtime win, even seemed Whalers-like.

"I remember after that game in Boston saying it depicts the Hartford existence," Forslund said. "Just good enough to compete, not good enough to beat them; tough place to go with those colors on; tough for the fans to walk into that building. Many did."

Whalers Night once again was a theme during 2019–20, with Carolina hosting the Los Angeles Kings, this time on January 11. Hartford's longtime mascot Pucky the Whale was the master of ceremonies, and the Hurricanes made a Whalers-themed "Storm Surge" celebration—with images of whales leaping through water projected on the ice as "Brass Bonanza" blared from the PNC Arena speakers.

The Hurricanes further leaned into their history in 2020 when they unveiled their Reverse Retro jersey, a gray Whalers jersey that was an homage to the uniform Hartford sported from 1992 until their move to Carolina in 1997. They sold hats, jerseys, sweatshirts, and T-shirts with the logo, then sported the jersey on ice during the 2020–21 season, debuting it during Carolina's game against the Chicago Blackhawks on February 19, 2021.

"This was very much a league campaign," Forman said. "We looked at two or three different ways to take this, and all three had a Whalers tie-in. . . . The light gray does connect our two brands—it's the one shared color we have—it's a distant connection but it is a connection.

"Sometimes you have to go by feel, and it felt right to us to not explicitly blend the two brands together in a way that would upset everyone."

The Hurricanes capitalized on the Whalers Nights with jerseys, hats, and T-shirts sold and a boost to their national profile. But they didn't leave Connecticut out in the cold. The Hurricanes auctioned the game-worn jerseys and donated proceeds from Whalers Nights to Learn to Play initiative at Champions Skating Center, a rink in Hartford owned by former Whalers forward Bob Crawford.

"We wanted to make sure we were doing it the right way," LaTorraca said. "A lot of planning went into content production, the different themes but also a lot of the community outreach in terms of creating fundraisers to donate money back to Hartford youth hockey. There was a lot that went into it."

But the stunt was not without controversy. Some Whalers fans were irate with the green-jersey return, seeing it as a naked cash grab from the Hurricanes organization that was struggling to find an identity. Others, including NESN broadcaster Jack Edwards—no fan of the Whalers—were outraged that defenseman Dougie Hamilton wore his #19, which had been retired by Hartford to honor Johnny "Pie" McKenzie—a Hall of Fame forward who'd played in Boston and Hartford.

Ironically Hurricanes fans didn't seem particularly excited for the throwback nights either, since they didn't ask for a history lesson.

Perhaps unsurprisingly, minority owner Peter Karmanos, who moved the team from Hartford to Carolina, hated it too.

"I don't like it," Karmanos said frankly in 2019. "People in Hartford aren't going to like this, but there's nothing special about the Hartford Whalers."

But the Whalers logo won't stop any time soon, and members of Carolina's team are at least considering Connecticut fans as they capitalize on their only major pro team's identity.

"We have to be sensitive to the feelings of the people of Hartford," LaTorraca said. "This is not just a cash grab. This is an opportunity to celebrate one of the most historic, unique and beloved brands in hockey."

Plus there were definitely Whalers fans who were more than happy to see the uniforms back on the ice in the NHL.

"I have no problem with [the Hurricanes] bringing back our iconic uniforms for a couple of games," said Peter DeMallie, a Whalers Booster Club member. "In my view, it brings further attention to the team we lost."

Why do the Whalers continue to resonate? Nostalgia is certainly a part, and as sports fans of a certain era grew up so too did the trend of throwback hats, shirts, and jerseys—as brands like Mitchell & Ness grew into multi-billion-dollar enterprises. Like Hodgman said, it's easier and cheaper to wear a hat or T-shirt than it is to buy a ticket or fight for the team's return.

The Whalers no longer exist, in part because of fan apathy, but there is still a small and loyal base of supporters that died more than a little when the team left for North Carolina after the 1996–97 season. They essentially are hockey nomads, lost without a team, who can't stomach supporting the Hurricanes, Bruins, New York Rangers, or any other NHL team.

It is the reason the Whalers were such a hit to begin with.

Chapter 2

The WHA

The startup World Hockey Association decided to go head-to-head with the NHL when it was looking for markets when it launched in 1971.

So, uniquely, the story of the Whalers begins in Boston.

Boston is one of the most prominent US hockey hotbeds and Massachusetts has produced more NHL players than any other state.

A new era of hockey talent was just being turned onto the sport, largely thanks to the Bruins' success in the early 1970s. Defenseman Bobby Orr had just broken into the NHL in 1966 and was taking the city by storm, leading to a slew of locals pretending to be #4 in the spoked B sweater.

Despite Orr's wizardry—which included a magical "flight" during his game-winning goal in overtime that lifted Boston to the Stanley Cup in 1970—the Bruins toiled in mediocrity for decades. Orr's magic captured the city's imagination, but between 1941 and 2021 Boston won the Stanley Cup only three times, 1970, 1972, and 2011.

The NHL was far behind the other three pro team sports in the United States. Sure, the Original Six was huge, and hockey became a big part of the four American markets, New York, Detroit, Boston, and Chicago, but before cable TV or the internet, the rest of the country was open for business.

The WHA aimed to sell hockey in underserved US markets. The league was the brainchild of Gary Davidson and Dennis Murphy, two California-based entrepreneurs who also founded the American Basketball Association. The ABA succeeded by innovating with a red-white-and-blue ball and a three-point line, and the WHA also sought to challenge the old-hat league.

The league struck television deals in both the United States and Canada, unheard of at the time, then got to work poaching some of the NHL's brightest stars. Bobby Hull signed with the Winnipeg Jets during the summer of 1972 to a 10-year, $2.5 million deal that included a $1 million signing bonus. Hull got to play for the Jets, but each of the league's teams paid $100,000 to soften the financial blow.

Hull was a star forward with the Chicago Blackhawks at the time, coming off a 50-goal season and his 11th consecutive All-Star honor when he signed the deal. Chicago dared him to leave, which he did when the fledgling league made him one of the highest-paid athletes in pro sports.

Hull jumping to the WHA, in his prime, was a seminal moment in hockey history, but he wasn't the only superstar player to do so. The Philadelphia Blazers signed Derek Sanderson, the top center on the Stanley Cup champion Bruins, to a $2.6 million contract—the richest in pro sports at the time—and Frank Mahovlich later left the Montreal Canadiens to join the Toronto Toros in 1973.

Meanwhile in Boston, a foursome of local 20-somethings helped the WHA take off in New England. As the league founded, it put out an ad in newspapers around the country looking for prospective franchise owners, and Howard Baldwin answered an ad in the *Boston Globe*.

Baldwin had been co-managing a sports-apparel store with his friend John Coburn in Wareham, Massachusetts, and they were fundraising to found an Eastern Hockey League franchise in the gateway to Cape Cod. But when Coburn read the ad to Baldwin, he suggested his friend call league cofounder Dennis Murphy to pitch him on putting a team in Boston.

"Murphy said 'We don't have a team in New England,'" Coburn recalled, "'do they play hockey in New England?'"

Baldwin called his longtime friend and former college roommate Godfrey Wood, who was an investment banker in New York. None of the three had means to front the $25,000 entrance fee, but they pitched Bob Schmertz, who had just taken controlling ownership of the Boston Celtics and was interested in expanding his Boston-sports portfolio. Schmertz fronted the money, and the New England Whalers were born.

"[Owning the Whalers] seemed an attractive prospect, although I've never seen a hockey game," Schmertz told the *New York Times* that year. "There's a real satisfaction in creating something, and as for making money, you give a lot of it away anyway. . . . If you were primarily interested in profits, don't go into sports. As for money, you can only eat three meals a day."

Wood ran the financial side and aimed to get more investors. Baldwin was the president, and Coburn, the lone founder who hadn't played hockey, was VP.

Fortunately Baldwin was blessed with business acumen, plus hockey ran in his blood. His father, Ian, was a hockey player at Harvard University and won the program's Angier Trophy for most improved player in 1932. Howard himself played at the prestigious Salisbury School in Connecticut, then was on the freshman hockey team during a two-year stint at Boston University.

But by age 28, Baldwin had entered and exited the military, dropped out of college, and failed as a minor-league baseball player for the Detroit Tigers.

"I needed to do something with myself," he said.

In 1967, Baldwin joined the expansion Philadelphia Flyers' front office as the business manager of the team's minor-league affiliate in Cherry Hill, New Jersey. He climbed the ranks in the Flyers organization until 1970 when he returned to New England. Baldwin ran the Whalers as their managing general partner for 16 years. He exuded enthusiasm and passion for his beloved hockey club, treating it like a family member.

"He has this personality that is easy to like," said Ray Ferraro, a Whalers forward from 1984 to 1991. "The team was like his baby. He was always around, and he was easy to talk to."

Baldwin held controlling interests of the Whalers, San Jose Sharks, Minnesota North Stars, and Pittsburgh Penguins, and even once had a 50 percent stake of the Russian Red Army team. Somehow he managed to do all this without a significant business holding—outside of his film studio Baldwin Entertainment Group, which produced films like *Ray* and hockey-related flicks *Mystery, Alaska* and *Sudden Death*.

But Baldwin dreams big and is something of a showman. He's never been afraid to innovate or promote, even despite his lack of means.

"He was a very brash and self-confident young man," said Wood. "He was persuasive and charming."

Schmertz initially gave the founders a $600,000 budget to spend on payroll, but that quickly ballooned to $900,000 as New England sought to keep up with the rest of the league. The Whalers may have existed in hockey-mad Boston, but they still were third in the city's hockey pecking order behind the Bruins and the AHL's Braves.

When the Whalers started play in 1972, the Braves had just come off a record-setting year when they finished atop the AHL standings. The Bruins were the defending Stanley Cup champions, and neither was close to the draw of Schmertz's Boston Celtics, and their 11 NBA titles between 1957 and 1969.

The Celtics, Bruins, and Braves all played at Boston Garden. So when the Whalers started up, they split their home games, playing 19 at the Garden and 21 at Boston Arena. The Arena, now known as Matthews Arena, still stands as the oldest active indoor ice hockey arena, just one mile southwest of Fenway Park on the campus of Northeastern University.

Northeastern purchased the rink and renovated it three times between 1982 and 2009. But at that time the Arena was archaic and had not yet been modernized.

"The Arena was a hellhole," Coburn said. "There were more mice than people in the building."

The Whalers were fourth in line at the Garden, and fifth counting the circus, which outdrew most NHL teams of that day. Somehow, New England still made it work that first season. The Whalers finished with 94 points, tops in the league, and even led the WHA in attendance, averaging nearly 7,000 fans per game despite the arena split.

Coach Jack Kelley steadily guided the Whalers that year, but he wasn't the only option New England considered as coach. The Whalers initially sought Harry Sinden, the longtime Bruins coach and exec who resigned only days after guiding them to the Stanley Cup in 1970.

Sinden sat down with the group at a secret meeting in Toronto, but turned New England down before later passing on the chance to become the New York Islanders' first head coach. He returned to the Bruins as general manager, and he's remained in Boston's front office since.

That left Kelley to run the show.

The Whalers may have missed out on the coup that would've been Sinden behind their bench, but with Kelley running the organization, New England didn't always swing at the NHL and miss. The Whalers poached defenseman "Terrible" Ted Green from the Bruins, and he became the team's first captain. The Whalers also got defenseman Rick Ley from the Toronto Maple Leafs, goalie Al Smith from the Detroit Red Wings, and forward Larry Pleau, a Boston native who bolted from the Montreal Canadiens less than two years after he won the Stanley Cup with them in 1971—after New England offered the 24-year-old a three-year contract worth $180,000—triple the salary he made with Montreal.

"I think basically everyone who jumped over did so because they wanted more ice time and more money," Pleau said in 2017. "I think a lot of what you have in the NHL today is because of the WHA."

Kelley also joined the Whalers with a winning pedigree. The United States Hockey Hall of Famer developed an exceptional program during 10 years at Boston University and was coming off back-to-back NCAA National Championships in 1971 and 1972 when the ownership group brought him on board.

"Results; character," said Wood when asked why the ownership had him in mind. "I think he was our first choice all along."

The Whalers had no trouble on the ice that first year. They won the East Division, and players enjoyed playing for Kelley, who adapted his style to deal with professionals.

"He had some firmness to him, but he was flexible," said Pleau. "That was the key in dealing with the pro-level athlete as opposed to the college game. He was flexible to adjust to the pro game on and off the ice, and that went a long way."

New England also had talent on defense, with Green and Ley leading the team as its most prominent duo. Smith won 31 games, plus 12 in the postseason, playing every minute of every playoff game as the Whalers beat Hull and the Winnipeg Jets, 4–1 in the Avco World Cup finals.

"You have to have that good goaltending, that steady goaltending to be a contender," Kelley said while recapping the season. "Al is a money player, and can really come through when the chips are on the playoffs."

Kelley was known more as a defensive innovator and is credited with being the father of the defensive triangle formation that has since become the standard of hockey for killing five-on-three power plays. But New England led the league in goals, with 318, and the line of Tom Webster, Terry Caffery, and Brit Selby carried the team. Webster and Caffery each notched 100-plus points, with Webster scoring 53 goals. Caffery chipped in 39 goals and claimed Rookie of the Year honors.

"We had more scoring power than we thought we were going to," said Kelley.

New England scored seven-plus goals in three of its four championship-round wins, including a 9–6 victory over the Winnipeg Jets in the decisive Game 5. Pleau had a hat trick, helping the Whalers claim the Avco World Trophy in front of 11,186 at Boston Garden.

"Everything went right for me," Pleau said of having a hat trick in the clinching win. "Being from Boston, it made it special."

Who knew it would be the franchise's only title until the Carolina Hurricanes won the Stanley Cup in 2006?

Certainly not Baldwin. After the game, he issued a public challenge to the NHL—in the vein of the challenge-cup era from the early 1900s—that the winner of its league play the Whalers in a one-game playoff for the Stanley Cup. Despite a respectful pass from the NHL, Baldwin was flying high off his team.

"I don't think I ever appreciated it," Baldwin said in 2011 about the WHA championship. "It's like winning an Academy Award on your first movie. I don't know that it is a good thing."

The Whalers carved out a niche in Boston too. New England had the league's highest-average and gross attendance in its first year, better than Edmonton, Winnipeg, Quebec City, and Ottawa—four Canadian, NHL-deprived cities. They also pulled in the most money that season.

"We were getting 9,000 or 10,000 at Boston Garden and three or four at the Arena," Baldwin said. "We won everything that year. We won the regular season, we won the championship, we were the highest revenue team."

But that didn't lead to profits. The Whalers, like most WHA teams, hemorrhaged money, losing $1.5 million the first year. Those results didn't improve in New England's second season, even as the Whalers moved into the Boston Garden for a scheduled full season after the AHL's Braves folded.

"There were no earnings; only red ink," said Wood. "I never looked into the attendance figures to see if they were real or not, but we got no concessions out of the building. We only paid rent."

Kelley moved from coach to the general manager full-time the second season. Even though the Whalers posted another 90-point season and again won the East Division under coach Ron Ryan, New England averaged only about 7,500 per game.

"We thought we'd get 9,000 people per night," Baldwin said. "But the bloom was off the rose."

So Baldwin did what he had to do to keep his team afloat.

New England is a region of fanatical sports fandom, with Boston as its hub; and like most regions, it does not like splitting allegiances.

The Red Sox are kings of the city in baseball, as are the Bruins, the NBA's Celtics, and the NFL's New England Patriots—who started in Boston before moving about 30 miles south to Foxborough, Massachusetts, in 1971.

Baseball in Boston actually started in 1871 with the National League's Braves, whose history predates the Red Sox's. But in 1952 the failing team, which was far inferior on the field and failed to capture the region, moved to Milwaukee before settling in Atlanta.

Howard Baldwin and his group quickly realized they were the Braves, and playing in Boston and losing money while competing directly with the Bruins would ultimately lead to failure.

So he moved them to Hartford.

A $70 million arena/hotel/mall complex was being built on the corner of Church and Ann Streets in Hartford, originally designed to attract an ABA basketball team. The deal that would've sent the Spirit of St. Louis to the Nutmeg State was never completed, leaving the Civic Center without a prospective tenant.

When that deal fell through, and with his team at stake, Baldwin came calling.

"I went down there to see the building and meet with the building manager," he said. "We had a deal done in half an hour.

"The gods were in our favor."

Baldwin raised more than $1.5 million from 16 Hartford-based companies to bankroll the Whalers operation, developing a consortium that lasted more than 14 years. But the Civic Center needed about 11 more months to finish, so the team moved from Boston to Springfield, Massachusetts—about a half-hour north of Hartford and 90 miles west of Boston—at the Eastern States Exposition Coliseum.

Springfield might be better known for its history of basketball. It is the home of the Naismith Memorial Basketball Hall of Fame, named for James Naismith, who invented the sport with a peach basket at the YMCA there in 1891.

But hockey also has a major presence in Springfield. The city has hosted an AHL team since 1954—and missed only seven years since the Eastern States Coliseum, or "Big E," was built in 1926.

Legendary Boston Bruins defenseman Eddie Shore owned the barn, which seated 6,000 and still sits on the New England Regional Fair Ground in West Springfield. It housed the Springfield Indians, a long-time AHL affiliate of the New York Rangers, and Western Massachusetts high school hockey in the late 1960s and early 1970s.

"They have a great hockey history there," said Barry Melrose, a TV analyst and former NHL defenseman who started his pro career with the Indians. "The building was just a beautiful old hockey building. It was weird because it had glass at both ends, and at certain times in the day, the sun would shine right into the rink, and we had a terrible time seeing so we'd have to practice entirely at one end."

But after the Indians moved downtown to the Springfield Civic Center, leaving the Big E vacant, the Whalers filled the void for a year until their home in Hartford was completed. They announced the move in February 1974 and left immediately, even playing four playoff games at the Big E.

The Whalers built a 2–0 advantage in their opening-round series against the fourth-seeded Chicago Cougars but lost four of the final five, including a 3–2 defeat in the seventh game that ended their sophomore season.

"It was upsetting," Baldwin said. "We wanted to repeat."

The loss was a stunning upset for the Whalers, even though they had been decimated by injuries—they played the series without their three top scorers. But the series was as close as could be with the Cougars scoring just one more goal in seven games.

"The saddest thing for me was that loss to Chicago," said Stan Fischler, who served as color commentator for New England's radio broadcast for two seasons. "I remember the Cougars getting on the bus moving on, and our guys were left holding the bag."

The Whalers thrived again in 1974–75, in spite of their arena's limitations and WHA expansion to 14 teams. They averaged 7,845 fans in 39 home games that season—split between Springfield and Hartford—which ranked third-best of the nine US-based teams in the league.

The Whalers still won their division and finished with 91 points, even though Kelley fired Ryan with only five games left in the regular season. But the Whalers again suffered an early playoff exit, this time against the Minnesota Fighting Saints, who outscored the Whalers 28–17 in their six-game series win.

"The Fighting Saints sure beat us up," Fischler recalled.

Minnesota outscored the Whalers 16–9 in three games in Minnesota, including the Fighting Saints's 6–1 drubbing in the decisive Game 6. Hotel conditions may have aided the team's struggles.

"There was a convention in Minnesota and all the good hotels were booked," Fischler said. "They put us at the Hotel St. Paul, and I saw the biggest cockroach I'd ever seen."

The Whalers were the only team to post 90-plus points in the WHA's first three seasons. They won the championship in year one and despite sharing arenas then moving to Springfield, the Whalers became one of the WHA's most successful organizations—one that was poised to further upset the NHL establishment.

By 1975, the NHL had a lot going on.

The Original Six is the NHL's core constituency and served as the league's lone franchises for 25 years between 1942 and 1967. But in 1967, the NHL added six more clubs, dubbed The Next Six, in St. Louis, Pittsburgh, Philadelphia, Minnesota, Los Angeles, and Oakland.

Six clubs were then added over the subsequent six years—with two teams joining per year, every other year. The Buffalo Sabres and Vancouver Canucks began play in 1970. The New York Islanders entered with the Atlanta Flames in 1972, and the Kansas City Scouts and Washington Capitals capped the league at 18 with their entries in 1974.

The league lined its owners' pockets with expansion money, and some of those teams found success relatively fast. With a roster of tough, skilled players known as the "Broad Street Bullies," the Philadelphia Flyers won the first of their consecutive Stanley Cups in their seventh NHL season under coach Fred Shero.

But as the NHL grew, it was challenged by other leagues. And in the 1970s, the World Hockey Association was that upstart operation.

The WHA founders Dennis Murphy and Gary Davidson were known for upsetting the proverbial apple cart. Murphy, a former mayor of Buena Park, California, and Davidson, a lawyer also from Orange County, negotiated a deal for Bobby Hull to play with the Winnipeg Jets in 1972.

Buoyed by that star power, the WHA drew about 2.2 million fans—an average of roughly 4,700 per game in its inaugural season. The next year, the league average increased—to about 5,900 fans per game—as teams in Houston, Vancouver, Minnesota, Quebec, Winnipeg, and Cleveland each averaged more than 6,000 per game.

Part of that attendance boost came when the Houston Aeros convinced Gordie "Mr. Hockey" Howe—who had retired from the Detroit Red Wings in 1971 because of a wrist injury—to join their team along with his sons Mark and Marty.

After successful wrist surgery Howe and his business-manager wife Colleen spearheaded the move to the WHA, joining Hull and Frank Mahovlich as stars who joined the rival league.

"The thing about the WHA that was memorable was you remembered the first time you played against certain guys," said Barry Melrose, who played defense for the WHA's Cincinnati Stingers. "You remember the first night you played against Bobby Hull or Gordie Howe or Frank Mahovlich. I'll always remember the first time I played against guys I grew up idolizing."

But the WHA couldn't survive just poaching former NHL players. Like so many upstart leagues, they revolutionized scouting methods. The Winnipeg Jets became a breeding ground for Scandinavian-born players. The New England Whalers developed European players and good college players from Massachusetts who may not have gotten a chance in the NHL.

"We couldn't hurt the NHL by taking their stars," said Howard Baldwin, a Whalers cofounder. "We had to hurt them by signing juniors and building good players."

By October 1972, there were 16 NHL teams, but only 28 players from outside of Canada. The WHA offered pro-level talent an alternate option, with good-paying jobs in hockey and ice time that could've been years away in the NHL.

"For me, it was simple mathematics," Melrose said. "I got drafted in the second round by the Montreal Canadiens and was the fourth player selected by Montreal at that time, and I got to thinking, Montreal had six defensemen, and three were all-stars. Halifax [Montreal's American Hockey League affiliate] had six defensemen, and four were all-stars, and I was thinking 'when in the hell would I get a chance to play for the Montreal Canadiens?'

"I had a contract offer from Cincinnati, and they had some good players but not all-stars at every position, so I figured I'd go there, work on my game and get better."

It was a boon for hundreds of players who would've otherwise been trapped in the American Hockey League or at desk jobs, and many took their shot at becoming professional hockey players—even at the risk of being blacklisted by the NHL.

Ironically, if not for the players who jumped to the WHA, some NHL stars may never have gotten the chance to become the legends they are today.

The Flyers lost eight roster players from their 1971–72 team to the WHA, opening the door for a slew of young players to join their roster, like Bill Barber. Barber might have been stuck in the AHL if not for the WHA; instead he helped Philadelphia win consecutive Stanley Cup championships and make three straight Cup finals appearances.

But the WHA's founding fathers weren't interested in helping the NHL. They were innovators who went toe-to-toe with the NHL in some cases, and became the new outlet for fans to fulfill their hockey fix. They created a 10-minute overtime to settle tie games after regulation. They catered to television audiences, even trying blue pucks as a way for fans to better see the biscuit on TV and in person.

The WHA played in shiny, new arenas, which enabled half the league to average 8,000-plus fans per game in 1975–76, including the New England Whalers, who played in the Hartford Civic Center.

The Civic Center was a brand new, state-of-the-art arena in 1975. The arena was part of a megastructure that included the Civic Center Mall and the Hilton hotel. According to a 1978 *Sports Illustrated* article, the architects and engineers created a delicate roof that was visually spectacular from above.

Whalers fans were mocked by rival fans because of the arena's proximity to the mall. But the Whalers team store—the first of its kind—was one of the hundreds of spaces that occupied the mall in the prime age of retail space. And companies rented more than 65,000 feet of office space inside the complex.

Before the 1990s arena boom, the Civic Center was the finest arena in New England. Even though the ABA never made it to Hartford, the Civic Center attracted arguably the most iconic brand in sports, the NBA's Boston Celtics. The Celtics regularly scheduled a handful of regular-season games in Hartford every season between 1975 and 1995, when Boston moved to the roomier Fleet Center, now known as TD Garden.

Four NBA championship teams played games at the Civic Center, which sold out the annual Celtics games. Boston, which played in the iconic but crammed Boston Garden, used the Hartford games as a way to branch out and make more money. The Civic Center sat more than 16,000 fans for basketball—far larger than the Garden's capacity of 14,890.

The Civic Center took nearly four years to complete, and its first event was a concert featuring Glen Campbell, Johnny Mathis, and the Hartford Symphony Orchestra on January 9, 1975. Two nights later, the arena's main attraction took the ice as a capacity crowd of 10,507 watched the Whalers host the San Diego Mariners at the Civic Center Coliseum.

Player-coach Don Blackburn scored the first goal in Hartford at 11:21 of the first period, and Garry Swain had the game-winning goal in overtime, lifting the Whalers to a 4–3 come-from-behind victory.

The Whalers made themselves at home in the Civic Center from the start. In 1975–76, they were the WHA's highest-drawing American franchise, trailing only the Quebec Nordiques as an average 9,308 fans per game walked through the turnstiles in New England's first full year at the Civic Center.

During the 1976 WHA playoffs, the Whalers used their new home to their advantage, winning seven of nine home playoff games, including a 6–1 win over the Houston Aeros in Game 6 of their semifinal series. New England ultimately fell in the decisive Game 7, 2–0, and the Aeros reached the Avco Cup finals.

Success followed New England in Hartford. Fans flocked to the Civic Center to see likable players like Dave Keon—the former Toronto Maple Leafs star who won the league's award for most gentlemanly player in back-to-back seasons (1976–77 and 1977–78). George Lyle, who signed with the Whalers instead of the Detroit Red Wings, scored 39 goals and 72 points in 1976–77 and was named the league's Rookie of the Year. Defenseman Rick Ley, who spent nine seasons with New England, was named the league's top defenseman in 1978–79.

The Civic Center hosted the league's All-Star Game, with Whalers goalie Louis Levasseur sharing MVP honors, and New England even beat the Soviet Union's prestigious Red Army team 5–2 in an exhibition game at the Civic Center in the Super Series in 1976.

And in 1977, the Whalers made the move that put them on the map when they signed Marty, Mark, and Gordie Howe.

Getting all three Howes was a coup, particularly since the Whalers were competing with the Celtics and Bruins for entertainment dollars in the region. After 25 seasons with the Detroit Red Wings, Gordie Howe abruptly retired from the NHL in 1971. But after his wrist healed, Gordie stunned the hockey world by joining Mark and Marty on the Houston Aeros as a 45-year-old in 1973.

The Howes spent four seasons in Houston but were granted free agency after the 1976–77 season. Gordie was considering retirement again, and Mark and Marty were assessing their NHL options.

"I almost ended up in Boston (with the Bruins) and Marty could've gone to either Detroit or Montreal," Mark Howe said in 2011. "If we had split up, I think dad would have retired."

But ever the showman, Howard Baldwin swooped in and kept the trio together in Hartford—something every other NHL and WHA team balked at. Colleen Howe, Gordie's wife and business manager, arranged to have Baldwin meet them in Michigan on the Howe ranch, where Baldwin endured a memorable meeting of a different variety.

"I arrived at a ranch, and Colleen had these two pet llamas," Baldwin told the *Hartford Courant*. "Everybody is waiting for me in the middle of a field, so I start walking. A goat charged at me and bit my leg."

Gordie Howe was the third-highest-paid player on the Detroit Red Wings his last season—he made only $100,000 that year—but signed a 10-year contract with the Whalers worth $400,000 annually as a 49-year-old.

"I couldn't say no to him," Gordie Howe told the *Hartford Courant*. "Once the negotiations started he was relentless. Hell, he wouldn't let us sleep.

"All I know is when all the cards were placed on the table, everything kept pointing to Hartford."

Mark and Marty Howe were great players, but Gordie was the draw. He was a veritable hockey god, and fans lined up to see the NHL's all-time leading scorer.

"Every building we went to the stands were full," Mark Howe said in 2019. "Everybody wanted to see Gordie Howe play."

The Howes became known as the first family of hockey. Even Gordie's wife Colleen became a star in central Connecticut.

"They were an entity in Hartford," said Owen Canfield, a former *Hartford Courant* sports columnist. "When you thought of the Whalers, you thought of the Howes."

Gordie Howe lived to play hockey, and his hockey IQ was second to none. He was a 50-year-old man who never lost his joy for playing or even being at the rink.

"We used to have practices on Saturday before games, and we could bring our kids down to the rink to watch," said Ley, who played with Gordie Howe his entire tenure with the team. "And Gordie would be scooping snow onto his stick and flipping it over the boards on the kids.

"He still thought he was 21. And he stayed in such great shape. I don't know if his weight fluctuated from Detroit to Houston to the Whalers at all."

Gordie had a sharp sense of humor too, and was known to recycle jokes, to the dismay of his teammates. He also showed an under-heralded intellectual side, particularly on the road, with a knack for doing crossword puzzles and playing bridge—sometimes at the same time—while passing time on airplanes.

"He was a very rough human, but he was very astute when it came to hockey," Canfield said. "On airplanes he would, as he referred to it, 'work crossword puzzles,' . . . it was almost paradoxical."

Howe looked like a monster on the ice, looming with his 6-foot frame and menacing elbows. He used that size to create space for his sons, especially Mark Howe, a Bobby Orr-type defenseman who enjoyed on-ice real estate with the threat of Gordie doling out punishment if opponents messed with him.

Calling Gordie Howe a teammate was the thrill of a lifetime for many Whalers, particularly the ones from western Canada since Gordie hailed from Floral, Saskatchewan. Even the parents of Whalers players, many of whom idolized Howe from his Detroit days, were amazed that he was there.

"I showed up to sign my contract, and my parents were with me, and the first teammate I saw was Gordie Howe," said Jordy Douglas, a forward who was born in Winnipeg and played for the Whalers from 1978 to 1982. "My parents were in awe. My mom and dad didn't know how to act, and he came over to shake hands and said 'Jordy Douglas? I'm Gordie. We're teammates now.'"

Gordie Howe played right wing on a line with Douglas and Hall of Famer Dave Keon during the 1978–79 and 79–80 seasons. Gordie may have been a welcoming teammate, and protective father to Mark and Marty, but he also had a way of parenting on the ice. It all was in the bounds of making the Whalers better.

"I had a propensity when Dave or Gordie got the puck, I'd take off up the ice, and unbeknownst to me, I'd be forcing the play," Douglas said. "I'd have to curl off at the blue line or I'd be offside, and Gordie said to me 'don't do this; don't force me to give you the puck, let the play develop.'

"He said don't cut across the middle, or I'm going to hit you in the back with the puck. I said 'sure, whatever.' So sure enough, up the ice I go, and he fired the puck at me, hit me right between the shoulder blades and dropped me, and he looks at me in the game and said 'I told you!'

"If he told you he was going to do something, he did it."

Howe had an incredible memory, which unfortunately deteriorated as he was stricken with dementia in his later years—he died in 2016 at the age of 88. But if a player crossed Mr. Hockey, especially on the ice, he wasn't going to forget it.

"We were horsing around during a scrimmage one time, and I run into him and give him a shot and he doesn't do anything," said Paul Lawless, a Whalers forward from 1982 to 1988. "So we get back on the ice a week later, and the next thing I know I'm on my back looking up at the scoreboard. Gordie had gotten me back.

"Gordie was suffering from dementia at the end. We had this Whaler event [in 2010], and they brought the players in, and I was standing next to the door and he sees me. I hadn't seen Gordie in years, but he came up to me and said 'And I'd knock you on your ass again.'"

Fans flooded the Civic Center to see the Howes, and the Whalers became the top-drawing US team. Fans across the WHA loved watching Gordie Howe, but his opponents were in awe of him, seeing firsthand the things that made him a legend.

"Gordie changed hands," said Melrose. "On the faceoff, he'd come in left-handed, then the next one he'd take right-handed. We'd all be on the bench asking 'did he just switch hands?' because no one else did that."

Gordie Howe led the team with an almost-unbelievable 96 points despite turning 50 on March 31, 1978, which New England celebrated with a cake. Mark Howe was second with 30 goals and 91 points. Marty Howe, a stay-at-home defenseman, chipped in 10 goals and 20 points in 75 games.

The Whalers were flying high, but that's when disaster struck.

One of the most infamous moments in Hartford history happened in the wee hours of one January morning, a moment that forever altered the Whalers.

On the night of January 17, 1978, the University of Connecticut men's basketball team defeated the University of Massachusetts, 56–49, earning New England bragging rights in front of about 5,000 fans in a largely forgotten game at the Hartford Civic Center.

Bruce Berlet was covering the game for the *Hartford Courant* and was putting the finishing touches on his game story for the next day's edition. He had only one thing on his mind as he sprinted from the arena as one of the last four people to leave at about 12:35 a.m. ET.

"I was trying to make last call at Gaetano's," Berlet said, referencing an Italian restaurant and bar on Civic Center Place. "I left the building and said goodnight to the security guard and ran up the street and made it to last call."

It would be the last time anyone would depart the Civic Center for a long time. A season's worth of winter storms, with another hitting earlier on the 17th, buried New England. Ice and snow weighed heavily on the Civic Center's overwhelmed structure, and on the morning of January 18, at 4:19 a.m. ET, the building's roof collapsed under the weight of the ice and snow.

Fortunately, no one was hurt as the arena was empty when the structure hit the ground. Whalers owner Howard Baldwin remembers hearing the news while attending the WHA All Star Game in Quebec City.

"I couldn't believe it," Baldwin said. "I chartered a plane out of [Quebec] to get home, and from the overhead view . . . I could see it was in real trouble."

The Whalers were in Edmonton starting a three-game Canadian road trip, and they feared the worst: the team would fold, and the players would be dispersed across the rest of the league.

"Within two seconds I phoned my wife and then my agent," said Mike Rogers, a center for the Whalers at the time. "We got to find a place to play, because we're going to fold."

Fortunately Baldwin sprang into action. He lobbied the city's corporate community to fund the renovation and negotiated a deal for the Whalers to play in Springfield, Massachusetts, in the interim. The team, which was in first place in the league at the time, announced it would complete its WHA season at the Springfield Civic Center downtown.

"It was tough," Baldwin said. "We were going from a real-nice, new building into a smaller one. It was tough for the fans; it was tough for everyone.

"We were damn lucky to have Springfield to go to, and we didn't miss a beat."

Ironically, if not for the roof collapse, the Whalers story might have closed when the WHA's did. At the time, the Civic Center Coliseum could seat only 10,507 for hockey and without major renovations, it would not be deemed a suitable arena by the NHL. The roof collapse mandated upgrades, which the corporate community helped pay for. Roughly 4,000 seats were added, making the Civic Center an NHL-caliber arena.

"It was a blessing in disguise," Baldwin said. "It allowed us to make the building bigger and better. If we had to renovate it, without the roof collapse, it would have been too expensive.

"The roof collapse, indirectly, helped us get into the NHL."

For two years, the Whalers called Springfield home while the Civic Center roof was repaired, and fans made the 27-mile trek up Interstate 91 and dubbed themselves "The I-91 Club"—a group of more than 4,000 members.

The Whalers reached the Avco Cup finals in Springfield in 1978 before the Jets swept New England in four straight. Then thanks to Mark

Howe's 107 points, the Whalers reached the postseason for the seventh straight year and won all five of its home playoff games at the Springfield Civic Center that year, including three against the WHA's top regular-season team, the Edmonton Oilers.

But ultimately the Whalers bowed out 6–3 in Game 7, and Edmonton advanced to the Avco Cup finals against the Jets in the WHA's final championship series.

Meanwhile, the Whalers prepared for their rise to hockey's biggest stage.

The WHA tried to compete against the NHL.

It did everything it could, from overpaying Bobby Hull and luring the Howes, to innovating and putting teams in untapped NHL markets. The WHA eschewed normal behavior, changing the puck from black to blue, something the old-hat league wouldn't dream of doing.

"The WHA was in a position to experiment," said Stan Fischler, the New England Whalers former color commentator. "The NHL was very staid."

But the league ultimately failed, like most upstart leagues, because it was unable to compete financially. Bobby Hull wasn't the only player making substantial money; big acts like Derek Sanderson and Frank Mahovlich also received payouts that crippled cash-strapped WHA owners.

The WHA started with 12 teams in the fall of 1972, but the league's foundation began to crack before the blue pucks dropped. The Miami Screaming Eagles, a charter franchise of the WHA, never took the ice at all. The club signed Sanderson and goalie Bernie Parent but could not find a suitable arena to play. The Screaming Eagles hemorrhaged money and moved to Philadelphia to become the Blazers.

The Screaming Eagles weren't alone. Other franchises in Dayton, Ohio, Calgary, Alberta, and San Francisco never took the ice either. Six charter franchises ended up playing in a different city than they were originally intended, including the Whalers, and two others—Chicago and Minnesota—folded within three seasons.

"It was the wild west," Baldwin said of the WHA.

And the moves didn't stop. The league office called Baldwin midway through the first season and asked if he could spare John Coburn to run the New York Raiders. Coburn's role was to find a buyer, which he did, and the Raiders became the Golden Blades. Halfway through the 1973–74 campaign, they went to New Jersey and changed their names to the Knights. After that season they bolted for San Diego and became the Mariners.

"When I went back to Philadelphia [joining the Blades] then they moved to Vancouver," said André Lacroix, who left the Chicago Blackhawks in 1972 to join the WHA where he became its all-time leading scorer. "Then I went to New York and I said, 'they have to have a team in New York, if they don't have a team in New York, there's no league.' Then we moved to New Jersey."

But the league forged on, peaking with 14 clubs for 1974–75 and 1975–76. But nothing was out of the question.

"I remember walking through the Minnesota airport the morning the Whalers were supposed to play against the Fighting Saints," Fischler recalled. "And we didn't know whether or not we were even going to have an opponent to play against that night."

It became evident that the WHA, while a novel concept, would never last on its own. The money was too tumultuous, and the markets were too fickle.

"The Indianapolis Racers said they weren't going to play one night unless they got paid," Cincinnati Stingers defenseman Barry Melrose said. "We were certainly aware of that stuff."

Plus it wasn't like the rival NHL was trying to help its upstart competition.

The Whalers got to play scattered games at Boston Garden before stopping in Springfield and settling in Hartford. The Philadelphia Blazers wanted to play at the brand-new Spectrum in South Philly, but the Flyers—the primary tenants along with the NBA's 76ers—didn't let them.

The Blazers were resigned to play in the dilapidated, 42-year-old Philadelphia Civic Center, near the University of Pennsylvania campus. Then when the Blazers actually began play, disaster struck—coincidentally on a Friday the 13th in 1972. The Civic Center's Zamboni first arrived late to the arena, then ripped the virgin playing surface, forcing the game to be postponed.

Fans received orange pucks as a consolation gift, but the disgruntled Blazers supporters, in true Philadelphia fashion, hurled the rubber discs back onto the destroyed sheet of ice.

Derek Sanderson, the Blazers captain and former Stanley Cup winner with the Boston Bruins, took the microphone in the penalty box to try to stop the carnage. But when the fans saw him, they started throwing the pucks at him instead, and he narrowly escaped unscathed.

But for all its failings, the WHA put a dent in the established traditional institution. It helped pave the way for overtime in the NHL and created a new standard in pay.

"Salaries," said Melrose, when asked the greatest thing the WHA did for the NHL. "Every player in the NHL should call five guys from the WHA and make sure to thank them for the increase in salaries. In the past the owners wouldn't let it happen and there was no place else for players to go."

Plus the NHL took notice of the markets that did work. Merger talks between the NHL and WHA went on for the duration of the junior league's existence. After adding six teams in 1967, then two more in 1970 and 1972, the NHL offered to take all 12 WHA clubs in 1974 for $2 million per team.

The offer was a bluff, since few WHA owners could swing the hefty expansion fees—particularly since many were on the hook for the high-priced contracts of former NHLers. The NHL could never add 12 teams all at once, even with the hefty sum they'd amass, because the WHA had teams in Toronto, Chicago, Vancouver, and Los Angeles, each of which were NHL cities.

But as things looked more and more dire for the WHA, Howard Baldwin was named league president three years later to do one thing.

"I was put in place to facilitate a merger," he said.

Baldwin had worked for Ed Snider during his tenure in the Flyers organization and had the influential Philadelphia owner's ear. The NHL began to play ball in earnest when John Ziegler took over as NHL president in 1977.

The WHA thought it had a deal that year for six of the eight remaining clubs to create their own division of the NHL, but the senior league voted down the expansion proposal.

"They weren't dealing in good faith, because the decision, on a business-like basis, was so incredibly simple that it's almost impossible to reject it," Baldwin told reporters after the failed merger. "It's a sad thing that you have four or five people in the NHL that are little thinkers."

Baldwin and the other WHA owners were heated by the failed proposal, but those negotiations laid the foundation for further talks as the NHL had finally started to seriously engage with the WHA on a potential deal.

"We thawed some of the ice between us and the NHL," Baldwin said.

The NHL wasn't quite ready to expand south, and the Houston Aeros folded after the 1977–78 season. The WHA created a single, eight-team league for 1978–79, which dipped to seven after the Indianapolis Racers folded 25 games into the season—four of which were charter members.

"I was afraid," said Mike Rogers, a center for the Whalers. "I was afraid my career was over. . . . I called my agent and asked if he was going to find a place for me if this didn't work out."

On March 8, 1979, just two months before the final Avco Cup finals, the NHL agreed to take on the Whalers, Oilers, Nordiques, and Jets. The league needed a three-fourths majority to ratify the four teams, or 13 of the 17 member clubs. But when five NHL teams voted no, including the Bruins who wanted no part of sharing New England with the Whalers, the WHA was cast aside again.

"I'm elated," said Harold Ballard, the curmudgeonly owner of the Toronto Maple Leafs, at the time. "It's like the North beating the South in the Civil War."

Ballard's Maple Leafs joined the Bruins, Montreal Canadiens, Los Angeles Kings, and Vancouver Canucks as the NHL clubs that voted against WHA expansion. Ballard vowed to fight the merger every chance he could—as he'd lost Stanley Cup–champion players like Dave Keon and Rick Ley to the WHA.

"Over my dead body will we merge with those bastards," Ballard told the *Chicago Tribune* in 1977, according to Vice Sports. "They stole eighteen of my players in the last five years. They cost me $5 million in legal fees, and they screwed up hockey. . . . Let 'em die on their own, and they will. If they want my vote to merge, or whatever the hell they want to do, they can forget it."

Aside from Ballard's grudge, Toronto also had a business stake for voting no. The Maple Leafs, Canucks, and Canadiens were the only three Canadian NHL teams at the time, and they split equal shares of the lucrative *Hockey Night in Canada* revenue. A WHA merger would double the number of Canadian teams, therefore cutting their TV revenue in half, which is why each voted against the deal.

Exacerbating tensions, the Nordiques were owned by Canadian beer company Carling O'Keefe, a rival of Molson, which has owned the Canadiens for decades. Molson also has been the title sponsor for CBC's hockey presentation for decades, and they drew the ire of Canadian fans—who deemed them responsible for keeping the WHA teams out. Fans called for a boycott, and a fan in Quebec called in a bomb threat at the Molson brewery there.

Winnipeg was particularly distraught by the news, since the Jets had a partnership with Molson during their WHA days. A Winnipeg newspaper editorial urged fans to write to their representatives in the Canadian capital of Ottawa to protest a vote, which many did. Meanwhile, the Jets canceled their partnership, and an incensed fan fired a bullet into a Molson facility in the Manitoba capital.

The bad public relations, coupled with pressure from the Canadian House of Commons, inspired the NHL to vote again. The Canucks, who also felt heat from the Molson boycott, reversed their initial stance and voted yes. The final vote, held on March 22, was 14–3 in favor of the four-team expansion.

The Whalers were in the National Hockey League.

Chapter 3

The Nutmeg State

Hartford, Connecticut may seem like a strange location for a professional sports team. But the Whalers' placement made some sense.

Connecticut marries the requisite affluence, population, and fanatical sports rooting to support a major professional sports team. Add its cold climate and history of on-ice prowess, and hockey seemed like the perfect athletic venture for the Nutmeg State.

"I think hockey is huge," said Howard Baldwin, the Whalers founder and former managing general partner from 1972 to 1988. "It gives the people of Connecticut a feeling of great pride and brings enormous value to our region."

Hartford was established in 1635 and named two years later, as it sits in the geographical heart of Connecticut. It was named the state capital in 1875 after it had shared the privilege with New Haven since 1701.

Insurance has been Hartford's leading industry—it is known as The Insurance Capital of the World because companies like Aetna, Travelers, and The Hartford either were founded or have had major presences there.

But Connecticut also has its own important place in hockey history. As of 2021, only four US-born NHL players had won the Conn Smythe Trophy (awarded to the playoff MVP), with two coming from Connecticut. Perhaps the greatest player from Connecticut was not actually born there, but there's no disputing Brian Leetch as one of the NHL's greats—and one of Connecticut's own.

Leetch was born in Corpus Christi, Texas, the son of an Air Force pilot and former Boston College hockey standout, Jack Leetch. Jack had grown tired of moving around the country, as the Leetches went from

Texas to California to Oregon before finally settling down in Cheshire, Connecticut, where Jack got a job as ice-rink manager.

"The truth is, it wasn't a great job for him," Leetch told the *Hockey News* in 2008. "He had to do everything there, all the paperwork, run the Zamboni, organize all the ice time. After about seven years there, he basically said 'this job is hurting my family, and it's killing me.'"

In Brian's formative years, he and Jack regularly made the 20-mile trek from Cheshire to Yale University hockey games at Ingalls Rink. Hockey flowed through Brian's DNA, and he became something of a folk hero in the state's hockey community after scoring 52 goals in his freshman year at Cheshire High School in 1983–84.

"This is where I have my roots," Leetch said of Cheshire to Whalers Sports & Entertainment in 2011. "This is where I learned to play hockey, where I skated on a pond for the first time, played all the way through my sophomore year of high school.

"Until I went to Boston College, I was a Connecticut kid through and through."

After two seasons of public school, Cheshire's home rink closed, which prompted Leetch to transfer to prep school and hockey factory Avon Old Farms—which also housed the Whalers' practice rink—under the tutelage of John Gardner, where he burst onto the NHL's radar.

"I heard great things about him. I'd seen him play at Cheshire High School," Gardner told Whalers Sports & Entertainment in 2012. "We had a practice, and I saw Brian take the puck coast-to-coast, and everybody on the bench sort of looked at each other and said 'wow, did he just do that?'

"We just said 'wow, this kid is really talented.'"

Leetch was named the New England Player of the Year for the Winged Beavers in 1986, and the Rangers selected him with the ninth pick of that year's draft. He spent a year at Boston College before dropping out to play for the United States in the 1988 Calgary Olympics, then joined the Rangers after the games.

Leetch won the Norris Trophy as the NHL's top defenseman twice, and claimed the Conn Smythe Trophy in the Rangers' only championship since 1940. He was inducted into the United States Hockey Hall of

Fame in 2008, then the Hockey Hall of Fame a year later, and Leetch's #2 hangs from the rafters at Madison Square Garden—one of only 10 such honorees in Rangers history as of 2021.

Jonathan Quick, Connecticut's other Conn Smythe Trophy winner, also spent some of his formative hockey-playing years at Avon Old Farms. Born in Milford on January 21, 1986, he grew up attending Whalers games but idolizing Leetch as a Rangers fan in Hamden in New Haven County.

Quick got his start playing street hockey on Tanglewood Drive and worked at a dry cleaners owned by Hamden High School hockey coach Bill Verneris. He was an All-State player as a freshman at Hamden High, and his #32 hangs inside the Louis Astorino Arena in Hamden—even though he played only two seasons for the Dragons before transferring.

"I remember he was an athletic, impressive freshman goalie, but geez he was just a tiny kid," Verneris told the *New York Times* in 2012. "Then as a sophomore, he started to grow and beat out the senior who had been the starter on the varsity team."

Many in Hamden cheer for the Los Angeles Kings, whom Quick has played with since 2008, and they still talk about the days when he backstopped the Dragons to the state playoffs in 2001–02.

"In his first game, against one of the best teams in the state, we're winning and Jon is playing great," Verneris told the *New York Times*. "With twenty seconds left in the game, a player on the other team gets a breakaway. He makes a couple of fakes and gets Jon sprawled on his back, but when he shoots, Jon reaches up and snatches the puck out of the air with his glove—pulls it back out of the net.

"That's where it all began. People in Hamden still talk about that incredible save."

After a 53–8 record and two New England prep championships over three years at Avon Old Farms, Quick was picked by the Kings in the third round of the 2005 draft. He became the starter in 2008, was a US Olympian in 2010, and became a household name by guiding the Kings to the Stanley Cup for the first time in 2012.

Quick was a Vezina Trophy finalist that season, helping the Kings sneak into the playoffs as the number eight seed in the Western

Conference—clinching a berth on the season's penultimate day. Then he outplayed each opposing goalie, including three-time Vezina Trophy finalist Roberto Luongo and Hall of Famer Martin Brodeur, posting an eye-popping 1.41 goals-against average and .946 save percentage while helping LA to a 16–4 postseason record and the championship.

Quick brought the Cup to his goalie academy in Stamford, then Greenwich where he celebrated with his ex–Avon Old Farms teammates. But two years later, he brought the Cup to Hamden for his second day with the trophy—after defeating his beloved Rangers in the Cup finals—and the whole town gathered at the school's football stadium to celebrate Quick's homecoming that year.

Quick had been the starting goalie for the United States at the 2014 Sochi Olympics, then helped the Kings win the Jennings Trophy for fewest goals allowed in the NHL. After an uneven first-round series against the San Jose Sharks, when he surrendered 17 goals in his first three losses and was pulled in Game 1, Quick sported a .963 save percentage over the Kings' final four wins, including a shutout in Game 5 of their seven-game series win—the first of three seven-game series wins en route to the Cup finals.

Then playing against his childhood favorite team, Quick regained his 2012 form by posting a .932 save percentage in the Cup finals. Thanks to three overtime wins, two of which went to double OT, and a Game 3 shutout, the Kings claimed their second championship in three seasons.

Quick is part of a star-caliber crop of Connecticut-born NHL players. Defenseman Kevin Shattenkirk, who was born in New Rochelle, New York, but played youth hockey in Fairfield County and high school hockey at The Brunswick School in Greenwich, and Max Pacioretty, a forward from New Canaan, joined Quick on the American Olympic team in 2014.

"If you look at the players that are developed in the state between the prep schools and the people who care about the sport," said NBC Sports commentator and New Canaan resident Pierre McGuire, "it's a state that should have never lost its team."

Pacioretty, like so many other Connecticut natives from Fairfield and New Haven Counties, grew up a fan of the Rangers, thanks to his dad

Raymond, and because of their magical run to the Stanley Cup in the spring of 1994.

Pacioretty was a fan of less-heralded Rangers, first wearing #16 because of Mike York and admitting that his line, with Theo Fleury and Eric Lindros that was known as the "FLY Line" during the 2001–02 season, was his favorite. After York was traded to Edmonton, Pacioretty switched to #93 for Rangers center Petr Nedved.

Pacioretty started his hockey career with the Norwalk-based Mid-Fairfield Blues, and he helped their U16 team win a national championship in 2005, alongside Quick and Shattenkirk. He went to Taft School in Watertown, where he initially moved from forward to defense to account for the program's lack of depth in the back end.

"He was a one-man breakout," said Dan Murphy, who coached Pacioretty at Taft, in 2015. "I said 'Oh my God, this kid is going to be special.'"

After moving back to forward, Pacioretty showed natural playmaking ability, and unlike his time in the NHL, was a pass-first player instead of a goal scorer.

"He'd beat the same guy three times, beat the goaltender and then pass off to his teammate for the goal," Murphy said. "He wasn't a sniper in prep school. He scored some great goals, but he created offensive chances for his teammates."

Pacioretty went from Taft to Sioux City of the USHL, then the University of Michigan. Shattenkirk, who played college hockey at Boston University, saw Pacioretty's game take off in his lone season with the Wolverines.

"He was always one of the bigger guys, and he used that to his advantage," Shattenkirk said. "But when he got to college you started to see him turn into this elite player and someone who completely bloomed and came out of nowhere. He became a top-end skill guy.

"We had a weekend early on in the season when we played at Michigan, and we got swept. That was when I started to see him as this emerging player."

Pacioretty jumped on the NHL scene as a young goal scorer and is third in points among players born in the Nutmeg State as of 2021. After netting his first NHL goal in front of his friends and family on January 2,

2009, in New Jersey, Pacioretty took off as one of the most lethal goal scorers in the league, posting six 30-plus-goal seasons as of 2021.

"His snap shot is one of the best in the league," Shattenkirk said of Pacioretty in 2015. "He has one of the quickest releases. It's hard to guard that. When he realized he had that weapon he had to find ways to get himself into a shooting position, and when he does that he doesn't really need that much time and space."

In 2015, he achieved a near-unheard-of accomplishment, becoming the captain of the Montreal Canadiens. Montreal generally saves its prestige for Francophone players, those who hail from the province of Quebec, but Pacioretty became the third American-born player to wear the C for Montreal.

As of 2021, Pacioretty plays for the Vegas Golden Knights, was named to his first All-Star team in 2020, and has been an NHL stalwart for more than a decade.

Cam Atkinson, who grew up in the Riverside section of Greenwich before attending Avon Old Farms, has been able to persevere despite his 5-foot, 8-inch frame.

"I've always been the smallest guy at every level, and everyone's always said I'd never make it to the next level," Atkinson told the *New York Times* in 2017. "Some people take that and get scared, but I take it as motivation to prove people wrong."

He posted back-to-back 30-goal seasons at Boston College, leading the NCAA in goals with 30 while guiding the Eagles to the college hockey championship in 2009–10. The forward, who was selected by the Columbus Blue Jackets in the sixth round of the 2008 draft, began turning heads in the NHL shortly after.

Like Pacioretty, Atkinson has become a dominant goal scorer. In 2016–17, he led Columbus in goals (35) and points (62) and helped the Blue Jackets to a 108-point season and a playoff berth. In 2018–19, he led the Blue Jackets with 41 goals and helped them to their first playoff-series win, an upset sweep over the Tampa Bay Lightning who finished tied for the most single-season wins in NHL history.

Pacioretty and Atkinson are NHL stars but haven't yet been able to hoist the Stanley Cup as of 2020. Shattenkirk added his name to the list of Connecticut-bred Cup champions in 2020 as a member of the Tampa Bay Lightning—joining fellow Nutmeg champions like Quick, Ryan Shannon, Ron Hainsey, and Nick Bonino.

Bonino took the Cup to Avon Old Farms twice—raising $40,000 for the Connecticut Children's Medical Center—after winning back-to-back titles with the Pittsburgh Penguins in 2016 and 2017. Hainsey brought the Cup to Bolton Ice Rink—another former Whalers practice facility—for a public gathering after his first championship win with Pittsburgh in 2017.

Shannon was a rookie on the 2007 Ducks and brought the Cup for a public gathering at Darien Ice Rink before a party at his parents' house.

"Anybody that makes it in hockey has to rely on a village to get them there," said Shannon, "and there's no better way to say thank you to the people that helped the individual get to that point than to share a day with the Stanley Cup."

The current batch of NHL stars had to learn their trade from somewhere, and Leetch wasn't the only superstar from the Nutmeg State. His good friend Craig Janney of Enfield is largely considered the greatest Nutmeg State–born hockey player.

Unlike Leetch, Janney grew up a Whalers fan and played four years of varsity hockey at Enfield High School—starting on varsity as an eighth grader then helping the Eagles win consecutive state championships in 1982 and 1983—and the school retired his #15 in 2011. He played his senior year at Deerfield Academy in Massachusetts, then was picked 13th by the Boston Bruins in the 1986 draft, after he was passed over by the Whalers for forward Scott Young.

Janney made the Whalers rue that decision, posting 751 points in 760 career NHL games—including 49 points in 38 career games against the Whalers. By the time Janney retired from hockey in 1999—prematurely due to blood clots—the Whalers had moved to Carolina.

Chris Drury ranks second on the all-time Connecticut-born players list, though he became a household name for his prowess on the baseball field. The youngest of three brothers, Drury became the star pitcher for the 1989 Little League World Series champion team from Trumbull, Connecticut, which still is revered statewide today.

Drury's reputation became synonymous with winning, which continued after his baseball career ended. The Fairfield College Preparatory School graduate was twice named Hockey East player of the year while at Boston University, and he helped the Terriers reach the Frozen Four three straight seasons between 1995 and 1997, winning the championship in 1995.

Drury still is the top goal scorer in BU history (113), and he won the Hobey Baker Trophy as college hockey's best player in 1998. Drury went on to a 12-year NHL career, winning the Stanley Cup with the Colorado Avalanche (2001), then representing the United States in Olympic play three times, claiming a pair of silver medals (2002 and 2010).

Drury's roots in Connecticut remain strong. He and his family continued living in the Nutmeg State while he oversaw all hockey-related matters for the New York Rangers' AHL team, the Hartford Wolf Pack, until he was named Rangers president and general manager on May 5, 2021. He also co-owns Colony Grill, a legendary Connecticut-based pizza establishment, with teammates from his Little League World Series championship club.

Connecticut continues to produce exceptional talent too. Darien native Spencer Knight was the first goalie drafted in the 2019 draft, then led the United States to the gold medal at the World Junior Championship in 2020—pitching a shutout over rival Canada in the final.

The Nutmeg State even has even produced some of the most recognizable women's hockey players. Three-time silver medalist Julie Chu is a native of Fairfield and a graduate of Choate Rosemary Hall in Wallingford, and Kendall Coyne-Schofield, a gold medalist for the United States in 2018, also played with Mid-Fairfield in her formative years. When the National Women's Hockey League started operation in 2015, it founded a flagship organization in Stamford, known as the Connecticut Whale.

Connecticut is even the hotbed for hockey's best training regimen. Some of the NHL's best, including Pacioretty, Shattenkirk, Quick, and members of the Rangers, flock to Stamford each summer to train with Ben Prentiss. Prentiss first pushed players to their limits at a gym inside a gas station before building a multi-floor facility adjacent to the Stamford Twin Rinks ice facility.

"Every summer we paid money to be tortured by this guy," recalled Shannon, who trained with Prentiss during his NHL days. "We were all going through similar pain and feeling. Like we were going to throw up on a daily basis, and I think we created really good relationships through that."

As guys like Quick, Pacioretty, Shattenkirk, and Atkinson have made names for themselves, others have emulated them. Hockey dreams start at many of the local rinks and with broadcast college hockey from the region.

"When my kid was young he liked watching hockey on NESN," said former Simsbury High School hockey coach Tom Cross, whose son Tommy was drafted by the Bruins in 2007. "I don't think it's any different now."

But college hockey actually started with a team from Connecticut as well. Yale University traveled to Baltimore to play Johns Hopkins University in the first intercollegiate hockey game in 1896. The first game finished in a 2–2 tie, but two weeks later, the Bulldogs earned the first win in intercollegiate hockey history, beating Hopkins, 2–1.

Thus, Yale has led the way in Connecticut's college hockey scene. Keith Allain, a former NHL scout and assistant coach, has been head coach for Yale's hockey team since 2006– when he took over for legendary coach Tim Taylor—and has guided the Bulldogs to the school's longest sustained period of excellence. As of 2020, Allain has more than 240 wins in just 14 seasons and won the National Championship in 2013.

But Yale's status as lead dog in Connecticut college hockey has been challenged by some upstarts, most notably from Quinnipiac University in neighboring Hamden, which sits just 10 miles north of Yale's campus in New Haven.

Quinnipiac has enjoyed a meteoric rise from Division II hockey to national prominence in less than 20 years—aided by the People's United Center, the gorgeous on-campus hockey rink/basketball arena that opened in 2007.

Led by head coach Rand Pecknold, Quinnipiac joined Division I in 1998, then moved from the Metro Atlantic Athletic Conference to the prestigious ECAC in 2005.

The Bobcats quickly developed a border war with Yale—fueled by New Haven and Hamden's history of bad blood in sports—and no year put that rivalry in the public eye quite like 2013.

Quinnipiac rode a roster of 12 seniors to the nation's top ranking that season, ripping off a 21-game unbeaten streak after a 3-4-1 start. The Bobcats finished the year an eye-popping 30-8-5 while also beating Yale in their first three head-to-head meetings—twice in the regular season and once in the ECAC Tournament.

Even as Yale middled through the regular season, it found itself in the NCAA Tournament as the West Region's number four seed. Yale stunned Minnesota in overtime in its tournament opener, then punched its first Frozen Four ticket in 51 years with a 4–1 win over North Dakota the next day.

Meanwhile, in the East Regional, top-seeded Quinnipiac came from behind for a 4–3 victory over Canisius before blitzing ECAC-rival Union College, 5–1, to reach the Frozen Four for the first time in program history.

Despite blowing a 2–0 lead against UMass-Lowell in the national semifinal, Yale still reached the championship game thanks to Andrew Miller's overtime goal. Quinnipiac followed with a convincing 4–1 win over Saint Cloud State in the nightcap, setting up the all–New Haven County final—and the schools' fourth meeting of the season.

The Bulldogs used a stifling defense to thwart the Bobcats at every turn, and Yale claimed its first hockey National Championship along with bragging rights with a 4–0 win over Quinnipiac.

The Bobcats have sustained success on the national stage even after the hangover of losing to their archrival. Quinnipiac made the NCAA tournament in 2014, 2015, 2016, and 2019, but haven't quite reached the summit, including a 5–1 defeat to North Dakota in the national-championship game in 2016.

But Quinnipiac has developed more NHL prospects than Yale of late. As of 2021, three former Bobcats—Connor Clifton, Matthew Peca, and Devon Toews—were active in the league, more than any other Connecticut school.

Quinnipiac and Yale ruled the Connecticut Division I college hockey scene for years while the University of Connecticut and Sacred Heart

University languished in the lower-tiered Atlantic Hockey Association. But the Huskies moved to the prestigious Hockey East in 2014–15, where they've played respectably under former Boston College assistant Mike Cavanaugh. UConn had its first player chosen in the NHL entry draft when Tage Thompson was picked by the St. Louis Blues with the number 26 pick in 2016.

Even Sacred Heart's program received a boost when it moved its home games from the tiny Milford Ice Pavilion to Webster Bank Arena in Bridgeport in 2016. The Pioneers received their first national ranking in hockey during the 2019–20 season, announced construction of a $60 million on-campus hockey rink—which broke ground on March 15, 2021—then earned bragging rights by beating Yale and Quinnipiac to claim the inaugural Connecticut Ice Festival in Bridgeport on January 27, 2020.

"It was a very important moment for this program," Sacred Heart coach C. J. Marottolo, a former assistant at Yale, told the *Hartford Courant*. "I was very proud of them. The work they put in every day, to see them rewarded and to see them be excited. The smiles on their faces, this is what you work for."

Connecticut Ice was founded as a four-team college hockey tournament meant to mimic The Beanpot in Boston. It also was a celebration of hockey in Connecticut, with youth players from around the state getting to play at Webster Bank Arena. More than 10,000 fans attended the weekend-long event at the home of the AHL's Sound Tigers.

The state's college hockey programs have risen in the ranks, but so too have the number of homegrown players on each team's roster. Seven Nutmeg State–born players graced the rosters of the state's four Division I schools in 2020.

College hockey is popular, but Connecticut views itself as a major-league state—despite a litany of minor-league options. That identity is part of why the Whalers are no longer there.

The State of Connecticut has 169 towns in only eight counties, and getting them all to work in cohesion is difficult.

Legendary Connecticut sports columnist Jeff Jacobs refers to the state as 169 petty fiefdoms, and sometimes individual towns can fracture further to individual villages or neighborhoods.

"Connecticut, because of where we are, is the king of the dabblers," said Jacobs, who now is a sports columnist for Hearst Connecticut Media Group. "I reflect that. I'm a correspondent for the dabblers."

Connecticut has become an embodiment of the ever-growing wealth gap in the United States. Port towns like New Haven and Bridgeport were originally import/export hubs that grew into the state's two largest metropolises. As they have fallen on hard times, economically—a 2013 *Business Insider* story named them and Hartford as three of the nation's 25 most dangerous cities—their suburbs have evolved into some of the nation's richest towns.

Athletically, the state cohesively supports the University of Connecticut, particularly in men's and women's basketball. But that was born mostly because of the Huskies' success. Connecticut has become one of the strongest women's basketball markets, thanks largely to the success of UConn women's basketball—which has dwarfed the success of its men's counterpart and frankly any other college program in sports.

Everyone loves a winner, and few programs in sports history have won more than Geno Auriemma's program. When Auriemma took over in 1985, UConn had had only one winning regular season in its history. Auriemma has had only one losing season in his 35-plus years at the university.

The Huskies burst onto the scene with an undefeated, National Championship campaign in 1995, led by guard Jen Rizzotti and forwards Rebecca Lobo and Nykesha Sales. When they defeated the University of Tennessee in the National Championship game, capping a 35–0 season, it was the greatest athletic accomplishment in Connecticut history.

Auriemma then won 10 more national crowns between 1996 and 2016 with five more undefeated seasons. The Huskies won 111 consecutive games between 2014 and 2017, a streak that was snapped only by a stunning loss to Mississippi State in the Final Four.

Huskies basketball may have captured the imagination of their state, but UConn basketball was largely an afterthought in the Nutmeg State until Jim Calhoun took over as the men's basketball coach in 1986.

Calhoun considered himself an underdog, and that endeared him with UConn fans through his 26-year tenure in Storrs. He became a legend first in 1990, when UConn won both the Big East regular season and conference tournament and reached the East regional final on Tate George's famous buzzer-beater against Clemson.

Nine years later Richard Hamilton, Khalid El-Amin, and the Huskies stunned the country by upsetting heavily favored Duke. Calhoun followed that with another championship in 2004, then a third title in 2010 thanks largely to guard Kemba Walker's incredible run through both the Big East and NCAA Tournaments.

In 2012, Calhoun passed the reins to Kevin Ollie, a former UConn player who guided the Huskies to their fourth national title in 2014 in only his second season on the job. UConn's success has brought the state together, particularly in 2004 when the Huskies became the first school to sweep the Division I championship in a men's and women's sport.

Basketball passion took off with UConn's jump to the national stage, and only then did it supplant hockey as the state's favorite cold-weather pastime. Plus, like many high-end sports institutions, there are few ties between UConn's players and the locals beyond on-court success. Former Huskies turned NBA stars, such as Ray Allen, Richard Hamilton, Emeka Okafor, and Rudy Gay, called Connecticut home only for those years they played in Storrs.

Aside from the Huskies, Connecticut has shown only a lukewarm interest in the athletic endeavors inside its borders.

Connecticut is something of a conundrum demographically when it comes to sports. It doesn't have a major pro team, but the New Haven-Hartford-Springfield, Massachusetts, market ranks 20th in the United States—with more than 2.2 million people—larger than St. Louis, Nashville, Cleveland, and Baltimore.

It is the largest market without a major pro team, and the state's residents have the kind of disposable income to make any sports organization drool. Yet unlike other states that are shut out by the four major pro leagues, Connecticut is close enough to two major pro markets, Boston and New York, and has the requisite rooting interest and wealth to support them.

Cable television has made supporting major pro teams easier than ever, and many in the state have access to both New York and Boston sports stations. Thus people in Connecticut can support their favorite major pro teams—legacy clubs like the Yankees, Red Sox, Giants, Patriots, Rangers, Bruins, Celtics, or Knicks.

"We were in a situation where around us we were competing with twenty to twenty-four pro franchises," former Whalers owner Peter Karmanos said. "Things like the New York Yankees, the Boston Red Sox. Iconic franchises. We had to compete against them for their time, sponsorship money, for people's money. On top of being the ultra small-market team, we also had all the giants to try to compete against."

Thus Nutmeg State fans will largely flock to teams and events that will put the state on the national sports radar and largely pass on small college and local minor-league teams and their cheap, fan-friendly attitudes. The Travelers Championship, the annual PGA Tournament event at TPC River Highlands in Cromwell formerly known as the Greater Hartford Open, regularly draws substantial crowds since it is the only major professional event inside the state's borders each year.

But the other major pro event, the Connecticut Open tennis tournament in New Haven, ceased to exist in 2018 due to lack of financing. The event was usually scheduled right before the US Open in New York, and many marquee players passed to prepare for the Grand Slam tournament. Thus the Connecticut crowds largely did the same.

Connecticans might've also overlooked the dozens of minor-league baseball teams that have come and gone. Since 2000 seven sub-MLB-level teams left the Nutmeg State, most recently the Norwich Sea Unicorns, who were not selected to continue playing affiliated baseball when Major League Baseball took over the minor leagues in 2020.

Those who live in the Nutmeg State might work or even identify themselves more by cities in different states or even alternate regions. Many Fairfield County residents still work in New York City and might identify as New Yorkers who moved northeast in search of quiet, lawns, and good schools.

Residents of northeastern Connecticut spend summer weekends on Cape Cod or Martha's Vineyard, eschewing some of Connecticut's scenic beaches. Others in northwestern Connecticut may vacation in the nearby Berkshires or go skiing in Vermont during the winter.

Thus, few in Fairfield County would go to Bridgeport to support the Atlantic League's Bluefish, but some will drive two-plus hours to Boston to see the Red Sox on a summer night. Those in New Haven County will fight traffic through two states and the George Washington Bridge to attend an NFL game at the Meadowlands in New Jersey, but wouldn't go to East Hartford to support the UFL's Colonials during their one-year stint in 2010—or even to Whalers games in Hartford when they were there.

Connecticut watched the Patriots toy with its psyche by proposing a move to Hartford in the late 1990s only to remain in Foxborough, Massachusetts. Still, the Patriots remain one of the most popular teams in Connecticut, due largely to Bill Belichick, Tom Brady, and six Super Bowl titles between 2001 and 2021, as well as Foxborough's centrality in New England.

The Giants, because of a longtime affiliation with Fairfield University and a two-year stint of playing games at the Yale Bowl in New Haven during the 1970s, rule southern Connecticut and even into central Connecticut and parts of Hartford.

Fans support the neighboring NFL teams in spite of the Nutmeg State's relative ambivalence to sub-NFL-caliber football. Connecticut's high school football teams are the last in the nation to begin play, as the tradition of meaningful games on Thanksgiving alters the schedule in the front end of the season.

Plus, the UConn football team has only one conference championship since joining FBS in 2000 and has become a laughingstock nationally—becoming one of the few FBS teams to opt out of the 2020 season due to the COVID-19 pandemic.

The Rangers and Bruins are two of the NHL's legendary Original Six, and their fan lineage gets passed down to future generations, and that also ultimately doomed the Whalers. The Whalers didn't get the requisite support because fans of the Rangers and Bruins, mostly based in southern and eastern Connecticut, would make the trip to the Civic Center only to see their favorite team play against Hartford. Rangers fans upped the ante by taunting Whalers fans with a "you play in a shopping mall" chant, referencing the Hartford Civic Center's adjacency to the Civic Center Mall.

"Every time the Rangers or Bruins would play the Whalers, all their fans would start fights," said Joanne Cortesa, a longtime Whalers season-ticket holder. "We'd always end up with triple the amount of police because of their fans, and there were more fights in the stands than on the ice."

The Whalers ultimately failed at capturing their entire state's fandom, but they tried their damnedest to move in on that territory after moving to Hartford. They even succeeded in Hartford and the surrounding area, mostly because of successful teams filled with highly visible players and a communal ownership situation where the city's major groups held minority shares in the team.

"If you go back even into the late 1980s, the buzz around Hartford was greater for the Whalers than UConn," said Rich Coppola, the sports director at Fox Connecticut from 1989 to 2019. "UConn wasn't that good."

The Whalers in turn created long-lasting memories for thousands of people—especially kids. They regularly held youth shootout competitions at their games's intermissions that featured kids from Hartford suburbs—places like Glastonbury, Avon, and South Windsor.

"It was the primary sport we followed growing up," said Sean Pendergast, who grew up in the Hartford suburb of Simsbury during the 1980s. "UConn was not even close to the power they are now in basketball; they had no football either."

It is this hockey background that inspired the World Hockey Association, Baldwin, and ultimately the National Hockey League to come to the Nutmeg State.

But once it arrived, things didn't go particularly well.

Chapter 4

The Failure to Launch

The Hartford Whalers' inclusion into the National Hockey League should have been when they "arrived."

The Whalers were one of the 16 teams the NHL added in only 12 years after it absorbed the four WHA teams who earned the right to pay $6 million to enter the fledgling league. The Whalers were the only team from an American market to reach the NHL from the WHA—a fact worth celebrating.

"All these [WHA] franchises were folding, and to Howard Baldwin's extreme credit, he was able to cobble his franchise as one of the four," said Jeff Jacobs, a sports columnist for Hearst Connecticut Media Group who covered the team for the *Hartford Courant*. "They were the only American franchise at a time when they were trying to expand. It was not easy. The Bruins definitely didn't want them in."

To outsiders, Hartford may have been another small Northeast city between New York and Boston—akin to Albany, Providence, or Bridgeport. But suddenly hockey's brightest stars would be embarking upon Connecticut's capital.

"Harry Sinden once said 'cities like Hartford and Albany, they're all the same to me,'" said Jacobs, referencing the Bruins' longtime front-office member and former coach. "Hartford saw itself as an important city, and it was, and it still is."

The Whalers made Hartford a major-league city, and at the time it was thriving. The Whalers' arrival coincided with a boom for many insurance giants, including Aetna, Cigna, Travelers, and others based in the

Connecticut capital. They helped build skyscrapers that created the city's skyline, which further added to its prestige.

Suburbs like Glastonbury and Simsbury became flooded with wealthy insurance tycoons who made their living in the city and hung around to take in Whalers games at night—after the Hartford Civic Center was rebuilt.

Reconstruction took longer than expected, but that didn't stop the Whalers from enjoying their first NHL season split between Hartford and Springfield, Massachusetts—a city roughly 30 miles north of the Connecticut capital.

With the new team name, Hartford altered its logo and color scheme from the green, yellow, and white color variety to the Kelly green, royal blue, and white logo that Peter Good had designed—the look the Whalers are known for today.

Merger rules stated that WHA teams could protect two players and two goaltenders whose rights were held by NHL teams, then each WHA team could round out its roster by selecting from a pool of unprotected players on NHL rosters—each NHL team could protect 15 skaters and two goalies.

The Winnipeg Jets and Edmonton Oilers were ravaged by teams from the elder league, but the Whalers only had to protect Mark Howe, Jordy Douglas, and goalies Al Smith and John Garrett to keep them away from their NHL rightsholders, the Boston Bruins, Toronto Maple Leafs, Buffalo Sabres, and St. Louis Blues.

The Whalers used their expansion draft choices to take players who had played in their WHA program, like Rick Ley, Blaine Stoughton, and Al Hangsleben.

The Whalers' entry also landed Gordie Howe back in the NHL. The Red Wings relinquished Howe's rights—as a condition Howard Baldwin negotiated in the league merger—which meant an entirely new crop of NHL players could say they played against the league's all-time leading scorer at the time.

"It was quite an honor to be on the same ice as 'Mr. Hockey,'" Hall of Fame defenseman Ray Bourque said on NHL Network in June 2016. Bourque was a rookie in Howe's last season and won the Calder Trophy in 1980, his first season patrolling the blue line full-time for the Boston Bruins.

Hartford became an instant draw because of the Howes. Mark Howe, who started the season on left wing on his dad's line, registered 80 points, third-most on the team.

The Whalers were bitten by injuries to their defense early in the season, dressing as few as four healthy defensemen. Coach Don Blackburn moved Mark Howe back to defense, where he ultimately became a Hall of Famer.

"They just decided they wanted me to play defense," Howe said in 2019. "It was a kind of learn-as-you-go thing. I always considered myself a team player, and I was asked to play defense."

Mark was a budding superstar, but the Whalers were legitimized by Gordie Howe. At the time, Howe was the greatest offensive player in NHL history. He'd scored 786 goals and 1,809 points in his 25 seasons with the Detroit Red Wings, both NHL records at the time.

And during the 1979–80 season, the player Wayne Gretzky himself has called the greatest player to ever lace skates played his home games in Hartford.

"That was the identifying symbol of the Whalers when they first entered the league," said longtime NHL commentator Mike Emrick. "The Howes gave all of us outside New England the quickest association with the Whalers."

The Montreal Canadiens had won the Stanley Cup four straight years but did not have Mr. Hockey on their team. The New York Rangers led the NHL in attendance, packing 17,400 fans per game into Madison Square Garden that season, but those fans weren't watching Gordie Howe—other than the two times the Whalers came to town.

Howe was something of a publicity stunt—he was 51 years old and the Whalers manipulated some of his ice time in hopes he'd score his 800th goal at the Civic Center. He was unable to showcase the same skill he had as a young player, but Gordie still was "Mr. Hockey," and somehow put up 15 goals and 41 points that season.

Gordie did manage to score his 800th NHL goal in Hartford—becoming the first player in league history to reach that milestone against the St. Louis Blues on February 29, 1980.

Howe may have been the lead draw for fans across North America when the Whalers came to town, but Hartford's first season proved Howard Baldwin wasn't crazy to challenge the NHL's champion in 1973 after winning the Avco World Trophy.

Unlike many expansion teams, the Whalers were good and had developed chemistry thanks to years of playing together in the WHA. The Howes had been playing together since Mark and Marty could lace up skates, but they weren't the only talented players on the roster. The "bash-dash-stash" line of Blaine Stoughton, Mike Rogers, and Pat Boutette combined for 249 points for Hartford.

Stoughton scored 56 goals, a single-season franchise record that still stands as of 2021, and he and Rogers each topped 100 points. He started the season on a line with his ex–Toronto Maple Leafs teammate Dave Keon but joined Rogers on January 12, 1980, in Detroit, where the duo combined for three of Hartford's six goals in a 6–4 win over the Red Wings.

"Blaine and I had never even skated together on the same line in training camp or anything," Rogers said in 2019. "All of a sudden we're together in that first game, and yeah it worked out."

The rest was history as Rogers, a 5-foot, 9-inch playmaking center, picked up a slew of assists setting up Stoughton's goals. Playing at that level surprised the Whalers, since Rogers had signed a two-way, bonus-laden contract before that season.

"I took a cut in pay, because even where I had successful seasons in the WHA, they were still not sure if I could play in the NHL," Rogers said. "I came to camp in the best shape I'd been in, and I came in with a purpose to make the team and show them they were wrong."

He had never topped 83 points in his five WHA seasons but put up 44 goals and 105 points in the NHL.

"My bonuses started at eighty points, and I said 'I'm never going to score eighty points in the National Hockey League,'" Rogers said. "I had a bonus at eighty, ninety and one-hundred points, and I achieved them all."

Stoughton, who joined the Whalers after the Indianapolis Racers folded, had 65 points in three NHL seasons with the Pittsburgh Penguins and Toronto Maple Leafs before jumping to the WHA. But he put up 100 points that season, silencing critics along the way.

"We wanted to prove we belonged," Rogers said, referencing himself and Stoughton. "There were a lot of question marks surrounding both of us, and I think we had a chip on our shoulder and had something to prove, and we got thrown together one game and it was magical."

Gritty forward Al Hangsleben started on the line with Rogers and Stoughton, but after Hartford acquired Boutette from Toronto in December, Blackburn added him to the line in February. He provided the "bash" with physical play and hard work to retrieve the puck for Rogers and Stoughton.

"I think we had the three elements of a line that makes a good line," Stoughton said. "I was a natural goal scorer. Mike Rogers was quick and a good passer, and Pat Boutette was a little rugged guy."

Boutette even chipped in offensively. After posting just four points in 32 games with the Maple Leafs, he had 13 goals and 44 points in 47 games with Hartford. Led by that line, the Whalers took off, going 16-9-4 in a 29-game stretch between January 12 and March 15.

"The three of us had a lot of pride, and we wanted to succeed," Rogers said. "Pat Boutette doesn't get near enough credit as he should because he was really that piece that we needed.

"When Pat got traded here, we were the highest scoring line in the National Hockey League for the rest of the year, and he was the guy we needed. He was the guy who would go in the corners and allowed Blaine and I to play our games."

Hartford finished eighth in the NHL in goals with 303 and had strong depth in goal scoring. Dave Keon's 52 assists were second on the team behind only Mark Howe. Line-mate Jordy Douglas scored 33 goals, as the Whalers had success playing an uptempo style.

"That year was terrific," said Douglas. "I scored goals. I played with Dave Keon. It was like I was playing in junior. I was part of [the team's success]."

The Whalers won 27 games in their inaugural NHL season, including seven of their first eight back at the Civic Center. Hartford averaged more than 12,000 fans per game, and created a veritable home-ice advantage, losing just four times there that first season.

"We surprised a lot of teams, I think," Douglas said. "We had an older roster that had experience, a lot of ex-NHL guys, and good young talent."

The Whalers were one of two WHA graduates to reach the playoffs their first NHL season. Ironically, the Whalers finished fourth in the newly founded Norris Division, 10 points better than Gordie Howe's former team, the Detroit Red Wings.

"It was a Cinderella year," said Chuck Kaiton, who started as the Whalers radio broadcaster in 1979–80. "The Whalers weren't just another expansion team. They had a pretty good hockey club."

With a keen eye on competing in the playoffs, the Whalers even acquired Bobby Hull from the Winnipeg Jets on February 27, 1980, in an effort to beef up their offense. He joined Howe as a tag-team of idols on Hartford's roster—and periodically played on a line with Howe and Hall of Famer Dave Keon.

"We loved it, just to get a chance to play with him," Stoughton said. "He was actually my idol growing up."

Unfortunately the Whalers scuffled down the stretch, winning just two of their final 12 games. Hartford finished with 73 points, tied with the Pittsburgh Penguins for 13th-most in the 21-team NHL. Yet, the Penguins earned the tiebreaker with three more wins.

Hartford was locked into the number 13 seed, and a potential date with the Bruins, but Pittsburgh came on late and the Whalers wilted. One of Pittsburgh's extra victories came late in the season against Hartford, a 6–4 win on April 2.

Instead of Boston, Hartford's first-round prize was a date with the Montreal Canadiens, the third seed and four-time defending Stanley Cup champions. The Canadiens registered 107 points for their sixth straight 100-plus point season, a streak which ultimately reached eight—made more remarkable given they played in an era without overtime and when teams only got one point for a tie after regulation.

But the 1979–80 Canadiens appeared slightly more beatable. The Whalers tied Montreal three times during the regular season as the Canadiens struggled to cope in the NHL without Hall of Famers and team fixtures goalie Ken Dryden and forward Jacques Lemaire, who had retired before the season.

Scotty Bowman, arguably the finest coach in hockey history, had a falling out with Montreal management and left to coach the Buffalo Sabres. Franchise idol Bernie "Boom Boom" Geoffrion replaced Bowman at the season's outset but was forced to resign after just 30 games when a stomach ailment limited his ability to stand behind the bench and skate at practice.

Montreal still had stalwarts like forward Guy Lafleur, a first-team All-Star, and defenseman Larry Robinson, who won his second Norris Trophy that season. Plus, Montreal entered the playoffs on a roll—closing the season on a 21-game unbeaten string that spanned from February 19 through the season's end.

The Whalers also were ravaged by injuries. Forward Jordy Douglas missed the playoff series with a separated shoulder, and Stoughton played only one period after breaking his leg in Game 1 at the Montreal Forum.

"I remember coming through the neutral zone and there was like ten seconds left [in the first period]," Stoughton recalled, "and I wanted to get a shot off before the buzzer went. I tried to shoot on one leg to get a shot off and I switched my leg to my shooting foot and shot it just as he hit me and went feet-first into the boards.

"It hurt real bad for about five minutes, just excruciating."

Montreal blitzed Hartford 6–1 in Game 1, then won 8–4 in the second game at the Montreal Forum, despite Gordie Howe's 68th and final playoff goal of his NHL career. After Howe scored from Mark Howe and Gordie Roberts, the crowd at the Forum gave Gordie a standing ovation just in case he and the Whalers did not make it back to Montreal for Game 5.

"The people in Montreal respect their hockey players as much as any city or any fan base," Mark Howe recalled. "It's a reputation and respect that my dad earned over thirty years of hockey, and the people knew that and respected him for it."

Mark didn't appreciate it at the time but now cherishes the fact he helped set up his dad's final goal.

"It was a bad goal," Mark Howe said. "I remember the score was pretty lopsided, so for me at the time 'yeah, dad scored,' and it was later in the third period so it's more or less a meaningless goal. But as you look back at it, it's cool. I assisted on dad's last goal."

The Whalers returned to Hartford for their first home playoff game at the Civic Center. Hartford played as if it had nothing to lose, scoring first on Boutette's first-period short-handed goal. The game see-sawed, and trailing 3–2 midway through the third period, Hartford pulled even on Tom Rowe's only playoff goal that forced overtime.

But as quickly as the Whalers had hope, Yvon Lambert scored 29 seconds into the extra session, lifting Montreal to a 4–3 win and a sweep.

Montreal was upset by the Minnesota North Stars in seven games in the subsequent series, and that postseason is still looked at as the beginning of a downward spiral—where regular-season success led to early playoff exits.

But a sweep at the hands of the Canadiens was the high point of the Whalers' first six seasons in the National Hockey League, as Hartford missed the playoffs for five straight seasons.

The New England Whalers were one of the most consistent WHA teams, guided by locals who felt right at home playing in Boston, Hartford, and Springfield. Then the Hartford Whalers shocked the NHL establishment by making the playoffs in their first season, 1979–80.

But Hartford failed to build any momentum despite box-office success in its subsequent two NHL seasons. The Whalers averaged roughly 11,700 fans in 1980–81 and 1981–82—on par with their Adams Division rivals the Boston Bruins who had reached the playoffs both seasons—but the on-ice product did little to capture the community's attention.

A lack of continuity and direction permeated the organization. The Whalers had six coaches in just seven seasons in the World Hockey Association and still made the playoffs every year. But consistency is key in the NHL, and managing general partner Howard Baldwin cycled through four coaches and two general managers in just four seasons.

"We made too many changes at the top," Baldwin recalled in 2013. "It was my fault and nobody else's. Things got a little out of whack, and we didn't have a good hockey program that we were sticking with."

Baldwin and the organization also alienated some of the star players that had put the Whalers on the NHL stage. Blaine Stoughton took the Whalers to court in September 1980 seeking $600,000 and the right to sign with any NHL team—a right he was ultimately granted before he re-signed in Hartford for three years and $160,000 per season.

Forward André Lacroix was just four points from 1,000 in his WHA/NHL career as he got set to enter the 1980–81 season. He showed up for training camp with three years on his contract, but the team no longer had a roster spot for him.

"I didn't appreciate the way they treated me at the end," Lacroix said in 2018. "When I came to training camp, I was in great shape, but I could tell something was wrong. During the preseason, they would say 'you don't have to dress, we want to see what the kids can do,' and I said 'undress somebody else. I need the ice time.' They knew I needed four points [for 1,000], and they never gave me the chance to do it.

"I ended up working a deal with them. I knew they didn't want me, and I didn't want to be somewhere I wasn't wanted, and I was getting too old to go play someplace else."

Gordie Howe was coming off a 41-point season as a 51-year-old and continued to live in Hartford after announcing his retirement on June 6, 1980. The Whalers gave him a front-office position to keep him visible within their organization—which he was invested in since his two sons were still on the team.

Gordie was clearly done playing NHL hockey, but he loved practicing with the Whalers and being on the ice gave him a sense of purpose.

"He was always in a good mood," said Ron Francis, who never played with Howe but skated with him during that time. "He was a bit of a prankster at times, which certainly was fun to be around."

Howe had a brain for hockey and was astute at diagnosing little things that led to big results—like when he taught Jordy Douglas about forcing the play. He didn't often teach lessons but when he did they stuck.

"I remember one day out in practice," recalled Francis, "and I was going down the chute, and the next thing you know my right hand is flailing around in the air, and I looked back, and he had the stick turned upside down and jabbed down on my glove.

"He said 'son, that's why you take the laces out of your gloves,' and I said 'yes, Mr. Howe,' and I went over to the bench and took the laces out and never wore them again."

But Whalers management of that day wasn't interested in Gordie Howe teaching their players lessons. They ostracized Howe by misleading him and sometimes even outright lying to him.

"I think he was more of an inconvenience for them," Mark Howe said. "Dad would ask 'where's practice?' and they would say 'we gave everybody the day off.' So dad would stay home, then he'd find out later that the team had a practice.

"So he'd say to them 'look, I know you're practicing, where are you practicing?' And they'd say, we're at the Bolton rink [outside of Hartford] and practice will be at twelve o'clock, so dad would show up at 11:30, while we were just getting off the ice. Practice would've been at ten.

"I'll guarantee you anything they thought he disrupted practice."

Mark Howe has since become a scout in the Detroit Red Wings organization, working for four Stanley Cup championship teams as of 2021. He's seen how smart coaches and managers get an edge through collaboration and by seeking advice from as many bright people as possible.

And he's dumbfounded that Whalers management wouldn't want what Gordie Howe could provide.

"Any words of wisdom from him were far more beneficial to any hockey player than any words of wisdom that the coaching staff had," Mark Howe said. "His words of wisdom [did] not [come] very often, but they were always dead-on."

"Eventually they had to come and tell him 'Look Gordie we don't want you here. We don't want you on the ice. You can ask any player there. Having Gordie Howe on the ice tell him just a little tiny nuance about what to do in a certain situation. He helped every single player.

"Can you imagine lying like that to someone who is such a great asset that you can use and to not use such a great asset? I find it quite foolish."

Mark Howe also watched the organization, in his mind, mishandle Marty Howe's career. Marty was a defenseman, and although he wasn't the playmaker Mark was, he still could hold his own in his day.

"I knew Marty wasn't an elite player, but I knew Marty was good enough to play," Mark Howe said.

Instead, Marty Howe was shipped off to the AHL in 1979 and played only six games in the NHL during the 1979–80 season. He played just 31 games over three seasons and was traded to the Boston Bruins in 1982.

"He used to get tapped on the shoulder and asked to go fight somebody, and that's not who Marty was," Mark Howe said. "Marty would fight at the opportune time for his team, but he wasn't wanting to go out and just drop the gloves and go after somebody."

Larry Pleau himself was reassigned five times in the three-year span. From 1980 to 1983, he went from Whalers assistant coach to head coach and general manager to general manager back to interim coach, then demoted to the coach of their American Hockey League team in Binghamton, New York.

The 34-year-old native of Lynn, Massachusetts, took over as the team's general manager after Jack Kelley finished his second tenure with the organization in 1981.

Pleau has ultimately enjoyed great success as an NHL executive. As assistant general manager of the New York Rangers, Pleau helped build a championship team in 1994, breaking a 54-year Stanley Cup drought. He moved to the St. Louis Blues after the 1996–97 season, and they made the playoffs eight times in 13 seasons there—including the team that won the Presidents' Trophy (awarded to the team with the most points) in 1999–2000.

Pleau held the longest tenure of any general manager in franchise history and mentored John Davidson during his transition from television to an NHL front office. He earned another Stanley Cup ring in 2019 as an executive in St. Louis's front office after the Blues claimed their first championship in their 52-year existence.

But Pleau's successes in St. Louis and New York came after growing pains while overseeing the Hartford Whalers front office. Pleau's staff was adept at finding talent, but their NHL product suffered because of impatience.

Baldwin pushed Pleau to part with important draft picks, which could've been used to deepen the organization's talent pool, and Pleau was too young to successfully handle the pressure and responsibilities of the dual role he was assigned.

"When I was hired, I was thirty-[four], and I was coach and GM and I had no idea what I was doing," Pleau said. "When you're a player, you make a decision that you want to get into management, and when you do, you realize it's not anything like what you expected it would be."

Pleau traded the Whalers' first-round selection twice in four seasons, including on July 3, 1981, when their 1982 first-round selection fetched forward Rick MacLeish from the Philadelphia Flyers.

MacLeish was a former 50-goal scorer who helped the Flyers win the Stanley Cup twice. He was coming off a 38-goal season in Philadelphia but spent just 34 games with the Whalers, scoring only six goals, before he was traded to Pittsburgh on December 30, 1981.

"Unfortunately, they started to do what I call the quick-fix method, which is to make trades," said Jordy Douglas, a Whalers forward from 1978 to 1982. "They start trading guys and thinking they can upgrade themselves, and that's a real short-term fix for a long-term solution."

By offloading that pick, Hartford picked 14th in 1982 instead of fourth, plus Hartford threw in Fred Arthur and Ray Allison, its first-round selections from 1979 and 1980. The Whalers essentially traded two first-round picks and swapped another for less than half a season of MacLeish.

Pleau also broke up the bash-dash-stash line shortly thereafter. When Pat Boutette was acquired from Toronto, he, Mike Rogers, and Blaine Stoughton pushed the team's offense into the postseason. But Pleau felt his team needed an upgrade in goal after watching John Garrett and Mike Velsor average more than four goals-against apiece in 1980–81.

Pleau signed goalie Greg Millen from Pittsburgh and was forced to give up Boutette as compensation. Pleau fought the move in arbitration, but ultimately ceded the winger in the deal, and Boutette posted consecutive 20-goal seasons on the lowly Penguins.

After parting with Boutette, Pleau capped his first offseason as Whalers GM by offloading Rogers, the team's leading scorer. After his second straight 105-point season in 1980–81, Rogers built a house in the Hartford suburb of Farmington for his wife and infant daughter, Dayna, which he hoped to live in for the rest of his career.

But hoping to sell high on Rogers' two standout years, and give Ron Francis an increased role, Pleau traded the Whalers captain to the New York Rangers for Chris Kotsopoulos, Gerry McDonald, and Doug Sulliman.

"I know Mike Rogers is a popular player with the fans, but there is no other way to put it," Pleau said according to a book published by the Whalers in 1987. "My job is to develop a team for three to four years from now. . . . We may never replace 105 points, but we can do things to improve our club for the future."

Rogers was incensed by the trade and publicly criticized the Whalers' lack of direction.

"I was really mad," Rogers told the *New York Times* after the deal. "I felt there was no reason for me to be traded.

"Then I realized you can't be satisfied with a team that finished eighteenth," Rogers added, "and I realized that with the Whalers I had no chance to play for the Stanley Cup."

Rogers had been voted Hartford's captain and lived in his house just a week until the trade. In 2019, nearly 40 years after he was traded, he was still searching for answers.

"I'm still not happy," Rogers said. "I guess the biggest thing for me was that question, why? We loved Hartford, my wife and I. We thought this is where we're probably going to settle."

Gordie Howe offered to drive Rogers from training camp in Binghamton to Hartford so Rogers could collect his belongings—he declined Howe's offer when the Rangers sent a plane for him so they could hold an introductory press conference. Howe's wife Colleen called Rogers's wife to console her about the move.

"It was probably the only good thing that ever happened about that trade," Rogers said. "That meant so much to me that Gordie cared so much about our friendship and about me that he would do something like that."

Rogers may have been bummed by the trade, but it never showed on the ice. He posted a 103-point season and helped the Blueshirts reach the second round of the playoffs. He scored 20-plus goals each of his four seasons with the Rangers, and they did not miss the playoffs during his tenure in New York.

Hoping to make up for what it had lost in Boutette and Rogers, Hartford traded three picks, including a first-rounder, to Montreal for forward Pierre Larouche in December 1981.

It was a bold move, as Larouche was a two-time former 50-goal scorer who was only 26 at the time of his deal. But Larouche was known for two things: scoring goals and partying hard. He had started his career in Pittsburgh, netting 53 goals with the Penguins in 1975–76, before being dealt to Montreal in 1977. There he helped the Canadiens win the Stanley Cup twice, and became the first player with a 50-goal season with two franchises, scoring 50 for the Canadiens the season they eliminated the Whalers in the first round.

Larouche had a goal-scoring touch, but his effort was questionable, particularly in the defensive side of the game, and early in his career he had a surly streak and was known for coming and going as he pleased.

Larouche was suspended by the Penguins for showing up late for practice and failing to accept a demotion to the AHL, then was traded to Montreal at the end of that season. Amid a frustrating season in 1981–82, and after being a healthy scratch in one of Montreal's games against the Whalers, Larouche got drunk during the game and boarded the team bus en route to Boston, and demanded a trade.

Irving Grundman, the Canadiens general manager at the time, had studied under Sam Pollock, Montreal's Hall of Fame general manager who was adept at convincing desperate opposing managers to offload high draft picks in quick-fix deals. He called up Pleau, who had played for the Canadiens for three seasons and may not have known that he was being played, to discuss Larouche.

"It got to the point where the running joke was 'if the Montreal Canadiens call, Pleau should hang up the phone,'" said Bruce Berlet, the Whalers beat reporter for the *Hartford Courant* at the time.

But those weren't even the organization's worst trades of its first five years in the NHL.

Mark Howe's Hall of Fame career was just taking off by December 1980.

Howe finished fifth in Norris Trophy voting in 1979–80, despite starting the season as a left wing, and in the NHL's post–Bobby Orr era, he was one of the most consistent defensemen in the league.

If Gordie Howe's play was about tenacity and brawn, Mark Howe was more of a finesse player. The *New York Times* once referred to him as a non-star, the type of player that coaches are forced to game plan against but also the one who was hardly noticed by the lay hockey fan.

"He was a top-five player I ever played with," said former NHL player Paul Lawless, who was a teammate of Howe's for one season with the Philadelphia Flyers. "He was such a professional. He wasn't just a great guy. He took so much pride in his game. He took so much pride in his skating."

He was one of the smoothest skaters and a player that teams of any era would drool over: A number one defenseman who could move the puck and slow it down as needed. He was entering his prime, but a freak injury coupled with the Whalers' treatment of it, quickly led to his exit from Hartford.

Howe endured a serious injury in a game against the Islanders on December 27, 1980, when he tangled with New York forward John Tonelli, lost his balance, and flew violently into the net.

"The first thing you think of when you're going into the net is 'I want to absorb some of the shock with my knees,'" Howe said. "I put my legs up, and I guess what happened was the net came up and ended up jabbing into me and ended up going in about five-and-a-half inches overall."

The net frame cut his posterior and thigh so deeply it nearly came all the way through to his hip. He suffered significant blood loss—only paramedics kept him from dying on the ice.

"I was in a panic because I know something dramatically wrong happened," Howe said. "I'm on the ice, and I'm just screaming for the trainers and I know something has speared me and I think I'm dying. . . . They stuck towels up my rear-side, and all I kept saying was 'am I going to live? Am I going to live?'

"And then dad got in the room and I remember he grabbed my left hand and said to the doctors 'I want to see the injury,' and the doc said 'no, I don't think you should,' and he said 'this is my son, I want to see the injury,' so they took the towels away and the next thing I knew I felt this squeeze on my left hand, I thought he had crushed it."

Gordie and Mark sat in a hospital waiting room for almost an hour before a doctor saw what had happened. Fortunately that was the only bit of bad luck.

"The doc came in one day, and all I kept asking him was 'am I going to play hockey again?'" Howe said. "He said, 'you're one of the luckiest human beings I've ever met in my life. All of the things that could've went wrong, if the center part of the net had gone in straight you would've been paralyzed, but it went in on an angle. It missed your spinal cord by about an inch.' Then he said 'It scraped your rectal wall, and if it was an eighth of an inch the other way, it would have torn your rectum right out.'"

Howe spent a week in the hospital and lost about 25 pounds after a bad reaction to Demerol, his prescribed pain medication. Three weeks after the injury, Howe suffered an infection in his hip, since his incision wrongly healed from the inside-out.

But Howe began to feel better after doctors cured the infection, and began skating to try to return to the ice. He missed only 17 games to the near-fatal injury and was a shell of the player he'd been.

"I played a game within six weeks, and that was horrible," Howe said. "The night I played I was 172 pounds, so I was down 25 pounds within six weeks, and I was weak and I was horrible but I wanted to get back and try."

The NHL was different during the Howe saga, as players were more apt to fight through injuries and ailments to stay on the right side of their employers. It wasn't right, and in Howe's case, the Whalers made things worse.

Coach Don Blackburn initially promised to ease Howe back onto the ice, but eschewed that quickly after his job became less secure. He was ultimately fired with 20 games left in the 1980–81 season, leaving Pleau as coach and general manager.

Howe still managed six goals and 22 points in 28 games after he returned, finishing the season with 65 points in 63 games. He then had 53 points in 76 games in 1981–82 even as the physical effects of the injury lingered that season.

"It took me every bit of a year to regain my strength," Howe said. "I'd be the first to admit how bad I was. I was not a good player for about a year."

But some within the organization feared Howe would never regain his original form and he was using the injury as an excuse to loaf. They began exploring a trade for Howe, and those rumors seeped into the public midway through the 1981–82 season.

"I asked Larry Pleau, 'Why do you want to trade me? I'm coming off a bad injury. I know I'm not playing well, but I'm still twenty pounds under what I should be,'" Howe recalled. "And he looked me in the face and told me 'We think that you've made enough money, and you've got your long-term contract and you probably want to sit on the couch. I can invest your money for you, and you never have to worry about playing again.'"

The perception stung Howe, who continued to play hard even after learning what his team thought of him. He submitted a four-team list where he'd accept a trade: the Rangers, Islanders, Philadelphia Flyers, and Boston Bruins.

Pleau told Howe, in front of the rest of the team, that he'd never play in a Whalers uniform for as long as he was around, then denied saying that when Howard Baldwin met with them at the Howe residence after the season. Hartford finished with 60 points for the second straight season, missing the playoffs by 22 points.

"I had always played on winning teams, and now we're losing and I hated it," Howe said. "I knew the coaches didn't like me. I knew the coaches thought I didn't try hard and didn't compete. But I was quite the opposite. I cared as much as anybody that played on that team.

"I said 'you don't want me. I don't want to play for you either.'"

Pleau obliged Howe by trading him to Philadelphia for Greg Adams, Ken Linseman, and two draft picks, including a first-rounder on August 19, 1982, just weeks before camp opened.

With a fresh start, and a healthy body, Howe became one of the sport's most dominant defensemen over nine seasons in Philadelphia. He finished second in Norris Trophy voting three times, and his face and #2 live on a banner in Philadelphia as one of six retired numbers in the organization's history as of 2021. He was inducted into the Hockey Hall of Fame in 2011.

Without Mark Howe patrolling their blue line, and in the run-and-gun 1980s, the Whalers surrendered 403 goals—more than five goals per game—in the 1982–83 season, a number that remains the fifth-most allowed in a single NHL season as of 2021.

The 1982–83 Whalers were a nightmare, fueled by terrible play and checked-out players—most notably Pierre Larouche.

Larouche produced his first year in Hartford, posting 25 goals and 50 points in 45 games playing alongside Ron Francis in Hartford after the trade, then posted six goals and 12 points in Hartford's first seven games.

But his sulking and penchant for partying won out. Early during the 1982–83 season, a season when Hartford finished 19-54-7, Larouche landed himself in the Whalers' doghouse after an incident in Los Angeles with first-year coach Larry Kish.

Kish, 40, had been hired before the season after Pleau had grown weary of juggling both the head coach and general manager roles. In a forward-thinking move, Pleau had tried to hire Alpo Suhonen, a coach of Finnish descent who would've been the NHL's first European head coach.

But Baldwin rejected Suhonen, instead picking the longtime American Hockey League coach of the organization's affiliate in Binghamton, New York. Kish had spent the previous 18 seasons in the AHL, guiding the young budding stars to the Calder Cup finals while earning Coach of the Year honors in 1982.

"The National League isn't the American League," Kish said before the season. "The principles and the rules are the same, but you need capable, skilled hockey players."

Unfortunately the Whalers didn't have enough of those. Kish worked well at teaching the game, as his lengthy career proved, but had a hard time dealing with NHL egos. He'd push buttons and talk about them behind their backs to the media. Players could see through the veneer, which one ex-Whaler called "phony baloney."

"I think he was a little naive," said Whalers forward Blaine Stoughton.

Things went south for the Whalers in a hurry—they lost 32 of their first 49 games—and the frustration came to a head on October 22. Larouche had been out in Los Angeles the night before the Whalers' game with the Kings and returned to the team's hotel drunk with just a sport jacket on and no shirt at 11:10 p.m. PT, 10 minutes past the team's curfew.

Kish was sitting in the hotel bar and saw Larouche stumble through, making sure to note the forward's lateness. Larouche fired back that he was only 10 minutes late for curfew and told Kish to "fuck off." The Whalers sent Larouche back to Hartford, suspending him indefinitely, which ultimately lasted just two games.

"No one player is bigger than the team," Kish said after the suspension.

Larouche later enjoyed a consistent tenure with the New York Rangers after leaving Hartford that season. But his outburst highlighted the misery and lack of respect the 1982–83 Whalers had for each other and their place in the NHL. There was the bus trip in which veterans took rookie forward Ray Neufeld's entire paycheck in a poker game; the game in Buffalo on March 23 in which Hartford lost 8–3, but defenseman Chris Kotsopoulos proudly professed afterwards "I was only a minus-one."

"The 1982–83 team had the worst chemistry of any team in the history of sports," said Berlet. "It was a catastrophe. They were eliminated in December."

The Whalers fired Kish after only 49 games, and Pleau resumed the role of interim head coach. Pleau hung around for just 18 games before relinquishing the duties to John Cunniff for the remainder of the season to focus on the impending amateur draft.

Cunniff won just three of the 13 games he coached in Hartford. Adding to the organization's embarrassment, Cunniff lashed out publicly at Howard Baldwin, criticizing him for pressuring Pleau to offload Hartford's first-round pick. When Pleau refused to deal the pick, he was demoted to director of hockey operations in an organizational restructuring.

"If it were left to Howard Baldwin, we wouldn't have our No. 1 [pick]," Cunniff told the *Manchester Journal-Inquirer*. "He would have traded that a long time ago."

On the ice, Ron Francis emerged as the team's bright spot, scoring 31 goals and 90 points in just his second season. Stoughton added 45 goals and 76 points as each provided rare professionalism. But their attitudes were not the norm.

"There were guys who really cared," Berlet said, "and then there were guys who didn't give a shit.

"19-54-7 speaks for itself. It was a disaster covering a team like that."

It quickly became clear that the Whalers needed to hit bottom, clean house, and start from scratch.

And that's when a cat came to the rescue.

Chapter 5

The Cat's Arrival

The Hartford Whalers' first six years in the National Hockey League netted one playoff appearance and an enormous amount of embarrassment.

The Whalers actually drafted well thanks largely to amateur scouting director Bill Dineen. Missing the playoffs also led to early picks, which enabled Hartford to pick up good talent, despite their shortsighted trades and the primitive age of scouting.

Before the advent of the internet, organizations relied heavily on firsthand scouting. Plus, with tight budgets, limited technology, and no knowledge of European players, teams tended to focus on surefire Canadians and local Americans who would help sell tickets.

The Whalers front office aimed at selecting local talent, and that pool consisted mostly of players from Massachusetts. In 1981 they were also negotiating a television contract in Hartford, and in the interest of attracting viewers to a young and promising star, Whalers general manager Larry Pleau eyed standout center Bobby Carpenter, a high school player from the Boston suburb of Beverly, Massachusetts.

Carpenter had become the first American-born hockey player featured on the iconic cover of *Sports Illustrated*, which dubbed him "The Can't-Miss Kid." The 6-foot, 200-pound center from St. John's Prep in Danvers, Massachusetts, was deemed a prototypical NHL center of the future. He was supposed to go to Providence College on a hockey scholarship after a breakout performance when he had nine points in five games as a 17-year-old for the United States at the World Junior Championship.

"We had a lot of interest in him because we were trying to get a local TV deal," said Pleau. "If he was there, we probably would've taken him."

The Washington Capitals also were enamored with Carpenter and discovered him by reading the cover story published earlier that year too. Slated to pick fifth in that year's draft, behind the Whalers who were at number four, Washington general manager Max McNab also knew Hartford would covet Carpenter.

"Max McNab came up to me and told me he was going to make a trade with [the] Colorado [Rockies] to draft Carpenter, and what kind of deal would we be willing to make to prevent that from happening," Pleau said. "I showed him my draft board, and that we had [Ron] Francis 1a, and Carpenter 1b, and Max showed me his, and he had Carpenter at 1a and Francis at 1b."

So after Dale Hawerchuk and Doug Smith were selected with the first two picks, by the Winnipeg Jets and Los Angeles Kings, and realizing their consolation prize would be the player they preferred, the Whalers stood pat as Washington swapped top-five picks with the Colorado Rockies to select Carpenter number three overall.

Washington aimed to capitalize on Carpenter's celebrity by inviting him directly to the NHL squad straight out of high school. He posted three 30-goal seasons in Washington, including a 53-goal campaign in 1984–85, before falling out with management and bouncing between four other organizations.

The Whalers then selected Francis with the fourth pick, which became the greatest pick in franchise history.

Many believed Francis was an elite hockey player. But Dineen, who became familiar with Francis when he was a teammate of his son Gord in Sault Sainte Marie of the Ontario Hockey League, saw Francis's difference-making intangible: his hockey IQ. And it was Dineen who shaped Pleau's decision to stand pat instead of trading for what he felt was an inferior player in Carpenter.

"Billy Dineen was smart enough to see how good Ron Francis was," said Jeff Jacobs, the Whalers beat writer for the *Hartford Courant* from 1984 to 1993.

Francis had flirted with college hockey, after watching his second-cousin Mike Liut enjoy a standout career at Bowling Green, and would've gone to play at Cornell University, where he was being recruited by coach Dick Bertrand.

"In my mind I was going to play college hockey," Francis recalled in 2019. "I had been recruited heavily by Cornell, and pretty much everything was said and done."

But Greyhounds general manager Sam McMaster selected him in the second round of the 1980 OHL draft and enticed Francis to join the Greyhounds that fall. Francis changed his mind at the last minute, when the Greyhounds offered him the opportunity to play and attend St. Mary's College in Sault Sainte Marie.

"Sam said 'we've got a complete hockey player,'" said Terry Crisp, the Greyhounds coach at the time. "When Sam said that, I knew we had a kid who knew how to behave, had a good family, good background, knew what he had to do in the community as part of the team and what his role in the community would be also."

Francis for sure knew about his role in the community. He grew up playing hockey in The Soo, a town of about 75,000 people that sits on Lake Superior about 350 miles north of Detroit. He also knew there was immense pressure on him to perform in Sault Sainte Marie, since he was one of the few homegrown players on the Greyhounds. Most pro-caliber Canadian junior players leave home at 16 to play hockey and live with host or "billet" families.

The OHL's Greyhounds are the biggest sporting act around, and fans and residents flood the arena to get a glimpse at tomorrow's NHL stars.

"Certainly more pressure for a local kid because the Sooites want to see their people do well," Francis said. "They're rooting hard for you, and you don't want to disappoint them."

But if Francis felt the heat, he didn't show it.

"Ronny Francis was so well-grounded, and his family had him so well-grounded, and Ronny was mature beyond his years," Crisp said. "As a 15- or 16-year-old, Ronny Francis was far ahead of other kids his age, and his family knew what they wanted and knew where they were going, so there was never anything about 'you have to be a player' or 'you have to go to college.' It was a process. They didn't just jump aboard."

Francis helped his team with his 200-foot game and mature demeanor. He sacrificed points and some of the limelight to help the Greyhounds win, which they did often during his 89-game tenure there. In his first season, 1980–81, Francis only had 69 points in 64 games—far fewer than leading scorer John Goodwin's 166. But Francis helped the Greyhounds to a 96-point season and a division championship.

Francis may have been the best all-around player, but he certainly wasn't the only NHL-caliber talent on the team. Six of Francis's teammates in Sault Sainte Marie were drafted in 1981, including fellow first-round pick defenseman Steve Smith and goalie John Vanbiesbrouck, whom the New York Rangers selected in the fourth round.

The Soo may have been used to watching ex-Greyhounds reach the NHL, but Francis was a member of the community, and his selection triggered civic pride across the city. But when the joy of being drafted subsided, Francis remembered being in the dark about Hartford.

"I didn't know much about it," Francis said in 2013. "I came from a small town in Ontario, but I remember my agent telling me at the draft that it was good for me. Washington had traded up to get Bobby Carpenter, and I was left to go to Hartford.

"I went in there with an open mind."

Crisp and McMaster knew they wouldn't have Francis for his full junior tenure, and sure enough after 25 games with the Greyhounds in 1981–82, scoring 48 points, Francis left for Hartford, where he became the face of the Whalers for the next decade.

"We were playing in Oshawa, and we had four or five of these boys from Hartford watching the game," Crisp recalled. "Sure enough, after the game, they said we'd like to take Ronny home with us. And I said 'well, when would you like him?' and they said 'we were hoping to take him right now.' And I said 'now now?!'

"We called Ronny over, and I said these gentlemen want you to go to Hartford, and they said 'yeah, we just want you to go there for a week or two; we just want to acclimatize you to the city, we'll have him back at the very latest, two weeks.' And off they went, and every time I see Ronny I say 'you owe me a lot of hockey' because that was the last I'd seen of Ronny Francis in The Soo."

As of 2020, Francis was still the organization's leader in games, goals, and points, and his 821 points in Hartford still led second-place Eric Staal by more than 50. He ranked fifth on the NHL's all-time points list as of 2021, with his 1,798 falling in line behind only Wayne Gretzky, Jaromir Jagr, Mark Messier, and Gordie Howe.

"Special is the right word because if you look at his accomplishments in the history of the league he's right up there with the very best," said Ulf Samuelsson, Francis's teammate in Hartford and Pittsburgh from 1985 to 1995. "Having all that skill and the combination with the kind of humble leader that he was made him, to me, that special guy that you can always lean on, ask questions and he would arrange things and make sure everyone was included.

"He's just an incredible player. So smart, so gifted on both ends of the ice. It was so much fun to play with him."

Dineen and Pleau further laid the foundation for future success a year later at the 1982 draft, which was ironically one of Hartford's best. The Whalers had swapped first-round picks with the Flyers in the Rick MacLeish trade but still got Paul Lawless with the 14th pick.

"I was thinking 'where the fuck is Hartford,'" Lawless recalled in 2019. "My first interview was with [Hockey Hall of Fame commentator] Dick Irvin, and he said 'congratulations, Paul. Do you know where Hartford is?' And I said 'Hartford. That's in Connecticut!' I don't know where I pulled that out of my ass from."

He wasn't alone. Besides Lawless, Pleau also managed to bring in defenseman Ulf Samuelsson in the fourth round and forward Ray Ferraro in the fifth. Acquiring such a haul in the later rounds is unusual in the NHL, but the Whalers found diamonds amid the ashy soot.

"[The Whalers] got a pretty good bounty from that one draft," Ferraro said.

Samuelsson might've been drafted on June 9, but in the pre-internet age news traveled more slowly from Montreal—the site of the draft—to his hometown of Leksands, Sweden.

"I got a letter in the mail two weeks after the draft from the Hartford Whalers telling me I'd been drafted," Samuelsson said in 2020. "That's how behind the times we were in Sweden in that time."

Ferraro was drafted out of Penticton of the British Columbia Junior Hockey League after leading the team with 135 points in only 48 games. He fell to the fifth round because of his 5-foot, 10-inch stature but turned out to be a skilled and hard-working player—one who simply loved hockey enough to carve out a 21-season NHL career.

But like Francis and Lawless, a journey to Hartford might as well have been to Mars.

"I knew nothing about Hartford," Ferraro said. "The Whalers were this misfit team that had come through [the WHA] merger."

There was one pick who knew something about Connecticut: Hartford's third-round selection Kevin Dineen.

What might've seemed like a nepotism pick, with Bill Dineen drafting his son, ended up as one of the best picks in Hartford history. Kevin posted the second-most points in Whalers history behind only Francis, and fortunately Pleau was willing to put his faith into Bill Dineen, enough to select his own flesh and blood.

"I knew Billy, and I had no reason not to trust him," Pleau said.

Dineen helped build the foundation for a winning club. But they needed stability and consistency at the top, and they were about to get it when they brought in Emile Francis.

Francis, known as "the Cat," had an impact far greater than his 5-foot, 6-inch, 145-pound stature. The North Battleford, Saskatchewan, native was a goalie who spent much of his playing career trapped in the American and Western Hockey Leagues. After starting one season for the Chicago Blackhawks, Francis was traded to the New York Rangers where he was stuck behind Hall of Famers Lorne "Gump" Worley and Johnny Bower.

He played only 95 NHL games. But Francis had a brilliant mind for hockey, and at age 33, he quit playing and became head coach of the Guelph Royals of the Ontario Hockey Association. There he guided Hall of Famers Jean Ratelle and Rod Gilbert to the league championship, then was called up to the Rangers as an assistant coach in 1962 before becoming New York's head coach in 1965.

Francis coached the dormant Original Six team back to respectability. The Rangers had missed the postseason in 12 of 16 seasons but made the playoffs nine straight seasons under Francis, including a run to the Stanley Cup finals in 1972.

Francis was fired by the Rangers in the middle of the 1975–76 season, but joined the St. Louis Blues as coach and general manager for 1976–77. He was inducted into the Hockey Hall of Fame as a builder in 1982 and somehow built playoff teams under the looming threat of relocation as the Blues struggled through dire financial straits in the early 1980s—also saving hockey in St. Louis by finding a stable ownership group.

Francis lost his job midway through the 1982–83 season but was not unemployed long. He had attended NHL board meetings and became chummy with Whalers chairman and managing general partner Howard Baldwin.

"I told him, 'I'd love to work with you someday,'" Baldwin recalled. "And he said 'keep me in mind, things aren't so good here.'"

So when it came time to start fresh, after Hartford's miserable 1982–83 season, Baldwin hired Emile Francis as Hartford's general manager.

"We needed a lot of experience that people would take very, very seriously," Baldwin said. "He ran a couple of really good programs in New York and St. Louis, and we brought him in to take charge and do what needed to be done. And that's exactly what happened."

Francis changed the culture right away. Hartford had four head coaches in four seasons—three during the 1982–83 season alone—but Francis built a stable organization with people who helped him have success in St. Louis.

"The Whalers finally got their act together in 1983 when they hired Emile Francis," said Chuck Kaiton, the Whalers radio broadcaster for their entire NHL tenure. "He brought a lot of stability and experience."

The first connection was former Blues assistant Jack "Tex" Evans. Like Francis, Evans was also a former Rangers farmhand, and they already had a Connecticut connection by playing for the New Haven Ramblers of the AHL.

Evans had NHL coaching experience—leading both the California Golden Seals and Cleveland Barons during the 1970s. He had been coaching Salt Lake City in the ECHL when Francis called on him to coach the Whalers, a job Evans officially took July 7, 1983.

"We've known one another for a good number of years," Francis said at Evans's introductory press conference. "I've always had a great amount of respect for Jack Evans . . . he's not only a disciplinarian, he's also an excellent teacher."

Evans was intense and fiery, but chose his words carefully. He was an old-school, hard-nosed type who liked the team to police itself. He would not fill a reporter's notebook with quotes, and players seemed to respect him and his ways, which showed with the Whalers' on-ice success.

"Jack Evans was a father figure to a lot of players," Kaiton said. "There were a lot of great players on those teams, and Tex was smart enough to steer the ship."

Francis had overcome his limited physical capabilities by being a smart goalie, and committed to making the Whalers a family. He dispatched the many unhappy players who had graced the Whalers' dressing rooms and made personnel decisions based on hockey IQ and the player's commitment to the community.

Hartford finished out of the postseason for the fifth straight year in 1983–84, Francis's first season running the organization, but there were bright spots. After finishing 35 points behind the fourth-place team in the Adams Division, Hartford ended up just nine behind the number-four-seeded Montreal Canadiens.

Sylvain Turgeon, Hartford's first-round pick in 1983, posted a promising rookie campaign, leading the team with 40 goals. Ron Francis was second on the team with 83 points as the Whalers improved by 19 points in the standings.

On February 12, 1984, the eventual Stanley Cup champion Edmonton Oilers left the Civic Center with their tails between their legs after the Whalers delivered an 11–0 beatdown. Francis scored four goals in the drubbing fans still longingly recall today.

Still, like seasons prior, Hartford's undoing came on defense and in goal. Though they cut their goals-allowed totals by roughly a goal per game, the Whalers were still lousy, surrendering the Wales Conference's third-most goals (320). Greg Millen led the team with a 3.70 goals-against average and .878 save percentage, and backup Ed Staniowski allowed 74 goals in just 18 games. The Whalers won only four of 27 games between December 6 and February 1.

The Canadiens and Quebec Nordiques duked it out for the Adams Division crown again in 1984–85, but Hartford once again was doomed by its inability to keep pucks out of its net. A 1-12-2 stretch that spanned more than a month—in which Hartford surrendered 80 goals—assured the Whalers of a sixth straight year out of the postseason.

"We had a tough division back in the day," Whalers defenseman Joel Quenneville said.

Emile Francis watched his goaltenders stop just 18 of 28 shots in a 10–4 loss to the Nordiques on February 10, 1985, and realized enough was enough. Less than two weeks later, he changed the course of franchise history by going back to his St. Louis roots and giving the Whalers their first legitimate NHL goalie.

Francis traded both his captain and leading scorer Mark Johnson and his starting goalie, Greg Millen, to the Blues for goalie Mike Liut.

No goalie played more minutes between 1981 and 1984 than the 6-foot, 2-inch, 195-pound netminder from Weston, Ontario. Yet when St. Louis acquired Rick Wamsley from the Canadiens on draft day 1984, Liut had lost his starting spot. Liut played in just 32 games in St. Louis in 1984–85 before being traded to Hartford, and was offloaded as the highest-paid Blues player.

It was technically Liut's second stint with the Whalers—New England picked him in the second round of the 1976 WHA draft before trading his rights to Cincinnati—but he regained a starting role and was reunited with Tex Evans and Emile Francis.

The trade was about to invigorate the veteran netminder, but Liut was anything but refreshed by the deal.

"I was disappointed at the time of the trade, because I put so much into the St. Louis organization and it was the first time I experienced being traded," Liut recalled. "Hartford had missed the playoffs for several years, and they were not going to make the playoffs that year. In St. Louis, we were in first place so coming to Hartford was a bit of a shock to say the least."

It may have negatively shocked Liut, but the trade signaled the team's arrival.

"They had a pretty good team," *Hartford Courant* beat writer Bruce Berlet said. "But then they got [Liut] for Johnson and Millen. That was the final piece of the puzzle for them becoming a contender."

Francis trusted Liut because of their time together in St. Louis. Plus, he liked Liut's playoff pedigree and quiet fire, which quickly came out in his early days in Hartford.

The Whalers were 21-34-7 and running out the string of games when the Vancouver Canucks came to Hartford on March 3, 1985. The Canucks were scuffling too, en route to a 59-point season in which they fired their coach Bill LaForge after just 20 games.

The Whalers built a 4–1 lead in the first period and maintained the advantage amid a string of Canucks rallies. When Turgeon capped his hat trick, giving the Whalers a 6–4 lead with just 1:10 remaining, it appeared that Hartford would send its fans home happy on that Sunday afternoon.

But Vancouver coach Harry Neale, a Whalers coach during their WHA days, was trying hard to win that day. He pulled his goaltender for an extra attacker, and the Canucks struck for two goals 22 seconds apart, tying the game in the final minute and forcing overtime. Vancouver stunned the home crowd on Jean-Marc Lanthier's goal at 2:47 of the extra session that gave the Canucks an improbable 7–6 win.

Liut was incensed by the loss, and living in a hotel at the time, he ordered room service for his postgame meal. The thought of the loss plagued him, and maddened with rage, he flipped his tray over and onto his hotel-room floor.

The move symbolized the Whalers' turnaround, as neither their netminder nor team would accept the failings of the past. Liut played 12 games, sporting a team-best .908 save percentage and 2.97 goals-against average. Hartford went 9-3-2 in its final 14 games that season, including an 8–7 win over the eventual-champion Oilers, turning around three two-goal deficits on March 29.

"Cat did a real nice job," Quenneville said, referencing Emile Francis. "Getting Liuty, who was around winning . . . that brought experience and leadership to the room. He was a solid and improving goaltender."

Liut's acquisition ultimately became a steal. One Blues blog rated it the eighth-worst trade in team history because Millen never had a save percentage above .890 and only once sported a goals-against average below 3.38 in five seasons with the Blues. Johnson recorded only 10 points in 17 games and was traded to New Jersey after the 1984–85 season.

But the trade wasn't the only important move of the final weeks of the 1984–85 season. With the Whalers out of contention, Emile Francis called up a slew of players from the AHL—including Paul MacDermid, Ray Ferraro, and Ulf Samuelsson—who helped the Whalers to that hot finish.

"We had an unbelievable run," said Quenneville, one of the few veterans on the roster by year's end. "We called up all those guys from Binghamton, and it seemed like we got more speed and more skill."

For those younger players, simply playing in the NHL felt good enough.

"We were all so young," Ferraro recalled. "We didn't have any grand designs about our organization. Had we been with a good team, we probably wouldn't have gotten that opportunity."

There was cause for optimism as the 1985–86 season approached in Hartford, and the team could sense it.

"We had a very young team starting the 85–86 season, and we were developing a sense of ourselves so there was no expectation as to what we might accomplish," Liut said. "We did, however, have the team that played well together, and we very quickly realized that we could become competitive in the Adams Division."

Still, while there was reason for optimism, the hockey media wasn't yet buying. Despite Liut, a young and dynamic group of forwards, a budding defense, and consistency behind the bench in Tex Evans, Hartford was widely predicted to finish last in the Adams Division for the fifth consecutive year.

Whether the Whalers succeeded or not, 1985–86 was poised to be a big year for Hartford. The Whalers were hosting the All-Star Game, and the NHL's brightest stars descended on the Insurance Capital on February 4.

•

After a 10-10 open to their season, the Whalers reeled off a 16-10-1 stretch. Capped by a five-game winning streak, the Whalers sat in fourth place in the tightly packed Adams Division, and within striking distance of home-ice advantage when the calendar turned to February.

ADAMS DIVISION STANDINGS ON FEBRUARY 1, 1986
(Top four reach playoffs)

	W	L	T	Points
Montreal	29	17	5	63
Quebec	28	19	3	59
Boston	25	18	7	57
HARTFORD	26	22	1	53
Buffalo	23	23	5	51

But injuries in January nearly doomed the club. Kevin Dineen broke his knuckle in a fight and lost seven games. Ron Francis, who had played in all 80 games in 1984–85, injured his ankle, which cost him 27 games and an appearance in the All-Star Game at the Civic Center that year.

"Unfortunately I got to watch it on crutches with my foot in a cast," Francis said in 2019. "It was a pretty disappointing moment in my career, not being a part of that game.

"I think anytime you get to play in an All-Star Game, it's great, but when you get to play in one in your hometown, in front of your own fans, you'd love that opportunity. I was so looking forward to it and that happened and didn't get that chance."

But even as injuries nearly sabotaged the season, Emile Francis tinkered with his roster. He acquired Wayne Babych from Quebec for Greg Malone. Babych was another who had played under Francis in St. Louis, scoring 54 goals in 1980–81 with the Blues.

"[Francis] found character guys and upgraded our depth," said Quenneville.

The injury bug continued to bite during the cruel month of February. Without its stars on the ice, Hartford suffered a 2-13-1 stretch between January 27 and March 1. Rumors swirled that Evans's job was in jeopardy, which was made worse after he shoved *Hartford Courant* reporter Randy Smith after a loss.

"We were solidly in playoff contention but incurred several key injuries in January," Liut said. "The month of February was the worst month of hockey I ever experienced."

Still Liut remembers Evans and Emile Francis keeping Hartford from falling into the abyss again—even as the vocal crowds at the Civic Center called for Evans's head.

"The most positive memory was the support that Emile Francis and Jack Evans continued to show the team," the goaltender recalled. "Never once did they waver, never once did they deflect blame onto the team; if anything they absorbed the brass of the fans as much as they could. It showed true leadership."

Hartford was in a full-on freefall in the days leading up to its big moment on the NHL stage. The Whalers built a 4–0 lead against the Washington Capitals in their final tuneup before hosting the All-Star Game, but allowed five third-period goals, including Larry Murphy's with just 1.15 in regulation, losing 5–4 for their fourth straight loss in a drought that ultimately became seven.

"We had this great event," Whalers managing general partner Howard Baldwin said, "and we came into it on such a low. Everybody there thought we were going to miss the playoffs again."

Hartford bookended February with another four-game losing streak capped by a dismal 5–1 loss to the Pittsburgh Penguins in the Steel City on March 1. Hartford sat in last place in the Adams Division and trailed the fourth-placed Buffalo Sabres by eight points entering the season's stretch run.

When the Babych deal didn't net enough results Francis tinkered some more, dealing defenseman Risto Siltanen to Quebec for John Anderson—the second of Hartford's three midseason trades with its division rival.

And while a horrible month of hockey seemingly put them in a hole, the Whalers would still have life if they survived a five-game Adams Division stretch that started the next day at home against the Boston Bruins.

"We were eight points out of playoff position, so clearly the next week would decide the season," Liut said.

ADAMS DIVISION STANDINGS ON MARCH 2, 1986	W	L	T	Points
Montreal	35	23	6	76
Quebec	34	27	4	72
Boston	31	26	7	69
Buffalo	30	28	6	66
HARTFORD	28	33	2	58

Kevin Dineen, one of the Whalers' emotional leaders, had had enough and when he saw the opportunity to take retribution from Bruins defenseman Mike Milbury, and also light a spark under his team, he did so.

Milbury was a burly player, known mostly for the time he jumped the glass at Madison Square Garden to beat a New York Rangers fan with his own shoe. He had a reputation as an arrogant player, with a particularly punchable face, and had drawn Dineen's ire when he sucker punched him during a Bruins-Whalers game in Boston on March 7, 1985.

"We'd had a scuffle the year before," Dineen recalled. "I kind of got hit when I wasn't looking."

Dineen thought he'd lost all chance for retribution when Milbury announced his retirement after the 1984–85 season. But when the Bruins blue line was bitten by a rash of injuries in 1985–86, Milbury returned for one last run at the Stanley Cup.

Dineen was playing his first game in two weeks while nursing a sprained knee, and after Hartford built a 3–1 second-period lead against the Bruins, he ignited his teammates by knocking Milbury out with one punch during a fight midway through the frame.

"I think I landed a lucky one," Dineen recalled. "You don't think you're going to get another opportunity when somebody retires, and then he opens up to come back and play, and that was kind of an open invitation.

"There was another confrontation on the ice, and I went up to him and asked if he wanted to settle some unfinished business."

Dineen said he's spoken with Milbury about the fight in recent years, and seemed embarrassed when asked about the event more than 30 years later.

But the punch galvanized the rest of the Whalers.

"Kevin was a really nasty fighter," said Whalers defenseman Ulf Samuelsson, a heavyweight in his own right. "He'd dig deep down and find that big haymaker and sometimes it connected . . . and when it connected someone usually fell asleep."

"If there was karma, that was the day," said Dave Babych, a defenseman whom the Whalers had acquired from the Winnipeg Jets midseason. "I don't know Mike Milbury, but I did not respect him when I was playing against him.

"You can be tough when you've got tough guys around you, or you can be tough when you're by yourself. I think Kevin figured that out, and it was a joy to everyone."

Dineen's knockout of Milbury was a seminal moment in Whalers history, and the highlight of Hartford's 4–1 win on March 2. It also was symbolic that the Whalers were done being a punching bag to the Adams Division and the rest of the NHL and would start delivering some blows of their own.

"When we were playing the Bruins for home games in Hartford, more than half the building was Bruins fans," said Whalers forward Paul Lawless. "The place was packed with majority of Bruins fans, and [Dineen] one-times him, and it was absolutely gorgeous."

Hartford took off from there, winning each of a home-and-home series with the Buffalo Sabres by a combined score of 11–3. After a loss to the Quebec Nordiques, the Whalers authored an historic and convincing 5–2 win over the Canadiens.

In more than six seasons in the NHL, the Whalers were 0-16-4 in 20 regular-season games at the Montreal Forum and had lost their only two playoff games there as well.

The Whalers fell behind 1–0 in the first period, but John Anderson's goal in the final second of the first frame started a run of four straight goals that pulled the Whalers within four points of Buffalo for the division's final playoff spot.

"Somehow, from somewhere, as a group we found a way to win a Sunday afternoon game against Boston and that Monday evening game in Montréal, which was the first Whalers win in Montréal," Liut said.

That 4-1 stretch became a 12-3-2 spurt, as the Whalers' offense exploded for 60 goals in their final 11 games. Meanwhile, the Sabres lost four of their final five games, and Hartford edged out Buffalo by four points for the final Adams Division playoff spot.

"The month of March was probably the best month of hockey I ever experienced," Liut recalled.

Thanks to time spent playing with Ron Francis and Dineen, Anderson came up huge, recording 25 points in just 14 games.

For the first time in six years, Hartford was playoff bound.

"We played like one of the elite teams," Baldwin said. "After the years of doom and gloom, it was like winning the Stanley Cup."

1985–86 ADAMS DIVISION FINAL STANDINGS

	W	L	T	Points
Quebec	43	31	6	92
Montreal	40	33	7	87
Boston	37	36	12	86
HARTFORD	40	36	4	84
Buffalo	37	37	6	80

The Whalers' regular-season script flipped thanks to some wisdom and maturity from the young bunch, which would end up being a precursor to a calling after many playing careers ended.

"There was a lot of wisdom in that room to figure out things and get them going the right way," said forward Dave Tippett, who has since enjoyed a lengthy NHL coaching career. "Look back now how many players were coaches from that team. Managers fix problems, and early in our career, that's what we were doing in that room."

Meanwhile, the folks in the Nutmeg State were so elated, they weren't quite sure how to celebrate.

"We almost didn't know how to handle it when they made the playoffs," Whalers fan and Connecticut native Sean Pendergast recalled. "We slept out for playoff tickets partially because we wanted tickets, but also because we just thought that's what you do in playoff cities."

And it was about to get even crazier for fans in Hartford and around the NHL.

The 1980s were an extraordinary time for the National Hockey League.

The decade featured both the greatest players and dynasties in league history. The New York Islanders won an unfathomable 19 straight playoff series, claiming the decade's first four Stanley Cup championships before passing the torch to the Edmonton Oilers, who went on one of the most incredible runs in league history.

Coached by Glen Sather and led by Wayne Gretzky, Edmonton was a veritable machine that smashed the offensive record books and owned the Smythe Division and Campbell Conference for most of the decade.

After falling to the Islanders in the Stanley Cup finals in 1983, Edmonton turned the tables on New York in 1984, claiming its first of five titles in a seven-year stretch. Edmonton's run of dominance included 1985, when the Oilers knocked off the Philadelphia Flyers in five games for their second championship in as many years.

Many expected the 1985–86 Oilers to cap the three-peat. They were loaded, scoring 426 goals by playing an uptempo brand of hockey that exhilarated fans. Wayne Gretzky set NHL records with 215 points and 163 assists, marks that still stand and likely will never come close to being broken again. Edmonton had four 100-plus point producers, including Jari Kurri, who led the league with 68 goals, and defenseman Paul Coffey, who registered 138 points and 90 assists.

Edmonton rolled to 119 points and the inaugural Presidents' Trophy, then swept the Vancouver Canucks—who finished 60 points worse in the regular season standings—in the best-of-five Smythe Division semifinals.

But the Oilers were unseated in 1986 by their provincial rivals who finished 30 points worse in the standings.

After the Calgary Flames stole Game 1, 4–1, in Edmonton, the teams split the next five games, setting up a do-or-die Game 7 at Northlands Coliseum. With the score tied at 2 in the waning stages of the third period, Edmonton defenseman Steve Smith tried to start a breakout from behind his own net, but his pass clipped goalie Grant Fuhr's skate and bounced into the net, propelling the Flames to a stunning, and now-infamous, 3–2 win.

The victory marked Calgary's only series win over the Oilers in four head-to-head playoff meetings during the decade, and the Flames followed with a seven-game win over the upstart St. Louis Blues to reach the Stanley Cup finals.

In the Wales Conference, the Flyers were flying high under head coach Mike Keenan. The Flyers had moved on from the Broad Street Bullies teams of the 1970s and were remade with offensive stars like Brian Propp, Peter Zezel, Murray Craven, and Rick Tocchet. Propp led the Flyers with 97 points, Tim Kerr scored an eye-popping 58 goals, and former Whalers defenseman Mark Howe finished third with 84 points.

Contrary to Edmonton's run-and-gun style, the Flyers were more balanced, surrendering a league-low 241 goals en route to a 53-23-4 record. Philadelphia ripped off 15 of its first 17 games, including 13 straight wins at one point. The Flyers bookended their 110-point regular season with an 11-2 stretch to finish three points better than the Washington Capitals for the Patrick Division regular-season championship.

"There was a constant drive to finish high, employed by the Flyers organization, and most visibly by their coach Mike Keenan," said Mike Emrick, the team's play-by-play broadcaster at the time. "They blasted through the regular season."

The Flyers achieved all that with heavy hearts. After winning the Vezina Trophy as the NHL's best goalie in 1985, goaltender Pelle Lindbergh entered the 1985–86 season aiming to lift the team over the top.

But Lindbergh was driving from a team party through southern New Jersey and lost control of his Porsche and crashed into a wall at 5:41 a.m. Lindbergh was declared brain dead and was taken off life support November 11. It was later discovered that Lindbergh had a blood-alcohol level of 0.24—still nearly two-and-a-half times the legal .10 limit at the time, and three times the current standard of .08.

The Flyers donned sewn #31s on their shoulders. But with hockey to be played, Bob Froese took over the starting role and went 31-10-3 with a 2.55 goals-against average.

As the postseason opened, Washington looked like the only squad that could unseat the Flyers in the Wales Conference, and the Caps met the advanced billing, rolling to a three-game sweep over the Islanders in the first round.

Yet Philadelphia's hockey faithful had its eyes fixed well beyond that.

"Expectations in Philly were for a showdown with the only other team to get that many points, Edmonton," Emrick recalled. "Just like '85, just like '87."

But the mighty Flyers had their hands full with Vezina Trophy winner John Vanbiesbrouck and the upstart New York Rangers.

New York and Philadelphia share a rivalry in every sport, and the NHL was no different. The rivalry between the Rangers and Flyers was really taking off, as the teams had met in five of the previous seven postseasons—including Philadelphia's dominant three-game sweep in the 1985 Patrick Division semifinals.

The players, fan bases—even the front offices—hated each other. When longtime Flyers coach Fred Shero, who led Philadelphia to consecutive Stanley Cup championships, resigned to join the Rangers in 1978, Flyers fans scorned him for more than 30 years. Shero's replacement Bob McCammon famously dubbed the Rangers "smurfs" because of their small players in blue shirts.

The Flyers had home-ice advantage in 1986 by finishing 32 points better than New York in the standings. Still, the Rangers' shocking 6–2 Game 1 win at the Spectrum set the defending conference champs on their heels.

"The Rangers came in totally relaxed and had nothing to lose," Emrick said.

Philadelphia rebounded to win Game 2, 2–1—outshooting the beleaguered Rangers 44 to 12—then built a 2–1 advantage in Game 3 in New York. But the Blueshirts rallied with four third-period goals, taking a 5–2 victory. The Flyers's 7–1 rout in Game 4 forced a do-or-die Game 5 in Philadelphia, one that many predicted would go to the home team.

But New York refused to wilt. Despite a raucous crowd spurred on by Renée Veneziale's rendition of "God Bless America," the Rangers were the aggressors from the opening faceoff. Pierre Larouche's first-period goal, his third of the series at 11:52, put New York ahead.

Willie Huber snapped a 1–1 tie midway through the second, and Vanbiesbrouck's 34 saves keyed New York's series-clinching, 5–2 win, that sent the heavily favored Flyers home.

Vanbiesbrouck stopped 150 of 163 shots faced (.920), and Ted Sator's defensive style stymied some of Philadelphia's big guns, limiting the club to three power-play goals in 27 man-advantage opportunities.

"Vanbiesbrouck was incredible in that series," said Propp in 2018.

Propp had just two points, a pair of assists, in the series, and the pressure of a do-or-die game against an upstart opponent got to the Flyers.

"Mark Howe was not playing well in that series; he wasn't as sure-handed as he'd been," Hackel recalled. "Expectations got to [the Flyers], and they found themselves in a Game 5 on home ice. And you could feel it in the building. They were booing the Flyers."

But according to Howe, he and the Flyers had run out of steam after a season's worth of drama.

"By the end of the year, I think [Lindbergh's death] took its toll on the whole team," Howe said. "The Rangers played well. You've got to give them credit, but we lost a goalie who had gotten to the playoffs and the finals the year before, . . . and I just think our team was worn out.

"I'm not blaming our goaltending by any means, but I just think we were more confident with Pelle in the net because he had proven to us that he was capable of doing the job and he had gotten us through the year before."

The series closed the doors on the Spectrum for that season, and anger turned to shock as the speed of the exit dawned on the fans.

"I recall the silence in the Spectrum after the handshakes and then the anger and yelling," Emrick said. "They were used to better. And in a week, after a spectacular season, thanks to Pierre Larouche, Barry Beck, Mike Ridley and others labeled as 'smurfs' in an earlier part of the decade, they were gone."

The Rangers then stunned the Capitals in six games in the Patrick Division finals—becoming the first sub-.500 team to win back-to-back series against 100-point opponents—leaving New York one series win from the Stanley Cup finals.

New York would meet the Adams Division champion, and with four teams packed within eight points, that crown was up for grabs.

In the 1980s, the Adams Division may not have been the NHL's best division, but it was the sport's most competitive. Four different teams won the regular-season crown in a four-season stretch, as only the Buffalo Sabres failed to finish first between 1982 and 1992.

The division featured an array of superstars. The Whalers of course had Kevin Dineen and Ron Francis. Buffalo featured forwards Dave Andreychuk and Gilbert Perreault. The Montreal Canadiens still had Hall of Famers Larry Robinson, Guy Lafleur, Guy Carbonneau, and Patrick Roy in goal. In Boston, there was Raymond Bourque, Cam Neely, Craig Janney, and Andy Moog. The Quebec Nordiques had the highly feared Stastny brothers.

In 1985–86, every team posted at least 80 points. The Nordiques were that season's division champions, and they were loaded. The top line of Anton and Peter Stastny and Michel Goulet combined for 300 points, and Quebec potted 330 goals—an average of more than four per game. Peter Stastny had 122 points himself, sixth most in the NHL.

"The Stastnys were really smart players," said Whalers defenseman Ulf Samuelsson. "I kept trying to go hard against them like violent, but those guys were so far ahead of me in their thought process that they changed my whole approach in how I defended against them."

Many expected the Adams Division to be decided again between Quebec and Montreal. The provincial rivals had met each of the previous two postseasons, including in 1984 when in Game 6—later known as the Good Friday Massacre—Montreal came back from 2–0 down to win 5–3 in a game that featured 222 penalty minutes.

The Canadiens, thanks to a 4–2 win in their final regular-season game, finished one point ahead of the third-seeded Boston Bruins and earned home-ice advantage in the other division semifinal. The Canadiens won three close games, two by one goal, to sweep Boston and advance to the division finals for the third straight year.

The Hartford Whalers were the number-four seed, gearing up for their first playoff series in six years. To win their first postseason series since their WHA days, the Whalers would have to supplant the Nordiques—the division champion and their former WHA rivals.

"We had real tough games," Quenneville said. "We had a real tough draw. They were good in their own building."

Few knew much about the Whalers at that time, and many thought Quebec would send Hartford a swift playoff exit. After all, the Nords were loaded with playoff experience. Quebec had been to the playoffs in five of its first six NHL seasons and had reached the Wales Conference finals twice in that stretch, including 1985 where it lost to the Flyers in six games.

The Whalers organization had never won a playoff game, let alone a playoff round, and only six players on the team's roster had even skated in a postseason game.

"I'm sure someone on our team must have had some playoff experience," Ferraro recalled with a laugh in 2013.

Yet the Whalers were confident as they took the ice for Game 1 of the Adams Division semis at Le Colisée in Quebec. With 11 players in their Game 1 lineup age 25 or younger, they felt they had little to lose. Plus Hartford entered the postseason with just one loss in their final 11 regular-season games.

"We were playing a level where you seem invincible," said defenseman Dave Babych. "It gets contagious."

"We entered that series on a roll," Baldwin said.

The Whalers and Nordiques split their eight regular-season meetings, but Quebec came out with renewed fervor in Game 1, and only Liut kept Hartford in the game. Quebec peppered shots on Liut and the shellshocked Whalers—posting seven in the first four minutes and 16 in the first frame—then struck first on Anton Stastny's power-play goal less than three minutes into the game.

The Whalers were outshot badly, but Liut helped Hartford find its way.

"They outshot us like 10–0," Ferraro said. "Mike was terrific, and somewhere in there we found our game."

When Dean Evason tied the score late in the period, the Whalers started to believe. And as the high-powered Nordiques failed to convert on six of their seven power plays—including a third-period, two-man advantage—or any of the 37 other unsuccessful shots on goal, Hartford took the chance to seize the game.

Anderson broke the tie on a power-play goal in the third, and even though the Whalers blew the advantage, they still felt good as the teams went to overtime tied at 2 in the series opener.

And then they stole the home-ice advantage early in the extra frame.

Wayne Babych forced a turnover behind the net, and Sylvain Turgeon beat Quebec goalie Clint Malarchuk to the short side at 2:36 of the extra session, boosting Hartford to a 3–2 win in Game 1.

It was the first playoff win in team history and put them in the proverbial catbird seat. Exacerbating tensions for the heavily favored Nordiques, Game 2 was the next night. Mere hours after its Game 1 upset, Hartford went for the throat in Game 2 and gained it.

"The heat was really on them in Game 2," Ferraro said. "Before they realized they were in a series, they were down 2–0 at home."

In Game 2, it was the Whalers who posted the fast start. Hartford outshot Quebec 16–8 in the first period, and Stew Gavin scored just 3:53 into the game. Paul MacDermid potted the first of his two goals, and the Whalers enjoyed a 3–0 edge they would not relinquish.

Mike Liut's 26 saves lifted the Whalers to a 4–1 win that boosted them to a commanding 2–0 advantage that left Le Colisée and the Nordiques stunned.

"We needed some goaltending, and we got it," Quenneville said. "Winning those games in their building was huge for momentum."

After claiming the first two in Quebec, Hartford went home to claim its first NHL playoff series. The city was pent up with excitement, preparing to host its second-ever playoff game in the NHL with the added exuberance of a potential clinching game.

After playing a tight, defensive style in Quebec, Hartford aimed to breakout, and the raucous crowd spirited Hartford early. The club fed off the energy, and after John Anderson drew a penalty 81 seconds into the game, Kevin Dineen's power-play goal gave Hartford the lead just 2:29 in.

Dave Tippett's short-handed goal, less than four minutes later, further incited the Hartford faithful. The Nordiques answered on the power play and cut the lead to 2–1, but defenseman Randy Moller was given a game misconduct midway through the first, leaving Quebec with just five defensemen.

The first was an end-to-end, penalty-marred period—with more than 50 minutes of time assessed. Each side scored short-handed and on the power play, and it appeared the Nordiques would exit in the first period within a goal as the seconds waned.

But Ferraro's power-play goal with 40 seconds left, Hartford's second with the man advantage, sent the Whalers to the locker room with a 4–2 lead.

"It got a little crazy there in Game 3," Quenneville recalled. "We had a lot of penalties, and we had a great start, which put us in a great position."

Evans and Co. had not allowed the Stastnys a first-period goal and went to work on slowing the Nordiques' role players. Meanwhile, facing backup goalie Mario Gosselin instead of Malarchuk, the Whalers dominated in period two.

Malarchuk allowed 11 goals in just seven-plus periods, but Gosselin was no match for Hartford either. The Whalers scored three second-period goals, taking a 7–3 lead into the second intermission. As the advantage became 8–4, then ultimately 9–4, and the seconds waned, the Whalers faithful grew louder. They roared, waving towels and serenading Quebec with the "Na na na. Hey hey hey. Goodbye!" song chant as the game entered the final minute. They counted down the seconds to zero until the Whalers were victorious.

"I don't think people had a handle on how good those Whalers were," Hackel said. "They had good players, a good goaltender, a balanced system and were more balanced than Quebec."

Posterity showed that Quebec was a great collection of talent, but a shallow one. And injuries decimated them, particularly on their blue line. Besides losing Moller in Game 3, Nordiques defensemen Normand Rochefort and David Shaw both missed the series with injuries.

"The Nordiques weren't healthy," Hackel said. "The Nordiques were a one-line team. If you could shut down the Stastnys, you could beat them."

For the first and only time in their NHL history, the Hartford Whalers were moving on.

Chapter 6

The Quebec Failures

If hockey in Quebec is a religion, the Montreal Forum was the region's house of worship.

The Forum was a pilgrimage for hockey fans around the world, and Les Habitantes have been blessed by their sweater, dubbed La Sainte-Flanelle—or The Holy Flannel in French.

The Forum, with its ghosts of playoffs past, had been the site of Canadiens miracles since 1926. By the spring of 1986, no road club had the audacity to claim the Stanley Cup at the expense of the Canadiens inside the Forum's hallowed walls, while Canadiens fans had watched their own team clinch 11 of their record 21 Cup titles there.

It was an intimidating place to play, with its aura and the most passionate and knowledgeable fans looming over the rink. Plus you never knew if Jean Béliveau, Yvon Cournoyer, Maurice Richard, or any of the other all-time greats would return to stare down from the rafters.

Even if you conquered all that, which most NHL teams didn't, the Canadiens themselves were always a daunting foe.

"The Forum was just an incredible atmosphere, and really had this aura about it and mystique," said Kevin Dineen, a Whalers forward who was born in Quebec City. "So many Cups won, and so many incredible players that have gone through there, but as much as it was the building or the jersey, you know, we were playing a pretty good team."

Led by coaching mastermind Scotty Bowman, the Canadiens lost just 46 regular-season games in a four-year span between 1975 and 1979, with just 13 coming at the Forum. Montreal lost only four home playoff games in that stretch, as the Habs cruised to four straight Stanley Cup championships.

The infamous "Too Many Men on the Ice" game in 1979, in which the Boston Bruins were assessed that penalty while leading 4–3 with less than three minutes left in Game 7 of their NHL semifinal series, fed the Forum's lore—ultimately leading to Guy Lafleur's game-tying goal, Montreal's stunning Game 7 win, and its Cup championship over the New York Rangers.

But by 1986, the Canadiens seemed less intimidating. Bowman had stepped down after the 1979 championship, and goalie Ken Dryden, just 31 years old at the time, retired to pursue a law career. Bowman's successor, Bernie Geoffrion, lasted just 35 games before a stomach ailment forced him into retirement. The Canadiens won the Norris Division in 1979–80, finishing with 107 points, but after a sweep of the Whalers, they were stunned in the NHL quarter-finals by the Minnesota North Stars in seven games.

And thus started a six-year doldrum period for Montreal. The Canadiens finished with at least 98 regular-season points, then were ousted in the playoffs' first round in three straight years. In 1983–84, they finished with just 75 points—their fewest in 31 seasons—and although budding bench boss Jacques Lemaire led them to a surprise trip to the conference finals, they were dispatched by the New York Islanders in six games.

When Lemaire stepped aside after a seven-game series loss to the Nordiques in 1985, the Canadiens were rife with youngsters like 24-year-old defenseman Chris Chelios, 19-year-old Petr Svoboda, and rookies Stéphane Richer, Brian Skrudland, Claude Lemieux, and goalie Patrick Roy. Even head coach Jean Perron was in his first year as bench boss.

Defenseman Larry Robinson, who anchored their blue line, and center Bob Gainey were the lone holdovers from the dynasty days, and it wasn't expected to be a banner year—even as stars like Mats Naslund and Bobby Smith put up gaudy numbers, and the Canadiens allowed the fourth-fewest goals in the NHL.

Yet when the top-seeded Quebec Nordiques were swept out of the playoffs, the Canadiens suddenly became the favorite to claim the Adams Division championship.

Montreal was loaded with depth on defense, at center, and in goal. Gainey and Guy Carbonneau created a veritable one-two defensive punch, plus they were set up in goal with Patrick Roy.

Roy, just 20 at the time, had a 23-18-3 record in 47 games played in 1985–86 and was just beginning to revolutionize the goalie position.

By the time his 19-season NHL career was finished, Roy would finish with three Vezina Trophies as NHL's top goalie, three Conn Smythe Trophies, five Jennings Trophies, 11 All-Star Game appearances, and the most wins in NHL history (551)—a mark that has since been surpassed only by fellow Hall of Famer Martin Brodeur.

But Roy's biggest contribution was pioneering a new era of goaltending. While many netminders were still playing the stand-up, blocking style in goal, Roy's goalie coach Francois Allaire was an expert and visionary in the craft, teaching Roy the butterfly style—one that was just becoming en vogue.

The butterfly is all about positioning. When a goalie goes "into the butterfly," he is on his knees, keeping his legs spread in opposite directions to block the net's lower quadrants. A butterfly goalie's upper body meanwhile is spread wide to defend against high shots—ultimately, resembling a butterfly while in this position.

The butterfly works because goalies give shooters very small holes to aim for and remain positionally sound to stop the puck even when they can't see it. Hall of Famers Glenn Hall and Gump Worsley had actually played the butterfly in their heydays, but both were smaller than the 6-foot, 2-inch, 185-pound Roy—an athletic freak at the time.

"Roy would go down on every shot, and you couldn't beat him," former NHL director of communications Stu Hackel recalled. "If you watched him during practice, he worked very hard on his technique, on squaring to shooters.

"Nobody knew what to think of him."

Montreal fans, some of the most conservative in the NHL, had their minds blown by Roy's antics, which ran contrary to Dryden's demure nature.

"He was very charismatic," Hackel said. "He would talk to his goal posts; he would eat fast food all the time. He did all these strange things that were the opposite of Dryden."

But Roy was fiercely competitive and refused to back down from a challenge. He twice fought Detroit Red Wings goalies, first squaring off against Mike Vernon in 1997 before throwing hands with Chris Osgood a year later. He would talk trash, either on the ice or in the media, and famously beefed with Blackhawks forward Jeremy Roenick during the 1996 playoffs when Roenick quipped about Roy's poor play earlier in their series.

"I can't really hear what Jeremy says because I've got my two Stanley Cup rings plugged in my ears," Roy told reporters.

Yet like Dryden, Roy endeared himself to the Montreal faithful in his first postseason. Roy had stopped 72 of 78 shots faced (.923), and Montreal swept Boston with three straight wins.

The prospect of playing for a division championship was exciting for the Hartford Whalers—a franchise coming off both its first three playoff wins and the first postseason series win in its NHL history. But playing Game 1 at the Montreal Forum added an emotional background to the Whalers' run to the Stanley Cup.

"Anytime you get to play a playoff series in Montreal, it's a very special event," Whalers goalie Mike Liut said. "We felt we were good enough to compete."

"It was magical," said Whalers defenseman Ulf Samuelsson. "That's one of the most famous places to play in the hockey world. To be able to play in front of those fans and in that whole city everything was geared toward that series."

On the surface, the confident Whalers entered their Adams Division final showdown against the Canadiens with little to lose. But in hindsight the series served as a crossroads for the franchise's future, mostly because of how it played out.

The Forum was fired up for another dramatic playoff series, and they outplayed Hartford from the start—outshooting Hartford 14–4 in the first frame. Only Mike Liut kept the Whalers afloat as they went to the dressing room scoreless after one.

Hartford settled in and gained confidence, then Stew Gavin broke the ice at 4:24 of the second period—the first of his two goals in the game and the Whalers' three second-period goals against Roy.

Liut stopped 26 of the 27 shots Montreal threw at him, and Hartford claimed a 4–1 victory in Game 1 for the Whalers' fourth straight playoff win.

"We had a lot of confidence coming out of that first-round series," forward Dave Tippett said. "We felt we were underdogs, then we went into their building and stole Game 1."

The Whalers had the chance to take the series by the throat but were outplayed again early in Game 2. Montreal outshot Hartford 15–2 in the first, and this time they cashed in twice. Guy Carbonneau's second of the game made it 3–0 early in the second period, and even as the Whalers peppered 23 shots at Roy in the game's final two periods, the goaltender stood strong, claiming a 3–1 win that sent the series to Hartford even.

The series swung back in Montreal's favor in Game 3 in Hartford. Liut was injured during the first period, forcing backup goalie Steve Weeks into action. The Canadiens smelled blood and built a 3–0 lead midway through the second period and won the game, 4–1, taking a 2–1 lead in the best-of-seven series.

Liut was not available again, thrusting Weeks into action again for the all-important Game 4 on home ice.

"It was a tough spot for a backup goalie," Liut said.

The Scarborough, Ontario–born goalie was an 11th-round pick of the New York Rangers. He was a veteran of five NHL playoff games and even fought Islanders forward Duane Sutter in Game 1 of the 1982 Patrick Division semifinals.

As backup to Liut, Weeks had played only 27 games during the regular season, but he was magnificent in Game 4, allowing only Mats Naslund's third-period, power-play goal. After Torrie Robertson's apparent go-ahead goal late in the third was waved off, the Whalers entered overtime even at one needing a boost.

And that's when one of their team leaders delivered.

If Ron Francis was the face of the Whalers, Kevin Dineen was the team's heart.

Francis was a skilled forward who put up points in the high-flying 1980s, but Dineen was the traditional Canadian hockey player—who played with skill, tenacity, and grit and was a thorn in the sides of opponents for his nearly two-decade NHL career.

"I think Kevin was a heck of a player," said Francis, the Whalers captain and Dineen's line-mate for much of their tenure in Hartford. "He worked hard every period, every shift, every game. He was tenacious on hunting down pucks. He wasn't going to let anyone stop him from getting to the front of the net or get in his way of having the chance to score a goal."

Dineen scored 355 career NHL goals in 1,188 games, yet his penalty-minute totals were a more accurate assessment of his style of play, as he averaged about one minor penalty per game with 2,229 career minutes in the box.

Dineen was born in Quebec City but raised in Toronto. His father Bill was a hockey lifer. The former Whalers scout and coach, who spent the bulk of his career in the American and Western Hockey Leagues, played 323 NHL games then carved out a coaching and scouting career.

Thus Kevin Dineen became a hockey lifer too, who moved around the country with his dad, mom Pat, and brothers Peter and Gord. Peter, Gord, and Kevin essentially grew up in hockey locker rooms, and it showed as each enjoyed a decade-plus NHL career.

"You see it in the NHL now, and so many players, their dad may have played, and part of that is the way they grew up around the locker room," Dineen said. "Hanging out with the guys and drinking sports drinks and eating bubble gum and skating with a bunch of guys is a pretty neat thing to be able to do. So it was a natural progression."

Kevin was the most skilled hockey player in his family but also benefited from being the youngest. He didn't back down and wouldn't put up with nonsense from any opponent—as proven by his famous midseason fight with Mike Milbury.

Despite his family name and pedigree, and summer training at the Okanagan Hockey School in Penticton, British Columbia, Kevin only ascended to Junior "B" hockey in the greater Toronto area, mostly because he was living in Houston—with his dad coaching the WHA's

Aeros—around the time he'd gotten picked to play junior hockey. Some of the Toronto-based junior "A" players play in the Ontario Hockey League and get drafted in the first round by an NHL team, but Kevin fell through the cracks, instead landing at the University of Denver on a hockey scholarship as a defenseman.

Kevin watched Peter and Gord get drafted by the Philadelphia Flyers and New York Islanders, then became the third Dineen drafted in as many years when the Whalers selected him with the 56th pick in 1982. His brothers still don't let Kevin forget that he was the only family member picked by the patriarch.

"My brothers used to love to tease me about that," Dineen said. "They used to say 'the only reason you got drafted is because of dad.'"

Kevin had immense pride and took being drafted by his dad's team almost as an insult. Henceforth, he played hockey like he had something to prove, and the results followed. He moved to forward during training camp before the 1983–84 season and spent that year playing the wing for the Canadian national team at the Sarajevo Olympics. He started the 1984–85 season with the Whalers' AHL affiliate in Binghamton but was called up December 3, 1984, as the start of Hartford's youth movement that season.

A shoulder sprain, broken knuckle, and sprained knee cost him 23 games and the opportunity to finish first on the team in any statistical category in 1985–86. But Dineen still did it all in his sophomore season, scoring 33 goals and 68 points. He even posted 124 penalty minutes, fifth-most on the team, and longtime Connecticut sports reporter Jeff Jacobs has referred to Dineen as "John Wayne on skates."

"He was a sparkplug," said Whalers defenseman Joel Quenneville. "When the team needed a boost, it felt like Kevin was always in the middle of it all."

Dineen had two shots on goal and had taken two minor penalties by the end of regulation for Game 4 of the 1986 Adams Division finals. But sitting in the locker room at the Hartford Civic Center waiting for overtime he felt he hadn't yet put his stamp on the game.

"I had a pretty solid series up to that point but had a pretty quiet night," Dineen said.

But that's when he rose to the occasion and further cemented his legacy in Hartford.

Thanks to a pesky forecheck, the Canadiens had trouble exiting the Hartford zone, and the right-hand shooting Dineen picked up the puck at center ice, turned on a dime and carried it into Montreal's zone on his off-wing with speed.

Patrolling the right-defense position for Montreal was Larry Robinson, aptly nicknamed "Big Bird" for his 6-foot, 4-inch stature that loomed over opposition. Robinson was a two-time Norris Trophy winner as the sport's best defenseman, and though he was 34 at the time, he was still dominating his craft. In 1985–86, Robinson had 63 assists, led all Canadiens defenders with 82 points, and was a team-best plus-25 during the regular season.

But in overtime of Game 4, Dineen showed little respect for the stalwart defender. Robinson was caught flat-footed and tried to cut Dineen off at the half-wall, but Dineen sped past him on his backhand, then quickly stickhandling to his forehand, and flipped a shot past Roy's stick and over his shoulder.

"You kind of see an opportunity, and sometimes the easiest guy to beat, even if it's one of if not the best player that's ever played that position, when somebody's coming at you it's pretty tough to start backtracking," Dineen said. "To be able to make that turn and then just get it on net and get a pretty good shot off, that was a pretty cool moment to say the least."

Dineen celebrated the series-knotting goal by leaping into line-mate John Anderson's arms. It was his first overtime game winning goal in the Whalers' first playoff overtime win at the Civic Center, and the place went into delirium.

"My fondest single memory in the building was Dineen's OT goal against the Canadiens in Game 4 1986," said Sean Pendergast, a Simsbury, Connecticut, native and Whalers fan. "Loudest hockey arena I've ever been in when that happened."

The noise even emanated on the Whalers bench.

"That was as loud as I'd ever heard the Hartford Civic Center," Tippett said.

The pandemonium spilled out onto the streets as 15,000-plus departed with their team two wins from the conference finals. Dineen's winner also made Steve Weeks a victorious netminder. The backup keeper stopped 18 shots to pick up his second career playoff win and knot the series at two.

"Steve was outstanding in Game 4," Liut recalled.

The series shifted back to Montreal for a pivotal Game 5 where Weeks aimed for a duplicate performance.

Instead, the Canadiens' aura took over.

Boston Bruins general manager Harry Sinden notoriously griped about the officiating in Montreal, saying "death, taxes and the first penalty at the Forum" were the list of life's certainties. In the crucial Game 5, sure enough, Hartford's Dean Evason was cited for tripping 1:52 into the game, and just 13 seconds later, Claude Lemieux put Montreal up, 1–0.

The early goal sent the Canadiens to a dominant first period as they outshot the Whalers 16–8 and netted three early goals.

The Whalers scratched back behind two goals from Dineen. Yet every time Hartford clawed closer, outshooting Montreal 12–5 in the second frame, the Canadiens had an answer. First, it was low-scoring defenseman Mike Lalor's only goal of the postseason, less than two minutes after Dineen's second marker, that ballooned Montreal's lead back to 4–2.

Then the Canadiens shut it down. Even as Dineen picked up his third point of the game, the secondary assist on John Anderson's goal, the Whalers managed just three shots on Roy in the third period. The Canadiens claimed a 5–3 win in Game 5 that sent the series back to Hartford with the Whalers facing elimination.

Weeks stopped just 25 of 30 shots in Game 5, and with Liut healthy enough, coach Jack Evans went with his number-one goalie in the elimination game. With a berth in the Wales Conference finals at stake, Montreal went for the jugular, swarming the Whalers' cage and peppering Liut with shots.

He stopped 14 in the first period and 32 with his team's season on the line. Meanwhile, the Whalers managed just 17 shots on Roy but found the one that mattered most. Dineen's goal, his team-leading sixth of the playoffs at 7:30 of the second period, pushed the Whalers within minutes of a Game 7.

"He had a flair for scoring the big goal," Quenneville said.

Liut and the Whalers hung on for a 1–0 victory, and the Civic Center faithful serenaded the Canadiens with a "Na, na, na, na. Hey, hey, hey. Goodbye!" Taking the Canadiens to a seventh game was cause for celebration, but Whalers fans were hopeful they'd get to see their team against the New York Rangers in the conference finals.

The series shifted back to the Forum, and the Whalers were suddenly confident, even without leading-scorer Sylvain Turgeon. Turgeon had scored 45 regular-season goals and two more in the playoffs, but after taking the warmup before Game 7, he could not overcome an abdominal ailment that forced him to miss the series finale.

Turgeon's career ultimately was doomed by the abdominal ailment that stemmed initially from a groin injury. Yet some believe he should have been able to go in Game 7.

"Turgeon pulled himself out of game seven," *Hartford Courant* beat reporter Bruce Berlet said.

Hartford could have used its leading scorer in the early going as the Canadiens outshot the Whalers for the sixth time in seven games. It also could have used Turgeon on one of its four first-period power plays as the officiating favored the Whalers.

But not only did the Whalers not score, extending their lengthy man advantage drought to 21, they let the Canadiens take the lead, as Mike McPhee beat Liut on a short-handed breakaway with just 1:13 in the first frame that whipped the Forum into a frenzy.

Liut kept the Whalers in the game, stopping 30 shots in the crucial game including 12 in the third period as Montreal tried to put the game away. On the other end, Roy refused to relent, making key saves especially early in the third.

The Canadiens held the slim 1–0 lead as it reached crunch time in Game 7. Yet, Hartford wasn't ready to wilt just yet.

With less than three minutes in regulation, the Canadiens were peppering the Hartford net in search of the goal that would put the game out of reach. But after a pass handcuffed forward Mats Naslund, the Whalers picked up the puck and counterpunched.

Dean Evason carried the puck through the neutral zone on a seemingly innocuous play. Three Canadiens defenders were back, including Robinson, and the winger crossed the blue line and dropped a pass for Dave Babych.

The Whalers had acquired Babych from the Winnipeg Jets for Ray Neufeld on November 21, 1985, and the defenseman scored 53 points in 62 games in Hartford. As the calendar flipped to the postseason, Babych became less of an offensive factor, posting just three assists through nine games.

"I think Emile Francis was trying to piece some things together," Babych said in 2018. "When I got here, the team was terrific. We were young, and maybe missing a few pieces, but not a lot."

But as the clock ticked toward midnight on the Whalers' Cinderella hopes, Babych struck. He smoked a shot from just inside the blue line, and it eluded Roy's glove and tied the score, stunning the Forum into silence and sending the Whalers bench into bedlam.

When the siren sounded, ending regulation, the clubs went to their respective dressing rooms tied at 1. Montreal was 1-6-7 in overtime during the regular season—and 0-1 in the playoffs in extra time—and had its chances dampened further by losing top-line forward Stéphane Richer to a leg injury with just 48 seconds remaining in regulation.

The Whalers looked like a team of destiny.

"To a man, we thought we were going to win in overtime," Liut said.

The Whalers were confident, but could not muster a shot on goal after Babych's game-tying goal—more than eight minutes of game action—and the overtime did not last long.

Less than two minutes into overtime, Dineen tried to be the hero yet again. He carried the puck across the Montreal blue line and dropped a pass for Ferraro, who faked a slap shot then deked around Robinson and skated in on Roy.

John Anderson was cutting toward the goal, and Ferraro tried to slip him a pass that could've been the game-winning goal.

"I should've shot it, and I passed it," Ferraro recalled.

Less than four minutes later, a new hero in Canadiens lore was born.

Claude Lemieux was a pest for his entire 21-season NHL career.

Lemieux's nickname was "Pepe"—playfully nicknamed for his surname's similarity to the cartoon skunk Pepe Le Pew and also after his tenacious and irritating style. Lemieux was a Kevin Dineen clone, only he somehow managed to be even better at it.

"He was just an agitator with a lot of skill," Whalers defenseman Ulf Samuelsson said. "He could play any game. He was really skilled and he was physical and pretty sound positionally. He was also a really good hockey player, but he ended up getting mixed up with some extra activities, which made things more interesting."

Through six games of the Whalers series, he scored three goals and racked up 18 penalty minutes and mixed it up with Samuelsson in both Games 4 and 6 at the Civic Center.

Lemieux was not one to back down from a challenge, and it showed again in overtime of Game 7. After Samuelsson nailed him with a cross check from behind, Lemieux got up and delivered a hit on Whalers defenseman Tim Bothwell.

Lemieux's physical play allowed the Canadiens to keep the puck in their offensive zone, and he went to work with line-mates Brian Skrudland and Mike McPhee, Stéphane Richer's replacement on that line.

McPhee drove the net on Bothwell, pushing him into Liut, and while that was happening, Lemieux shook off Hartford forward Paul MacDermid from behind the goal, took the puck on his backhand, and walked to the front of the net.

Bothwell lunged at the right-handed shooter, but Lemieux curled around the barreling defenseman to the right circle and flung a backhand shot at Liut. Ordinarily, Liut would have covered the top corner, but because of the heavy traffic, Lemieux's shot eluded the netminder and found the back of the net for the game-winning goal at 5:55.

"Lemieux's goal was a bit of a fluke," Liut recalled. "We had a great chance, and the puck came back into our end. One of their players and our defenseman crashed into me at the post just as Lemieux came out of the corner with the puck. He was about to backhand it as I was caught against the post. I don't think he looked. It just found the net."

While Lemieux exalted by diving at the feet of his exuberant teammates, the dejected Whalers were left to wonder what might have been.

"We were stunned, no doubt," Liut said. "We thought the game was ours . . . they got the break, and we didn't."

That sentiment pervaded Hartford's dressing room. Some shook off tears after the harrowing loss.

"We played so good," Samuelsson said. "There was almost disbelief when they won the game because I thought for sure we were capable of doing some damage that year."

Lemieux went on to score four more postseason goals, capping the playoffs with a team-best 10, and Roy took the first of his record three Conn Smythe Trophies as they forever cemented their places in Canadiens lore. The Whalers had pushed the Canadiens to the brink, but Montreal did not sweat after that, winning eight of its next 10 while claiming the franchise's 23rd Stanley Cup title.

Even Montreal appreciated what it had overcome against Hartford.

"When they won [in Game 5 of the Stanley Cup finals] in Calgary, Bob Gainey was talking about the fact that the Whalers were the toughest out," Jacobs said. "They were as good as anybody. They took the Stanley Cup champions to seven games and overtime."

Emile Francis addressed the Whalers on their team bus, declaring his pride for their work and that they would be back in the years ahead. About three decades later, many from that team still appreciate being a part of the Whalers' greatest series.

"And Montreal went on to win the Cup," Quenneville said. "That game seven could've gone either way. We played really well."

"The games were so competitive," Tippett said in 2013. "It was an unbelievable series to be a part of."

Some are certain they'd have brought the Cup back to Hartford if they simply would have scored in overtime.

"We beat the hell out of the Rangers during that year, and even when we played Calgary we beat them too," defenseman Dave Babych said in 2018. "We'd have gotten to the finals."

Ron Francis had cracked two ribs in Game 3 of Hartford's series with Quebec but played all seven games against Montreal. He did not have a point in the series and felt like he let his teammates down.

"It was a frustrating series for me, even more so in the sense that you're banged up and you don't feel like you can contribute like you know you can," he said. "That's frustrating because you go to war with these guys each and every night, and you want to be part of them having success and winning games, and when you can't do that it's frustrating."

Even though the Whalers were stung by the sudden exit, the community celebrated their successful season. Some went to Hartford's Bradley Airport to greet the team upon their return. Others even showed up at Mike Liut's house simply to offer condolences after the loss.

But the biggest move came from managing general partner Howard Baldwin and the city of Hartford, which threw the Whalers a parade mere days after their elimination—and while the playoffs were still going on.

About 20,000 Hartford fans lined the route with blown-up whales and signs to celebrate the Adams Division's fourth-place finish. Some point to the downtown parade as proof of the organization's minor-league trappings. Years later, Peter Karmanos, then the organization's owner, mocked the parade. Even Baldwin, 25 years later, cringed at the thought of it.

"I thought it was a very nice gesture but inappropriate," said Chuck Kaiton, the Whalers radio announcer who did not attend the parade in 1986. "It had never happened before—a parade for reaching the second round—and I'm an old-school type that believes a parade should be for the Cup winner.

"Nobody twisted my arm and said I had to be there. I remember watching it on TV, happy I didn't have to participate. It was a principle thing. Unless you win it all, you look like idiots."

But it was a hit with the players.

"The parade was somewhat misunderstood," Liut said. "Hartford was essentially community-owned, and I think the fans merely wanted to show appreciation to what was a very exciting two months of hockey. It could've been a rally. It could've been a luncheon. Someone decided on a parade. We had fun with it."

"I think it was certainly sincere, meaning everybody's heart was in the right place," said Kevin Dineen. "There was a passion there, and I think people really wanted to show it. I think it is something that, to me, I look back at it with fond memories as one of the good memories in Hartford that showed that people were engaged and enthused and didn't want [the season] to end."

That fun spilled over into the 1986–87 season. The same core was intact and as the season approached, the Whalers were met by an unusual guest: expectations. And on opening night, the Whalers gave their fans a sign of what was to come throughout the regular season.

Hartford trailed the Calgary Flames 5–2 in the third period but scored four third-period goals. Joel Quenneville, who had just three goals that season, improbably scored the game-winner with just 20 seconds in regulation to secure a wild 6–5 win in Hartford's opener over the reigning Campbell Conference champs.

The 1986–87 Whalers played exactly to Jack Evans's identity. They were strong in goal, disciplined, and good defensively, with enough of an offensive punch to keep them in games. The Whalers' 270 goals allowed were the third-fewest in the NHL, and their 1,496 penalty minutes were a league low.

The Whalers had strong balance too. They had eight players score 20-plus goals, led by Kevin Dineen's 40. Ron Francis posted 93 points, with 63 assists, and although Sylvain Turgeon was sidelined half the campaign with that abdominal ailment, John Anderson picked up the slack, posting 75 points.

"What I remember was how balanced we were," Quenneville recalled. "We had three lines that could score, and we had a lot of depth in the back end and had a good goalie."

The Whalers also finally enjoyed good health in 1986–87. Eleven players played at least 70 games. Hartford did not dominate any single long-term stretch but was the Adams Division's best team from start to finish.

"We had playoff success the year before, and our team continued to grow from those experiences," Tippett said. "We played very well on a consistent basis."

Hartford finally had a winner on its hands, and the crowds came in droves. The Whalers finished 13th in the NHL in attendance, averaging more than 14,230 fans—the Civic Center capacity was 15,126. The Whalers even celebrated forward Doug Jarvis that season, who broke the NHL's ironman streak by playing in his 915th straight game in front of a sellout crowd at the Civic Center on December 26.

But ever trying to attract more area support, the team commissioned a music video, "Whalermania," during the season. Each player appears in the awesomely cheesy, and totally 80s, pop video clad in a white shirt that says "Whaler Mania" in blue font while sporting his finest blue jeans.

The 1985 Chicago Bears had risen to the top of the charts with their now-famous "Super Bowl Shuffle," and since sports are a copycat business, the Whalers tried their hands at making a music video too.

Forward Paul Lawless served as the lead singer—or more accurately lead lip syncer—clad in aviator sunglasses and an electric guitar around his neck. Captain Ron Francis was behind him, also with a black electric guitar but with black Wayfarer-style sunglasses. Kevin Dineen delivered an epic saxophone solo as general manager Emile Francis stood at the front of the team, conducting as the rest of the team pretended to sing the chorus:

Be a part of Whalermania.
Be a part, a part of the fun.
Come see the Hartford Whalers become hockey's number one.
Be a part of the excitement.
Be a part, a part of the team.
Bring the Stanley Cup to Hartford.
It's the Hartford Whalers dream.

"The Bears had done a video, so we said we can do it too," Lawless said. "We were just lip syncing, and they had just told us that's what we're going to sing."

Defenseman Joel Quenneville admitted to the *Chicago Sun-Times* in 2016 he wasn't in "Whalermania." There are definitely other ex-Whalers who wish they weren't.

"I think that was a pretty sheepish moment for all of us," Dineen said in 2019. "I think we all realized that we were not at our best in that kind of environment."

"I tried to block that one out," Francis said. "In a perfect world you're probably hiding in the back row; unfortunately I was more towards the front. At least I wasn't the lead singer."

The video can now be quickly discovered with a simple YouTube search, but at the time, the Whalers threw it in as the final scene of their video yearbook, which they sold in their team store.

There was no sweating a playoff berth in 1986–87. Hartford finished fourth in the NHL in points with 93—only Philadelphia, Edmonton, and Calgary finished the regular season with more. Although it took until the season's penultimate day, the Whalers claimed their first and only Adams Division crown, edging out Montreal and its 92 points.

"It was a nice feather in our caps," Tippett said of winning the division championship.

For the first time, the Whalers would open their playoff season at the Civic Center. They'd also meet a familiar opponent.

The Stanley Cup playoffs are perhaps the most unfair postseason tournament in all of North American sports.

The 1986 postseason proved this when all hell broke loose and each division winner failed to reach the final four. Although the best team in each conference reached the Stanley Cup finals, the 1987 playoffs reinforced the unfairness.

For the second straight year, the Whalers squared off against the Quebec Nordiques in the Adams Division semifinals. Unlike the previous four seasons, the Nordiques were in shambles entering the 1987 playoffs.

Quebec still boasted some of the most feared offensive players in the game: Peter and Anton Stastny and Michel Goulet. Yet, like the Whalers of 1985–86, injuries and inconsistent play bit the Nordiques. Quebec finished just 20th in goals in the 21-team NHL after losing star forward Peter Stastny for 20 regular-season games with a variety of injuries.

Michel Bergeron managed to last the season, but Quebec's 31-39-10 record ultimately cost the head coach his job.

The Nordiques goaltending also was inconsistent. Starter Clint Malarchuk was just 18-26-9 and had been supplanted by backup Mario Gosselin, who was 13-11-1 after taking over starter's duties in January.

The Nordiques still had pedigree—1987 was their seventh straight trip to the postseason—and they entered their playoff year seeking revenge. They were confident they could hang with the heavily favored Whalers, even though they finished 21 points behind Hartford in the standings. Gosselin boasted that he'd "bet the farm" on a Quebec win.

What many didn't know was Bergeron had a trick up his sleeve. He remembered how undisciplined the Nordiques had been the year prior and how it had doomed them, particularly in the penalty-marred Game 3. He sought to get under Hartford's skin in the same way the Whalers had done to the Nordiques in 1986.

After Peter Stastny put the Nordiques ahead just 1:59 into Game 1, Whalers defenseman Scot Kleinendorst and Quebec's Mike Hough—who got the secondary assist on Stastny's marker—each got six minutes in penalties as they scuffled while the Nordiques celebrated. Kleinendorst and Hough's duel incited a penalty-marred first period, which set the tone for the series.

"We had penalty problems," Whalers defenseman Joel Quenneville said. "They were a division rival, and we took some uncharacteristic penalties."

At 3:06, all 10 on the ice were sent to the penalty box when a full line brawl broke out. Whalers defenseman Ulf Samuelsson was issued a game misconduct for being the third-man in on Randy Moller's fight with Dave Tippett.

"I didn't have a good series," Samuelsson said in 2020. "I was not as disciplined as I would like to have been, and I think that had something to do with the outcome of the series."

Thirty-eight penalties, resulting in 92 penalty minutes, were assessed in the game's first period, including Samuelsson's ejection, yet the Nordiques led 1–0 after 20 minutes. Quebec made it hurt further on the scoreboard when Robert Picard made it 2–0 at 6:32 of the second.

Things looked bleak until Hough's major penalty for cross-checking gave the Whalers a five-minute power play, and when John Anderson struck late in the man-advantage, the Whalers had life.

Hartford peppered Gosselin with shots, outshooting Quebec 13–4 in the third period, and when Dean Evason beat the beleaguered netminder with 12:12 in regulation, tying the game at 2, the Civic Center's 15,000-plus went mad.

The Nordiques tried to beat the clock before overtime, but John Ogrodnick's chance crossed the line after the clocks ticked zero, and just like Game 1 of 1986, the clubs went to an extra session.

And just like Game 1 the previous year, the Whalers took the series lead early when Paul MacDermid redirected Randy Ladouceur's shot past Gosselin, claiming Game 1 for the home team, 3–2.

Despite Gosselin's 38 saves Bergeron went to Malarchuk in goal in Game 2 the next night. And although the second game was more to Jack Evans's liking in terms of Hartford's discipline, the Nordiques once again led by a goal after the first period.

But the Whalers struck for four straight goals, three in the second period, to take a commanding 5–2 lead.

Yet, also on-par with the series's themes, Quebec scored a pair of goals in the third, cutting the lead to one. And while Hartford held on for a 5–4 win, the series's tide swung drastically, thanks in part to the NHL's playoff-format change, which Quebec had directly influenced.

The Whalers had stolen the first two games at Le Colisée in the 1986 postseason. They and the New York Rangers enjoyed success in winning three games to advance, but that year wound up being the last in which the first round was a best-of-five series.

Flyers owner Ed Snider was furious about his team's early exit. He and Nordiques owner Marcel Aubut decided to cook up change.

"If you lose Game 1 in a best-of-five series at home, you're in trouble," former NHL director of communications Stu Hackel said. "The Flyers and Nordiques had two of the big mouths at the Board of Governors meetings. They were innovative guys who were behind the playoffs, and it would not surprise me if they were the forces behind ending the best three out of five."

The 1986–87 season was the first to go best-of-seven in the first round, as the owners had no problem agreeing to at least one more home playoff game box-office gate. In the postseason, players only earn bonuses based on the rounds they win, and with zero for expenses and near guaranteed sellouts, home playoff dates are extremely lucrative for owners and their bottom lines.

So with a 2–0 series lead, the Whalers went to Quebec City needing to win two games instead of one to advance. Getting home, Bergeron stirred up some chaos, and the sleeping giants in Quebec awoke thanks largely to its special teams.

"Those games could've gone either way," Tippett said, referencing Games 1 and 2. "They were a desperate, desperate team."

The rough stuff started just 30 seconds into Game 3 when MacDermid and Nordiques tough guy Basil McRae dropped the gloves, earning McRae 17 minutes in penalties. The Whalers' power play had netted man-up goals in each of the first two games, and hopes were high when they got a power play just 47 seconds into Game 3, when Paul Gillis was charged with cross checking.

But the always-dangerous Peter Stastny was on the ice to kill the penalty, and when he saw an opening, he struck for a short-handed goal, giving the Nordiques the lead and whipping Le Colisée into a frenzy just 80 seconds in.

Stastny carried Quebec to a 5–1 win, capping the hat trick with a second-period, power-play goal. A night later, it was Goulet, the Stastny brothers' line-mate, who potted three goals as the Nordiques blitzed Hartford 4–1.

Suddenly, the series was even and shifting back to Hartford.

There were more than 330 penalty minutes in the two games in Quebec City, and that burned Hartford too. Top defenseman Ulf Samuelsson was suspended for the pivotal Game 5 in Hartford after picking up his second game misconduct of the series—after making an obscene gesture toward the Nordiques bench. More than 15,000 people packed into the Civic Center for the biggest game in Hartford since the previous year's Game 6 against Montreal.

And that was when Bergeron unleashed another trick he had up his sleeve.

Dale Hunter possessed two hockey gifts: a hellacious slap shot and a fierce knack for getting under his opponent's skin.

Nordiques coach Michel Bergeron famously referred to Hunter as "La Petite Peste," or "The Nuisance" in French. The Nordiques ultimately ended up trading him to Washington after the 1986–87 season—a move that many felt led to the franchise's relocation to Colorado in 1995.

As the NHL cliche goes, Hunter played to the edge, and sometimes went over it. Hunter's most famous playoff action came with the Capitals in 1993 when he separated Pierre Turgeon's shoulder with a post-goal cheap shot—an act that landed the enforcer a then-record 21-game suspension.

But like Claude Lemieux the year prior, the Nordiques forward also had a knack for scoring goals and points, and angering opponents at key times. Although a broken leg cost Hunter 44 games in the regular season, he returned no worse for wear come playoff time.

In the first-round series with the Whalers, Hunter became the most marked man. He also became an X-factor, which Bergeron used to wreak havoc on the Whalers. Hunter posted 56 playoff penalty minutes, and his Game 5 double-minor for high sticking led to Mike McEwan's power-play goal that gave Hartford a 2–1 lead in the first.

Hunter registered only an assist, a secondary helper on John Ogrodnick's game-tying, second-period goal, but he toyed with the Whalers' psyche in Game 5. The Whalers, playing without suspended defenseman Ulf Samuelsson, began to unravel, and the Quebec power play began to heat up.

"Dale Hunter was a smart player," Whalers defenseman Joel Quenneville said. "He knew what to do to draw us into taking penalties."

Hartford was caught in a web of penalties, and the Nordiques cashed in, spearheaded by defenseman Risto Siltanen. Siltanen endured a roller-coaster, three-and-a-half season tenure in Hartford before being traded during 1985–86 for John Anderson, then was dreadful in the Nordiques' playoff loss to the Whalers in 1986.

But a year later in the series's biggest game, the Finnish-born blue liner could do no wrong. Siltanen set a Stanley Cup playoff record for assists by a defenseman with five, four of which were primary helpers.

Quebec scored five power-play goals on nine man-up opportunities in Game 5, yet Hartford was still even thanks to Stew Gavin's goal at 11:19 of the third period. Gavin's goal sent the sold-out crowd into delirium, with many thinking the clubs would be headed to overtime again.

But Quebec was lifted by a third straight hat trick. This time it was Ogrodnick, who capped the hat trick by beating Liut with just 1:07 remaining. The Whalers outshot the Nordiques 43–24, but after Mike Eagles's empty-net goal, the Nordiques had their third straight win and first-ever playoff victory at the Civic Center, 7–5.

"When we came back to tie the game, I thought we would win it," Jack Evans said after the game. "It's a tough loss after coming back from a two-goal deficit, but we took penalties we shouldn't have and didn't contain their power play."

Facing elimination, Hartford built a 4–1 lead in Game 6 thanks to Dineen's second goal early in the second. The Whalers' power play, which was just two for 27 in their seven-game loss to Montreal the year prior—and entered Game 6 mired in a two-for-22 drought in the 1987 playoffs—had struck twice, and it looked as though a Game 7 would be coming in Hartford.

But Quebec goaded Dean Evason, Hartford's leading postseason goal scorer, into a game misconduct, which fired up the Whalers bench. Dineen lost his cool and took a penalty for interference, and Peter Stastny struck on the ensuing power play, cutting the lead to 4–2.

Stastny's goal opened the floodgates, as Quebec netted three straight and two on the power play. The frustrated Whalers couldn't stem the tide, and as the white-clad Quebec fans pumped energy into the Nordiques, they made Hartford pay just about every time—including Jason Lafreniere's power-play goal that tied the game at 7:05 of the third.

"Somewhere the Nordiques left us this scouting report that they could push us around and wanted to hit us," Whalers forward Ray Ferraro said. "I think we showed them how tough we were by taking a million penalties."

The clubs went to overtime tied at four, then Hunter made the Whalers pay again—this time with his skill. Just six minutes in, the Whalers set up a forecheck to try and force a turnover from David Shaw, who carried the puck behind his own net. Shaw quickly moved the puck to Randy Moller, who skated ahead at the half boards and found Hunter at the Nordiques' blue line.

Hunter stickhandled to his backhand and flipped a pass to the streaking Peter Stastny, who had gotten behind Whalers defensemen Joel Quenneville and Dave Babych. The Czech-born superstar closed in on Liut, deked from his backhand to his forehand, then snuck the puck past the beleaguered goalie's extended right leg.

Le Colisée went mad as the lights went out, spotlighting Stastny and the jubilant Nordiques, who flooded the ice to mob their superstar forward. In response to the Civic Center's unfriendly dismissal of Quebec a year ago, the crowd sang "Na na na na. Hey hey hey. Goodbye!" as the dejected Whalers lined up to shake hands with their slayers.

"When the momentum in a series starts, it's hard to slow the tide," Ferraro said. "We were a really good team, and we came apart at the seams."

Quenneville, Tippett, Samuelsson, Dineen, and many other Whalers players have become elite NHL coaches. Quenneville won the Stanley Cup three times as head coach of the Chicago Blackhawks, including in 2015 when Dineen was his top assistant. Tippett is widely considered one of the best coaches of his era, guiding upstart programs in Dallas and Arizona to the Western Conference finals before taking the Edmonton Oilers head coaching position in 2019.

Yet, this brilliant collection of hockey minds was somehow no match for Dale Hunter and the rest of the Quebec Nordiques' antics. Hartford was charged with 313 penalty minutes, and the Nordiques scored 12 power-play goals in six games.

"They looked like they were really good and really disciplined coming in," Jacobs said. "They had all these future coaches on the roster, and it all got out of hand when Dale Hunter got on the ice."

Just like that, the greatest season in Hartford Whalers history was over.

And that's also when things began to unravel in Hartford.

The Carolina Hurricanes took the ice in the Hartford Whalers' iconic uniforms for their game against the Boston Bruins on December 23, 2018, in Raleigh, North Carolina. Former Whalers great Mike Rogers dropped the puck for the ceremonial faceoff, and Hartford mascot Pucky the Whale also was back for the first of Carolina's "Whalers Night" celebrations. COURTESY OF THE CAROLINA HURRICANES

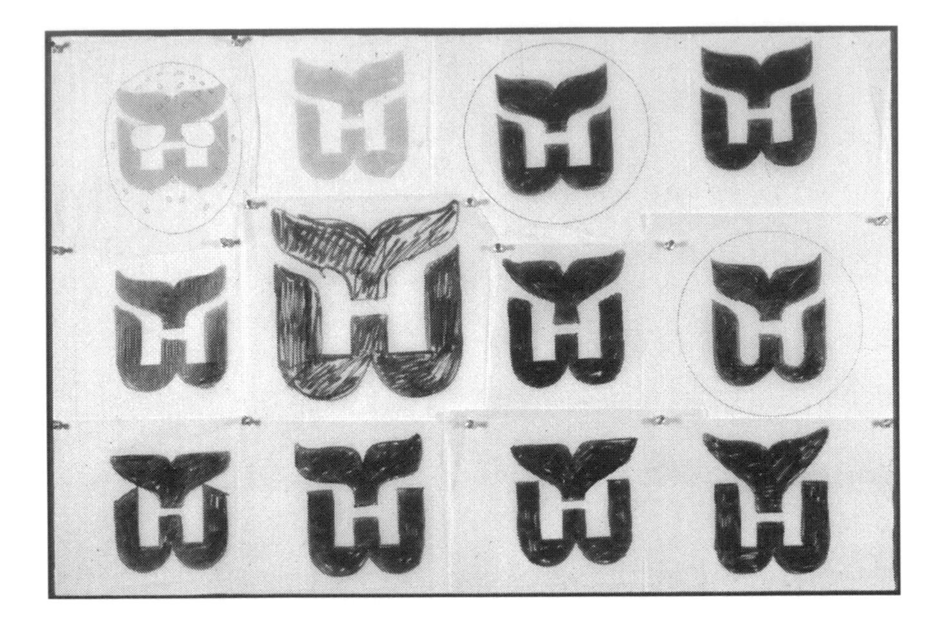

Connecticut-based artist Peter Good dabbled with a slew of options before developing the Whalers now-iconic logo. COURTESY OF PETER GOOD

Howard Baldwin put the WHA's New England Whalers on the map by signing Gordie, Mark, and Marty Howe, all pictured at their introductory press conference in 1977, which also helped the team gain entrance to the NHL in 1979. BOB CHILD/ ASSOCIATED PRESS

The Hartford Civic Center's famous roof collapse in 1978 nearly doomed the franchise but ironically helped them gain access to the NHL. Hartford's community leaders helped fund renovations, which also raised the arena's seating capacity and allowed the Whalers to play eighteen years in the NHL. BOB CHILD/ ASSOCIATED PRESS

Goalie Sean Burke was one of the brightest spots for the Whalers during the 1990s and started their final game in Hartford against the Tampa Bay Lightning on April 13, 1997.
COURTESY OF TIM PARRY

Coach Pierre McGuire guided the team for a half season during the 1993–94 season but had difficulty keeping the team under control. He was fired at the end of the season.
COURTESY OF TIM PARRY

FILENE'
SportsC

LOUISVILLE

Many credit the Whalers' trade of captain Ron Francis (opposite, top) and Ulf Samuelsson (opposite, bottom) to the Pittsburgh Penguins for John Cullen and Zarley Zalapski (above) as a major blow to Hartford losing its NHL team. COURTESY OF TIM PARRY

Pat Verbeek, dubbed "The Little Ball of Hate," was acquired via trade from the New Jersey Devils in 1988 then took over as Whalers captain for three seasons after Ron Francis was traded to the Penguins. COURTESY OF TIM PARRY

Wayne Gretzky's trade from Edmonton to Los Angeles in 1988, and subsequent preseason tour of the United States, helped expedite the NHL's Vision of the Nineties and hastened the Whalers' departure from Hartford. COURTESY OF TIM PARRY

Chris Pronger started his Hall of Fame career in Hartford and became the most famous No. 2 pick in hockey history when the Whalers chose him in the 1992 draft. But he had a rough time adapting to the NHL with the Whalers and was traded to the St. Louis Blues for forward Brendan Shanahan in 1995. COURTESY OF TIM PARRY

Peter Karmanos Jr. claimed he knew hockey when he bought the Whalers from the State of Connecticut in 1994. Although he moved the team from Hartford in 1997, his proclamation rang true when the organization won the Stanley Cup as the Carolina Hurricanes in 2006. COURTESY OF PETER KARMANOS

More than twenty former Whalers flocked to Hartford for the 2019 Whalers Weekend at Dunkin Donuts Park in Hartford. AUTHOR PHOTO

One of the many Whalers fans who attended the 2019 Whalers Weekend at Dunkin Donuts Park helps keep the memory of the team alive. AUTHOR PHOTO

Chapter 7
The Transition

Among the Hartford Whalers' greatest assets was their community involvement.

Years before landmark local and national television deals—and even before the cable TV boom of the 1990s and 2000s—season tickets were a team's top revenue source. The NHL was, and still is, largely a niche sport, particularly in the United States. Engaging in the community was one way small markets built fans and sold tickets.

Hartford does not have a robust downtown, and it wasn't particularly lively even during the "Whalermania" period of the 1980s. ESPN employees have cited their workaholic tendencies because Bristol, a suburb 18 miles from Hartford, and central Connecticut specifically, is not particularly exciting. But it's a stable environment for wealthy people with families, like hockey players.

"I'd just gotten married and started to have a family," former Whalers forward Blaine Stoughton told NBC Sports in 2012 when asked about his time in Hartford. "Although Hartford isn't New York or Boston, at that juncture in my career, I was kind of starting to settle down a little bit, so it was a good fit."

Emile Francis had discovered the formula for success in Hartford. He targeted high-character players who created a family-style atmosphere in Hartford, where players would bond on and off the ice.

"It was a pretty special group," Whalers captain Ron Francis said. "We got along and had a good time."

Players with children settled in wealthy suburbs like West Hartford, Simsbury, Avon, and Glastonbury, and enrolled them in some of the nation's best public schools.

"I had a young family, and I thought it was a good, safe and family-oriented place to have your kids grow up," said Pat Verbeek, who lived in both Farmington and Avon after the Whalers acquired him in 1988. "It was not a big town, so you got to know a lot of the people. It had a smaller, community feel, which was good."

Former Whalers forward Ray Ferraro was in Farmington—whose town center is just 10 miles from the Civic Center.

"I just loved it," Ferraro said. "It was very vibrant in those days. There were all kinds of people downtown at all times. For a bunch of young guys, it was a fun time to live there."

Being community owned meant giving back to the community, and mostly that involved work with local charities. The team most notably worked with the UConn Children's Cancer Center, which led to the Whalers Waltz for Children, a dinner-dance that was organized by players' wives. Francis met his wife Mary Lou while representing the Whalers at a blindness-prevention fundraiser. Kevin Dineen met his wife Annie, a former nurse at Hartford Hospital, through a mutual friend who was a firefighter. Both were born and raised in the Nutmeg State.

"We did a lot of charitable functions that I thought were fantastic," Francis said. "I've always been a big fan of giving back to the community, and I don't think an organization should ask the people who spend their hard-earned money to come in and root them on and not give something back to the community. That part I had no qualms about. I think we did an outstanding job in that regard."

The insurance industry was booming, but it was the Whalers that gave Hartford a morale boost—putting Connecticut in the big leagues. The state climbed to the top of the nation's earning scale, which enabled fans to flood the Civic Center. Hartford averaged more than 14,500 fans per game for two straight years in 1986–87 and 1987–88—roughly 600 fans shy of a sellout and far greater than their regional rivals, the Boston Bruins.

"It was a gate-receipt league at the time," said Jeff Jacobs, who covered the team for the *Hartford Courant* at the time. "The gate receipts in 1986 were really good. They were in the top echelon of the league."

Before social media and million-dollar contracts, hockey players, who generally are humble and down to earth, became part of an NHL city's fabric. The Philadelphia Flyers of the 1970s were so beloved in their city because they would drink at the same local taverns as many of their blue-collar fans. In the 1980s, members of the New York Rangers endeared themselves by recording songs and participating in commercials for Sassoon Jeans.

The Whalers were no different. They did charity work and shopped at the same grocery stores as their fans. They even had a recreational softball team during the summer.

"They bought homes there and spent considerable time there in the offseason," said Rick Peckham, the team's former television play-by-play announcer. "They became part of the community."

The players bonded off the ice, with lifelong friendships forged at post-practice parties and holiday gatherings at the Francis or Dineen households, or the farm owned by Joel Quenneville and his wife Boo, also a Connecticut native.

"We were a tight-knit group," said Francis. "Whether it was a Halloween party, a lunch after practice, a dinner after a game with the girls, it was a group that really enjoyed spending time together.

"There were a lot of things we did as a group I think that contributed to the success we had on the season."

Still, after their heartbreaking seven-game series loss to the Montreal Canadiens in 1986 and a premature playoff exit to the Quebec Nordiques in 1987, the Whalers plateaued. Emile Francis tinkered with their roster, trying to find the piece that would make them legitimate Stanley Cup contenders.

But Hartford regressed in 1987–88, falling back to fourth place in the Adams Division. After a 22-25-7 start, and after a 5–4 loss in Pittsburgh on February 6, 1988, Jack "Tex" Evans was fired and was replaced by Larry Pleau. Evans was set to enter the final year of his contract and told local media he would retire after the 1988–89 season. When that got out, Emile Francis fired him.

"I didn't know the politics," Quenneville said. "He was only going to be with us one more year, and I'm not sure if 'Cat' didn't want to have a lame duck or what."

Hartford was 13-13 under Pleau, but was one of the NHL's stingiest defensive teams. The Whalers allowed 267 goals, fourth-fewest in the NHL that season. Despite finishing second-to-last in the league in goals scored, Hartford still managed to surpass the Nordiques by eight points for the Adams Division's fourth spot, reaching the postseason for the third straight season.

But Hartford had no answer for dynamic Montreal Canadiens forward Stéphane Richer, who posted 11 points in the six-game series. The Canadiens won the first three games in the series, outscoring the Whalers 11–6 in the first two before scoring three goals in a span of 5:19 in the second period in their 4–3 win in Game 3.

The Whalers rebounded in Game 4 behind two goals from Kevin Dineen and Dave Babych to stay alive with a 7–5 win at home. Then goalie Richard Brodeur, replacing starter Mike Liut who was nursing a shoulder injury, made 22 saves, and Dineen and Francis each scored, leading the Whalers to a 2–1 victory at the Montreal Forum that forced Game 6 back in Hartford.

No team had blown a 3–0 playoff series lead in the NHL since 1975, yet the Whalers were just a home win away from forcing another Game 7 at the Forum. Montreal was without its top defensive forward Bob Gainey, second-leading scorer Mats Naslund, and starting goalie Patrick Roy for Game 6, as each nursed an injury.

Yet, Richer overtook the Whalers almost singlehandedly. The dynamic forward scored two first-period goals, and the Whalers managed just 20 shots on net in Montreal's 2–1 win.

Their second straight first-round exit sent the Whalers back to the drawing board. And in that 1988 offseason, the organization would undergo a seismic change—one from which it ultimately could not recover.

Howard Baldwin was by no means wealthy; in fact, he was quite the opposite. But that did not keep him from achieving his lofty ambitions.

Baldwin, who had helped found the New England Whalers in Boston, got them an arena deal in Hartford and negotiated their entrance into the NHL, and was the master of the Whalers' community involvement. He pushed his players to engage, and he did too.

After moving the Whalers to Hartford in 1974, in an effort to raise money to keep the team afloat, Baldwin sold shares of the team to the community—16 corporations bought in including the local electric company, Connecticut Power and Light, and even the local newspaper, the *Hartford Courant*, which owned a 0.1 percent stake in the team.

Because of this arrangement, Emile Francis referred to the Whalers as the Green Bay Packers of the NHL—citing the NFL team in that sport's smallest market that has survived for nearly a century by also selling shares.

Hartford didn't have a wealthy individual owner like Peter Pocklington in Edmonton or Bruce McNall in Los Angeles. Hartford did not have a single corporate backer like the New York Rangers did in Cablevision; the Whalers got by with investments from the corporate community.

Roughly 87 percent of the team was owned by five major Hartford-based insurance companies, with Aetna owning roughly 55 percent of the franchise—serving as the team's majority controller. They ceded the day-to-day operation to Baldwin, who was named the organization's chairman and managing general partner.

Yet as the Whalers improved, and their players became visible in the region, they became more popular in Hartford and across Connecticut. Whalermania was more than just a music video, and that phase of Hartford hockey has since been dubbed "Whalers Fever" by WFSB news anchor Dennis House.

The average attendance at Whalers games rose every season from 1984 to 1988, peaking at more than 14,500 in 1987–88—a near sellout every night—even though the Whalers finished as a sub-.500 team.

Hartford did the unthinkable, outdrawing the Boston Bruins, its regional rival, in three straight seasons.

The Hartford corporate community realized the Whalers value and wanted to capitalize on it. They instructed Baldwin to find a buyer.

Baldwin quickly scrambled to cobble together the money to stay in control of the team but ultimately couldn't come up with the necessary funds, and the duo of Richard Gordon and Don Conrad stepped in to take control, paying $31 million for the Whalers on June 28, 1988.

The transaction ended the Baldwin era in Hartford. He was the remaining founding member of the organization from its World Hockey Association days and had brought major-league sports to the capital of Connecticut. The Whalers were like his child.

Hockey was not quite out of Baldwin's system. Baldwin left for Hollywood to start a film company, which produced hockey-related films like *Sudden Death* and *Mystery, Alaska*—the latter of which he worked on with David E. Kelley, the son of the Whalers inaugural coach and general manager Jack Kelley.

Baldwin married Karen Mulvihill, a producer and former television host of the Whalers, and went on to manage multiple other NHL programs—winning the Stanley Cup as co-owner of the Pittsburgh Penguins in 1992. He lives in Los Angeles today.

"On the one hand we hated to leave," Baldwin said in November 2013. "But this is what the partnership and the owners had wanted, and we had started a film company and it was doing well."

Conrad and Gordon assuaged fears that the organization was in peril, proclaiming they would retain Emile Francis and that team would remain in Hartford.

"In many respects, the Whalers are Hartford, and they will always be playing in Hartford," Conrad told the *New Haven Register* after the sale.

Baldwin's departure was the first domino to fall in the dooming of Hartford's hockey club, but not for the reasons people generally think. Gordon came in as a quiet type who had made his money in the real estate industry, and Conrad, Aetna's boss, was backing him financially, which meant the Whalers went from a collection of corporate backers to just two men who were previously invested already.

Conrad had been instrumental in the Whalers' first coming to Hartford and then their entrance to the NHL. He and Baldwin had spearheaded the effort to renovate the Hartford Civic Center's roof when it collapsed in 1978.

"Howard Baldwin, Donald Conrad and the Hartford Whalers are the kind of people who make the National Hockey League one of the strongest leagues in professional sports," NHL president John Ziegler said in 1980. "The Whalers have made a commitment to their city, their fans and the NHL."

Gordon wasn't into hockey or sports, but he liked the limelight from owning the Whalers. He was from Rochester, New York, but had been a longtime lawyer and developer in Hartford and appreciated the Whalers' impact on the region.

"Richard's heart was always in the right place," said John Forslund, who worked for Gordon as the team's public relations director starting in 1991. "His hunger to win was huge. His loyalty to Hartford was equally huge."

As Gordon came to power he developed a brain-trust of high-profile athletes like former Dallas Cowboys quarterback Roger Staubach, and professional tennis players Ivan Lendl and Renee Richards. Gordon grew close with Bobby Orr, the former Boston Bruins defenseman, and named him a consultant with the Whalers.

Gordon wanted to be a hands-on owner but didn't have the requisite hockey knowledge that came with being such. He also couldn't stand relinquishing power to Conrad—or anyone for that matter.

With Conrad and Gordon sharing the majority ownership stake, a clause was written into their franchise purchase agreement that either could buy the other out after one year of ownership, and their relationship quickly became strained. Gordon launched the first grenade in March by threatening to buy out his co-owner.

Conrad fired back, saying he'd be bought out "over his dead body," then declared himself the buyer—which by the contract's right, he had 10 days to do. Ultimately Gordon reigned—Conrad sold his shares to Colonial Realty—and was declared majority owner of the Whalers on June 18, 1989.

Conrad loved the Whalers, and things may have been different if he had retained the controlling interest. Also Colonial Realty was later unveiled as a Ponzi scheme, which put Gordon behind the financial eight-ball. They scammed 6,800 people out of an estimated $350 million, including Gordon, and Colonial filed for bankruptcy in Fall 1990. Connecticut fell into a recession, and Ben Sisti, the realtor's founder and Gordon's financial backer, ultimately went to prison for nine years.

Economics may have screwed up the Whalers, but every fan and pundit has his own opinion about when things went south—including ex-Whalers forward Ray Ferraro.

"The first major blunder by management was leaving Stew Gavin on waivers," Ferraro recalled in 2013, 25 years after he'd been let go. "They were in a perpetual scramble from there. We thought we were a player or two away from competing, and we went the other way."

Gavin, a valuable yet unsung player who scored 57 goals in three seasons in Hartford, helped the North Stars reach the Stanley Cup finals in 1991, posting 13 points and playing all 21 games that postseason. To Ferraro's point, Francis continued to tinker in 1988–89, making five transactions, and three in-season trades, that did little to aid the on-ice product.

The financial debacle coincided with the University of Connecticut's meteoric rise in men's basketball. The Huskies had hired Braintree, Massachusetts, native Jim Calhoun away from Northeastern University in 1986, and in his second season, with future NBA players Clifford Robinson and Chris Smith, the Huskies posted a 20-14 record and won the National Invitational Tournament.

The Whalers still had a consistent team, but the Richard Gordon era was defined by organizational micromanaging and inconsistent goaltending—especially in the postseason.

Mike Liut missed more time with a shoulder ailment that forced Peter Sidorkiewicz into action. Sidorkiewicz filled in admirably, with four shutouts and a team-leading 22 wins, earning first-team NHL All-Rookie honors, but protecting the net would soon become a problem.

Liut's absence was part of a broad pattern of injuries for that season's team. A broken finger sidelined Ron Francis for 11 games, but he still finished as the team's second-leading scorer, scoring 29 goals and 77 points.

Only Ferraro and Dave Tippett dodged the injury bug enough to play all 80 games.

The team finished 37-38-5, still good enough to reach the Adams Division playoffs and meet the division-champion Montreal Canadiens for the second straight year.

Unlike the 1988 season, when they lost to the Boston Bruins in five games in the Adams Division finals, the Canadiens were a force. Coached by rookie Pat Burns, Montreal finished with 115 points, the most in the Wales Conference. They also were balanced, finishing first in goals-against (218) and fifth in goals scored (315).

The Whalers battled the Buffalo Sabres for third place in the Adams Division, and the right to play the Bruins instead of Montreal, to the regular season's bitter end. Hartford entered its final game two points back of Buffalo, but a 3–2 loss to the Bruins, coupled with the Sabres' win against the Quebec Nordiques, left Hartford in fourth.

Pleau went with rookie Kay Whitmore in goal for Hartford's playoff opener ahead of Sidorkiewicz, and starter Mike Liut who had battled through injury and inconsistency. Whitmore was the 26th pick in the 1985 NHL Draft, and the organization deemed him its goalie of the future. He'd played well in three games late in the year, winning two games and stopping 86 of 96 shots (.896)

But facing mighty Montreal, Whitmore struggled by allowing six goals on 33 shots in Hartford's 6–2 loss in Game 1. Pleau went to Sidorkiewicz for Game 2, and he didn't look much better, surrendering three goals on 17 shots before allowing five tallies on just 28 shots in a 5–4 overtime loss in Game 3 in Hartford.

The Whalers went back to Whitmore for the 4–3 overtime loss in Game 4 in Hartford, in which the goalie's brutal turnover led to Russ Courtnall's game-winning goal that capped a sweep at the hands of the eventual Wales Conference champions. However, more troubling than the swift playoff exit was the size of the crowds at the Civic Center. Neither of Hartford's home playoff games was sold out, and thousands of seats were empty for Hartford's season-ending loss in Game 4—official attendance was 12,245, the fewest attendees for a Whalers game since 1986.

The Whalers' average attendance dipped below 14,000 in that season for the first time since the 1984–85 season. After two straight first-round exits, then falling behind 2–0 in the series to the Canadiens, the bloom had come off the Whalers' rose as first-round exits are not exactly enticing.

Fans had become cynical, writing off the Whalers' chances against mighty Montreal. Although upsets have typically been the norm in the NHL playoffs, few wanted to shell out playoff prices to watch the Whalers lose to the Canadiens for a second straight season.

Gordon enacted further change. He fired Emile Francis after the playoff defeat and replaced him with Pittsburgh Penguins assistant general manager Eddie Johnston.

Johnston swiftly ousted Larry Pleau as head coach, ending Pleau's 17-year affiliation as a player, coach, and general manager for the team. Former defenseman Rick Ley took over as head coach.

Francis had built the club from scratch. He was the architect who had turned a 19-54-7 team into the Adams Division champion. Francis retained the title of president, but Johnston began calling the shots with personnel decisions.

"There was a transition there," former Whalers forward Dave Tippett said. "You went from Emile Francis and Jack Evans and Larry Pleau to a new GM and a new coach."

Many point to Francis's departure as another precursor to the Whalers' demise. Yet, at the time Johnston was widely known as the man who had drafted Mario Lemieux in Pittsburgh, so the move from the old-school Francis to the forward-thinking Johnston was considered a good one.

Johnston wanted the Whalers to be more accountable. Hiring Ley—the tough, stay-at-home Whalers defenseman in the WHA and NHL—was also keeping things in the family.

Johnston's first major move came on draft day, when he dealt oft-injured forward Sylvain Turgeon to the New Jersey Devils for Pat Verbeek. Turgeon was 11th on the team in scoring in 1989—he played just 42 games that season, registering only 30 points while dealing with his cranky abdominal ailment and a separated shoulder.

Verbeek was dubbed "little ball of hate"—years before Bruins fans gave forward Brad Marchand the same moniker—as he stood just 5 foot, 9 inches but got the most out of his frame by playing a fiery and tenacious style. He scored 46 goals but also posted 227 penalty minutes as part of the 1987–88 New Jersey Devils that lost to the Boston Bruins in the Wales Conference finals and fell one game short of the Stanley Cup finals.

"It was a really great trade," said Jeff Jacobs, who covered the team for the *Hartford Courant*. "Rick Ley loved Pat Verbeek. He was his type of player, and Pat became a leader [in Hartford]."

Verbeek was fishing in the woods of Ontario when the Whalers acquired him and didn't know he'd been dealt until hours later. He'd been the subject of trade rumors, and he was motivated by the trade to Hartford.

"It was a little bit shocking, I guess," Verbeek said. "It was unexpected but exciting. It was the start of a new chapter of my career."

The Whalers looked very different when opening night came against the Canadiens. Ley was behind the bench, and Johnston was in the rafters. New players like Verbeek and defenseman Adam Burt, the franchise's second-round draft pick in 1987, were in the lineup.

While the faces changed, the result, a 4–1 Montreal win, was the same, and so was a disappointing crowd at the Civic Center. Only 13,066, more than 2,000 short of a sellout, watched Patrick Roy stop 30 shots in the opener, continuing the Canadiens' ownership of Hartford.

Kevin Dineen and Ulf Samuelsson each missed the club's opener, but Hartford's goaltending, and Ley's use of it, became the story in the season's early-going. When starter Mike Liut injured his knee on December 7, his third consecutive season with a serious injury, Sidorkiewicz was thrust into action and would not relinquish the starting role.

After losing seven of his first nine starts, the 27-year-old lost just one of his first seven after Liut was shelved, and the Whalers trailed the Boston Bruins and Montreal Canadiens by just five points for home-ice advantage in the Adams Division on January 1.

The Whalers' playoff spot was never in doubt—the Quebec Nordiques posted just 12 wins in 80 games, and Hartford clinched a postseason berth in February. Liut returned on February 1, but was pulled in his third start back after allowing four goals on 13 shots in Hartford's 7–3 loss to the Canadiens on February 17.

Sidorkiewicz had earned the net. He posted good numbers as Hartford's starter, and that, coupled with Liut's injuries and management's wishes to find time for Whitmore, signaled the end to the great goaltender's time in Hartford.

On March 6, the Whalers traded Liut to the Washington Capitals for forward Yvon Corriveau. The move was met with almost immediate resistance from Whalers fans, and also Liut's wife, Mary Anne, who told the *New Haven Register* "We're very upset about the trade."

Liut, more than 20 years later, still recalled his disappointment about leaving.

"I was much more disappointed about the trade from Hartford," he said in 2012. "It was a really good place to play, and as a family, we enjoyed Hartford very much."

Liut's departure continued Hartford's transition from the Baldwin-Francis club to that of Gordon-Johnston. The core of Dineen, Samuelsson, and Ron Francis was still intact, but Liut was the netminder who had backstopped Hartford to its only NHL series win and the Adams Division championship a year later.

Still, like hiring Johnston, the move to get younger could not be second-guessed at the time. Sidorkiewicz and the Whalers finished with 85 points, their most since 1986–87.

Yet, playing in the NHL's toughest division—Hartford would've finished no worse than third in any other division and would have won the Patrick Division—the fourth-placed Whalers had to meet their regional rival and the Presidents' Trophy–winning Boston Bruins, in the Adams Division semifinals.

"We finished seventh overall in the league and were fourth in our division," Verbeek said. "We had a pretty tough division. We had a pretty good team and ran into some tough competition."

Boston loomed just 100 miles northeast of Hartford, and had long been a thorn in the Whalers' sides. They first tried to block Hartford's entrance into the NHL in 1979, then set up roadblocks in the Whalers' fight for success in the major leagues.

Boston had pushed for the New England Whalers to change their name to Hartford—since the teams shared the region in the NHL. Also despite the fact the Whalers started their NHL tenure in Springfield, Massachusetts, they were unable to market their team above the Connecticut border—since the Bruins claimed Massachusetts as their marketing territory. As time went by, major sponsorships in Springfield and western Massachusetts dried up in Hartford because of the region's loyalty to Boston.

Boston also is New England's regional hub, and hockey was the only pro sport where allegiances were divided at the time. Old rooting habits die hard, which means even though many Whalers fans were also supporters of the Patriots, Red Sox, and Celtics, hockey loyalties in Connecticut—particularly in the north, central, and east—still remained with the Bruins.

"It was one of the most underrated rivalries of that era," said Sean Pendergast, a Simsbury, Connecticut native. "It was very painful for us Whale fans. I'll always remember those arguments as one of the fun parts of my childhood."

Winning a playoff series against the Bruins in 1990 would've been a major score for the Whalers, as Hartford and Boston had not yet met in the postseason. The Bruins were strong. Coached by first-year bench boss and former hard-nosed defenseman Mike Milbury, led by goaltenders Reggie Lemelin and Andy Moog, and with a strong defense spearheaded by 29-year old Raymond Bourque, the Big Bad Bruins finished first in points and allowed the fewest goals in the NHL (232).

The Bruins' top line featured Bob Carpenter, Craig Janney, and leading scorer Cam Neely—who had 55 goals in 1989–90. That troika made up three of Boston's top-four scorers, with Bourque finishing second. The 1989–90 Whalers were good—probably the second-best team in their NHL history—but they'd have their hands full with such a dynamic and balanced team, particularly without Kevin Dineen, who missed Game 1 with a back injury.

The Bruins posed a mighty threat, but the Game 1 venue, Boston Garden, was less daunting than previous playoff arenas. The 1989–90 Whalers had set a franchise record by winning 21 of their 40 road contests that year, including two wins in Boston. Hartford had finished 3-4-1 in eight regular-season games against Boston, including Sidorkiewicz's 29-save effort in Hartford's 4–3 win December 7.

As it had in its opening-round playoff series against the Quebec Nordiques four years earlier, Hartford endured an onslaught from the tough and tenacious Bruins. Sidorkiewicz was tested early, stopping the game's first eight shots.

But Todd Krygier struck on the Whalers' first shot, and Hartford held that lead after 20 minutes. Then in the middle period, the Whalers potted three more goals, taking a commanding 4–0 advantage on Randy Ladouceur's goal at 9:19.

The Bruins battled back, scoring twice before the end of the second period. But Sidorkiewicz made 33 saves, earning his first career playoff win, and the Whalers stole home-ice advantage with their 4–3 victory.

Two nights later, with Dineen back in the lineup, the Whalers strived for a commanding 2–0 edge. The Bruins also countered with a move of their own, going to Moog in goal.

Krygier registered his second playoff goal, but as usual, Hartford's power play became a problem in the playoffs, failing to score on nine chances and boosting its man-advantage drought to 14 through two games.

While the Whalers' man-advantage floundered, Boston's soared. The Bruins scored three power-play goals, and Moog stopped 25 shots in Boston's series-evening 3–1 victory.

But Boston's win came with a cost. Bourque was injured when Whalers defenseman Grant Jennings delivered a hard, clean hit late in the third period.

"I dumped the puck in and nobody went to forecheck, so I was just like 'I'll go do it,'" Jennings recalled in 2019. "So I just went in there, and I ran him. It wasn't dirty or anything, but I just body checked him, and just messed him up."

Bourque's injury, initially called a hip pointer but later revealed as a blood clot in his hip, became a huge deal for the Bruins as the series shifted to Hartford for Games 3 and 4.

Bourque holds the NHL record for most goals, assists, and points by a defenseman and was the consensus top blue liner in hockey at the time. In 1990 he was 29 and entering the prime of his Hall of Fame career. He had 84 points that season and was about to win the third of his four Norris Trophies, annually given to the NHL's best defenseman, in a five-year span.

He also quarterbacked Boston's power play, which finished third in the NHL that season, and had a point on 47 of their 83 man-advantage goals (56.6 percent).

"He was their leader. He was their best penalty killer. He was their best power-play guy. Most years he was their best player," said Whalers defenseman Ulf Samuelsson. "He was a legitimate superstar. He played hard. He had skill. I always looked at him as one of the best players I've ever seen. He was a legendary good player."

Bourque was revered in Boston but also respected on the ice by opponents. He loomed larger than his 5-foot, 11-inch frame, particularly on the ice at Boston Garden, which was just 191-by-83—nine inches shorter, and two inches narrower than the standard 200-by-85 NHL rink.

"To me, he was always the best defenseman," said Dineen. "You can talk about a lot of different guys, but his game was just so well-rounded. He was a force on offense and big and hard to play against. Some guys were bigger, some guys were faster but to me he was the complete package."

With Bourque sidelined, the Adams Division regular-season champs were looking vulnerable as more than 15,000 packed the Civic Center for the pivotal Game 3.

"The whole room said 'well we've got to take care of business now'," defenseman Brad Shaw said. "'Hey, let's try and get things done while he's out of the lineup.'"

A year earlier, huge pockets of seats were empty for both playoff games in the Nutmeg State. But with the rival Bruins in town in 1990, fans of both teams flooded the box office to secure tickets for the games, creating a wild atmosphere.

The Whalers fed off the energy and skated circles around the beleaguered Bruins, who clearly were missing their all-world defenseman. For the first time all series, the Whalers outshot the Bruins, and Shaw posted four points and played more than 27 minutes in Hartford's 5–3 victory.

"Sometimes you just get a little lucky," Shaw said of his offensive outburst. "Sometimes things go your way, and you get in a groove and everything you put on net has the chance to go in."

With the chance to take a stranglehold on the series the Whalers went for the throat. Behind another raucous, sellout crowd, Hartford seized control, chasing Lemelin for the second time in four games. The Whalers again scored on their first shot when Dean Evason struck just 78 seconds into the game, whipping the Whalers loyalists into a frenzy.

The Whalers made it 2–0 on another goal from Shaw, and after trading goals, Yvon Corriveau blew past Garry Galley and beat Lemelin on the breakaway, making it 4–1 Hartford midway through the game.

The onslaught continued, as the Whalers beat the Bruins' shellshocked goalie five times on 22 shots, building a three-goal lead after two periods. By the time Ron Francis had beaten Lemelin at 16:15 of the second, "Brass Bonanza" was ringing in the ears of Boston and Bruins fans across New England.

The Whalers were 27-1-1 in the 1989–90 season when leading after two periods, and held a three-goal lead at home against the Bruins, who were without their best player. They had chased Boston's starting goalie again, and most of the crowd was behind them. Surely the Whalers would hold on and take the commanding edge to Boston with three chances to close out the Presidents' Trophy winners.

If fate were with Hartford, that's exactly what would've happened. The Whalers would have won Game 4, ousted the Bruins in five games, then rolled through the Wales Conference en route to the Stanley Cup finals. Maybe they would've even defeated their former World Hockey Association rivals, the Edmonton Oilers, and brought the Stanley Cup to Connecticut.

Unfortunately that's when things went sideways.

The collapse started so innocuously. Dave Poulin scored just 88 seconds into the third period to cut Hartford's lead to 5–3. Some curiously deem a three-goal lead the worst in hockey, so Poulin's goal should have served as a fine wake-up call for the Whalers.

But when Moog replaced Lemelin for the third period, something else snapped in the Bruins. Boston buzzed, and after Bob Beers made it 5–4 with 13 minutes left, Dave Christian struck just 70 seconds later to tie the game. Moog stopped each of the seven shots he faced, but as the game remained even into regulation's final stages, it appeared as if the Whalers had slowed the tide.

The Whalers were closing in on overtime, and with a full intermission between the third period and extra session, perhaps they could lick their wounds and find a way to persevere in overtime. Yet, Poulin's goal—off Randy Burridge's shot-pass—beat Sidorkiewicz, and the Bruins were ahead for the first time with just 1:44 left.

"I can't explain it," Whalers forward Pat Verbeek said. "Some of the goals were the weirdest goals you've ever seen. You can't stop it. Even if you try to stop it, it just keeps rolling against you."

The Whalers became the shellshocked team. They had allowed four goals on only 11 shots in less than 20 minutes to turn a sure series win into a deadlocked, best-of-three with two games in Boston. And before the Whalers knew it, they were facing elimination, as Moog's 20-save performance keyed the Bruins' penalty-marred 3–2 victory in Game 5.

Without Bourque, and after losing Carpenter and Janney to ejection and injury respectively, the Bruins still managed to persevere in Game 5, overcoming two more Hartford leads. Sidorkiewicz stopped just 15 of 18 shots and made a key gaffe on Cam Neely's game-winning goal that broke a 2-all tie late in the second.

Facing elimination, the Whalers returned home to try to extend the series. Janney and Bourque were both still absent for Boston, but the Bruins still managed to erase a 2–0 second-period deficit and kill off three more Whalers power plays. The teams entered overtime even at 2, with the Bruins eyeing a date with the Montreal Canadiens, who had dispatched the Buffalo Sabres earlier in the evening.

But Dineen had other ideas. He redirected Dean Evason's initial try between Moog's pads to give Hartford a 3–2 win that sent the series to Boston for Game 7.

The Boston Garden was electric for the do-or-die game, particularly when Bourque returned to the Bruins lineup. His presence alone left the Whalers shaken mentally.

"To know that he was back in the lineup, and as great a player as he was and what he meant for that team, it was a tough mental hurdle for that game," Shaw said. "It was a psychological sort of barrier when he came out for warmups, and it was 'we've got to go through this guy as well, not just the rest of the team.'"

Hartford outshot Boston 18–11 in the first period, but the Bruins hurt the Whalers on the scoreboard, scoring twice in the game's first 10 minutes. Only Francis's third-period power-play goal kept the Bruins from a Game 7 shutout. The Presidents' Trophy winners claimed a 3–1 win and the series 4–3 en route to the Stanley Cup finals.

Posterity showed the Bruins' toughest Wales Conference series came against the Whalers—just as Montreal's toughest test had come against Hartford four years earlier—as Boston rolled to the Cup finals before falling to the Oilers in five games.

But the moral victory still stung the Whalers, who were eliminated in the first round for the fourth straight year, leaving them wondering what they had to do to get over the hump.

And even though the Bruins fell short of the Stanley Cup, it became clear that theirs was the model to follow—particularly with Ley behind the bench. The Whalers entered 1990–91 with the same core as the club that had taken the Wales champs to the brink of elimination.

But Johnston's moves further disenfranchised the locals. On the eve of the season opener, Johnston dealt defenseman Joel Quenneville to the Washington Capitals for cash considerations.

"I didn't play much the year before," Quenneville said of the trade. "I wasn't young. I had the opportunity to go to Washington. It wasn't long after that that I was coaching."

Dave Tippett was also shipped off to Washington for a sixth-round draft pick. Later that year, Ray Ferraro was sent to the New York Islanders for defenseman Doug Crossman, who was then flipped later that same season for defenseman Doug Houda.

"The whole nucleus of the team got traded away," Tippett said. "When you don't win, changes get made, and that's what they did."

With the Quebec Nordiques struggling again, the Whalers easily reached the postseason for the sixth straight season. But it was an uneven season to say the least, as an eight-game winless streak in late October was followed immediately by a six-game unbeaten run in mid-November.

The Whalers were coasting along to the Adams Division number-four seed, and another date with the Bruins. But with the club suffering from a dearth in scoring, Whalers management decided to take action, and the move it made led to the death knell of the NHL in Hartford.

Chapter 8

The Detonation

By 1990, Ron Francis was clearly the face of the Hartford Whalers.

He had been the Whalers' captain for five years, since the Whalers unloaded then-captain Mark Johnson in the trade that sent Mike Liut to Hartford in 1985. He made his teammates better, helping Kevin Dineen become nearly a point-per-game player during their tenure on the same line together.

"I'd like to say we played off each other, but I played off of him," Dineen said of Francis. "I'd win a puck battle in our end, and my first thought was to try to find a way to get him the puck, and then off to the net you go, and you better have your stick on the ice because he always found a way to find you."

Francis was not just uber-talented; he also loved playing in Hartford—and did everything he was asked. He was the backup guitar player in the "Whalermania" video in 1987 and played comedic DJ in their video yearbook that year. He set the example for charity work and even met his wife Mary Lou at a Whalers function in Hartford.

"In a way I kind of grew up there," Francis said.

Mary Lou, a native of Stamford, was representing Connecticut Society To Prevent Blindness after winning a beautiful-eyes contest at a Tip-A-Whaler event, and according to the *Hartford Courant*, went on their first date at George's Pizza in the Hartford suburb of Unionville.

"Mary Lou was named 'Miss Connecticut Eyes,' and all you've got to do is take one look at her and you know why," Dineen said. "It was typical

Ronnie whether it was dealing with Special Olympics, he was a big part of that during his time in Connecticut.

"As good a player as he was, certainly the quality of the person matches that."

The couple was married in Farmington, Connecticut, in 1986 and Mary Lou gave birth to their first child, Kaitlyn, in Hartford on February 5, 1991. Francis built a family in central Connecticut and made a home there. The Sault Sainte Marie, Ontario, native had developed friendships with the core teammates in Hartford.

"We had an interesting group," Francis recalled in 2013. "We had a lot of younger guys who were trying to fit in. It was a pretty special group."

Those from that team still keep in touch and spend time together—even in Connecticut. Less than two weeks after Francis was named the first general manager of the Seattle Kraken expansion NHL team in 2019, he, Dineen, and Joel Quenneville got together in the Hartford region to celebrate.

"Still to this day, I have a lot of good friends there," Francis said in 2019. "I still go back almost annually and catch up with friends and stuff."

Like the Whalers, Francis endured ups and downs. His broken ankle nearly doomed the Whalers' 1985–86 season, and cracked ribs limited him in their playoff loss to Montreal that spring. Francis played a full season only three times during his tenure in Hartford and had good but not great playoff numbers—22 points in 33 postseason games with the Whalers—while the team was eliminated from the first round four straight seasons between 1987 and 1990.

Still, Francis was the model of consistency, and there's no debating the 1989–90 season was his best with the Whalers. The superstar forward was just entering his prime, registering 101 points and finishing fifth in the Selke Trophy voting as the NHL's best defensive forward. His six points in seven playoff games were second-most for Hartford, and the 27-year-old was hoping to cash in.

Salaries were on the rise, and Francis watched his line-mate Kevin Dineen receive a four-year, $2.1 million deal from the Whalers after the 1989 season. Then Yvon Corriveau—dealt for Liut at the 1990 trade deadline—was rewarded with a multi-year extension from general manager Ed Johnston.

Francis entered the 1990–91 season in the final year of club control. Johnston failed to reach an agreement on an extension over the summer—offering Francis only a one-year, $400,000 extension with an option for a second year.

"Ronny was looking for a new contract and a big contract," said John Forslund, who was broadcasting games for Hartford's American Hockey League affiliate in Springfield, Massachusetts at the time, "and Eddie Johnston was thinking along the lines of is he elite or is he very good? When you reach the second and third round, you know what you have. But they had been bounced from the playoffs in the first round all those years."

Francis declined the offer, and the 1990–91 season was set to become the final year of his contract. Unfortunately, it all coincided with owner Richard Gordon losing his financial backer Ben Sisti to prison in the Colonial Realty Ponzi scheme.

Things reached a head on December 7, 1990. The Whalers were just 11-13-4 through 28 games, and head coach Rick Ley stripped Francis of the captain's C, going to a three-player rotation.

"They took his C," said Grant Jennings, a Whalers defenseman at the time. "You want this quality of player, and you've got to treat them accordingly, and they didn't."

Ley told reporters before a game in Buffalo he was unhappy with the club's direction, and there are many who felt Ley was behind the railroading of Francis. Ley was a hard-nosed coach and player, who at times could be resentful of superstar players. He wanted the Whalers to be tougher to play against—in an effort to knock off the Big Bad Bruins, whom they were destined to meet in the first round of the 1991 playoffs.

Ley vehemently denies any accusation that he wanted Francis out of Hartford.

"That's all ownership that wanted to move those guys," Ley said. "That wasn't any trade that we would've made."

Even without the C, Francis played well in 1990–91, posting 76 points in 67 games for Hartford. Some inside the organization were interested in mending fences and had told him they'd begin negotiating a long-term contract to remain in Hartford.

"I got a phone call the week before the trade deadline saying that they wanted to sign me," Francis said. "I was told they weren't going to trade me, that they were happy with me, and I said 'fine, we'll do it after the [trade] deadline.'

"Our concern was that they signed me and then traded me at the deadline, so if that's the case, let's wait until after the deadline and we can talk about a contract then."

It then came as a surprise to Francis, and the rest of the hockey world, that on March 4, 1991, he was the centerpiece of a six-player trade that sent the face of the Whalers to the Pittsburgh Penguins along with defensemen Grant Jennings and Ulf Samuelsson for young forwards John Cullen and Jeff Parker and defenseman Zarley Zalapski.

"It was kind of shocking," Whalers forward Pat Verbeek said. "Ronny had been there a while. He was pretty entrenched in the community. He was a great role model for the younger players, and he was a good person."

Reports and rumors swirled that Francis had asked to be dealt, but that was never the case. Francis's extended family was still in Hartford, celebrating the birth of Kaitlyn, when he had to pack his things and fly to Pittsburgh.

Francis, like Ley, has since blamed owner Richard Gordon for the trade.

"I never wanted to leave Hartford," Francis said in 2013. "We had a new owner, and we didn't see eye to eye on some things . . . I never walked in there and said 'trade me.'"

Samuelsson, arguably still Hartford's best defenseman, had threatened to move back to Sweden and play after the 1990–91 season if he didn't get a change of scenery. He didn't want to be a part of a rebuild that he could see coming.

"Even though [the Whalers] had a young team, and a good promising team, I felt like it was a little way from being a contender," Samuelsson said in 2020. "At that time I'd been in the league a while, and I really wanted to go somewhere and have success and win whether it was in the Swedish league or NHL.

"I had some conversations with my agent—I didn't have any firm demands or anything."

The players were notified late in the evening that they'd been traded. Jennings, a hard-nosed defenseman who had been in Ley's doghouse, discovered that he was going with Francis and Samuelsson only when they met at Bradley Airport for their 6:00 a.m. flight to Pittsburgh for their game against the Vancouver Canucks on March 5.

"We were all quite surprised," Jennings said. "They said, 'you're going to Pittsburgh, be on a plane tomorrow at six, and there's other people going to be in the trade.'

"We all just kind of showed up, you know, not in shock, well I'm sure Ronnie was probably shocked."

Johnston and Ley have each been saddled with the responsibility of the trade, particularly the general manager. Some within the Whalers dressing room went as far as complaining that the trade was an act of collusion from Johnston's perspective—since he had come to Hartford and ultimately wound up coaching from Pittsburgh after he was fired following the 1991–92 season.

But according to Ley, Johnston's hands were tied. Gordon had ordered him to offload some of the highest-paid players on the roster, including goalie Mike Liut and forward Paul MacDermid, who were traded a year earlier. Low-balling Francis and ultimately trading him was Gordon's end game.

Ley said he is still resentful that he and Johnston are most remembered for running Francis and Samuelsson out of town.

"I would call it resentment," Ley said in 2018. "It wasn't fair because we bore the brunt of it and basically had nothing to do with it. Eddie had to make a call to save his job."

But in hindsight, Ley, Johnston, and Gordon all bear some responsibility. Gordon wanted to cut payroll, Ley stripped Francis of the C and gave no good reason for it, and Johnston, who had been the Penguins general manager from 1983 to 1988, thought Zalapski—whom he'd drafted with the fourth overall pick in 1986—brought an offensive element to the Whalers that they didn't have in Samuelsson.

"The owner got convinced that trading Ronny Francis was a good idea. Rick Ley was at the bottom of that, and Johnston went back to his Pittsburgh roots," said Jeff Jacobs, who covered the team for the *Hartford Courant*. "They were convinced that Cullen and Zalapski were better than Francis and Samuelsson.

"That is the Holy Triumvirate of the fuck-up."

If the men were duped, they weren't alone. Jimmy Roberts, who coached Hartford's AHL team in Springfield, loved that Hartford got Cullen in the trade, and the Whalers primary TV station, SportsChannel New England, took a sample of Whalers fans who had mixed feelings about the deal. Some had mistakenly placed trust in Johnston and thought Cullen, who had 94 points in only 65 games playing on the second line in Pittsburgh, was the next offensive savior.

"[Francis] was awesome but had never become the superstar that everyone wanted him to be," said Jason Mandell, a Whalers fan and Simsbury, Connecticut, native. "Cullen was lighting it up, and it was exciting to get a hot, young, high-flying offensive player."

Cullen also slipped up early, stating in his first public interview that he was "not Ron Francis." Making things even weirder, Francis and the Penguins came back to the Civic Center just five days after the trade for a game against the Whalers.

"I think it was one of the toughest games I had to play," Francis said.

Francis had been the Whalers' marquee player for nearly a decade, and the fan base celebrated him with signs and cheers in his return. He registered his first point with the Penguins in their 5–2 win over the Whalers at the Civic Center.

"The signs all over the place, and you're seeing people there for like six or seven years in the stands, and all of a sudden you're at the other end of the rink and they're not cheering for you," Samuelsson said, "and maybe most importantly the players you've been playing with and now all of a sudden you're supposed to run over them. It was really weird."

"That was really weird," Jennings said of his return to Hartford. "You could tell from the fans's response that they missed us big time."

The Francis trade resulted in the Whalers season-subscription base dropping from 11,000 to about 6,000 in a three-year span, as fans in the region quickly lost excitement without recognizable faces donning Whalers uniforms.

"My emotional investment went down the day they traded Ron Francis," said Sean Pendergast, also a Simsbury native, Whalers fan, and friend of Mandell's. "A big part of the team died with that trade."

Posterity showed that the trade was among the greatest in Penguins history, as Pittsburgh went on to win back-to-back Stanley Cup championships in 1991 and 1992. Francis and star center Mario Lemieux created an unstoppable tandem, as Francis chipped in 44 points in 45 playoff games those two years. Hockey analyst Barry Melrose called the deal the best trade-deadline move involving a forward in 2012.

"The trade changed our lives," Jennings said. "Ronny ended up being the best two-way center in the game, and he was out of the shadows and all that pressure on him kind of went on Mario. He got to be the player he was five years prior."

Samuelsson also played in 20 playoff games in 1991, posting three goals and a plus-seven rating. He also brought a physical element the Penguins sorely lacked and continued his ongoing war with Cam Neely—famously delivering a controversial knee-on-knee hit that damaged the Bruins superstar's career during Game 3 of Pittsburgh's upset win of the Bruins in the Wales Conference finals.

"This could be a perfect fit I was thinking right away," Samuelsson said. "I kind of had a rough idea about [Pittsburgh's] roster, but the fit was perfect for the three of us."

Conspiracy theorists, many without tinfoil hats, come out when the history of this trade is discussed.

"Eddie Johnston said he was trying to build a Stanley Cup champion, he just didn't say it was for Pittsburgh," Ray Ferraro snidely kidded in 2013. "It was an ill-conceived trade from the get-go. It wasn't just Ronny, it was Ulf Samuelsson that was the big piece to give up.

"At one point, [making the trade] was thought to be a good idea."

But for Hartford it was more than just offloading money, or even dealing on-ice talent for younger players. It was about stripping the face of the franchise from an organization that otherwise didn't have much of an identity.

"The Francis trade ripped the soul from the team," said Michael Arace, a former *Hartford Courant* sports reporter. "Let alone the fact that Francis is one of the greatest two-way centermen of all time, in Hartford, he was the face of the franchise and the embodiment of what was right about the teams assembled by Emile Francis.

"The trade of Francis, and Samuelsson, was the symbolic, and horrific detonation of the era."

The Whalers went 3-11-5 in their final 19 games, closing the year with just 73 points—the fewest of any playoff team in the Wales Conference. Their 238 goals also was a Wales Conference playoff low, as only the Nordiques and New York Islanders scored fewer.

But for the second straight year, Hartford's consolation prize was a first-round date with the Bruins, who again finished atop the Adams Division. Coach Mike Milbury's cast was largely the same: Bourque, Neely, Janney, and Andy Moog in goal. The Whalers entered the series as the underdog—finishing 27 points behind their regional rival.

For good measure, the Bruins blitzed the Whalers, 7–3, in each team's final regular-season game at Boston Garden. Then, just 23 seconds into Game 1, Jeff Lazaro put Boston up when he beat Sidorkiewicz.

But the new-look Whalers kept the Game 1 script the same as the previous year. Hartford scored three straight, one each from Verbeek, Dineen, and Rob Brown, and John Cullen posted three points, including a goal in Hartford's 5–2 victory.

The franchise was at another crossroads as it entered Game 2. Win another in Boston, and the series would shift back to Hartford with the division's top team on the ropes.

The Whalers did their damnedest to take that commanding series lead, building an early lead thanks to goals from Verbeek and Mark Hunter. Randy Ladouceur's goal late in the second gave the Whalers a 3–2 third-period advantage.

But Cam Neely stole the show and broke the Whalers' hearts yet again.

Neely willed the Bruins back, scoring the game-tying goal midway through the third. With just 3:22 separating Hartford and Boston from overtime, the superstar forward beat goalie Peter Sidorkiewicz on a two-on-one break that sent the Garden into delirium and the series back to Hartford tied at a game apiece.

It was Neely's second career playoff hat trick, and the final great playoff moment in the Hall of Fame forward's career. Two nights later, the Bruins stole home-ice advantage back with a 6–3 win at the Civic Center. The Whalers pulled even early in the third on Verbeek's third goal in as many games, but Boston roared back with four goals to break Hartford's heart yet again. Six different Bruins scored, with Janney posting a three-point effort just 20 miles from his childhood home.

Two nights later, the series see-sawed yet again, as Cullen and Zalapski each scored, and Hunter struck twice for Hartford's four first-period goals. The resilient Whalers hung on for a 4–3 win in Hartford, holding serve as the series shifted back to Boston.

In the all-important Game 5, Hartford struck first for the third time of the series on defenseman Brad Shaw's goal midway through the second and carried the narrow, 1–0 lead to the dressing room after two periods.

The Whalers had played an exceptional road game at the Boston Garden and were just 20 minutes from taking a 3–2 series lead back to Hartford.

But that's when the Whalers lost their cool.

The Bruins opened the third on a power play, and Bourque struck just 80 seconds into the frame when his dump-in try from center ice beat Sidorkiewicz, tying the game. While the shellshocked Whalers wondered what had hit them, the Bruins took the lead on Dave Christian's goal just 16 seconds later.

Boston's six-goal third period onslaught turned a close game into a laugher, and the Bruins even used intimidation to keep Hartford down. With the score 6–1, Randy Burridge checked Sidorkiewicz, and the frustrated Whalers came to their beleaguered goalie's aid. In all, 104 minutes in penalties were assessed, and with time to stew, the Whalers had an opportunity to regain tenacity and fight.

Instead, they fell victim to the Bruins again. Boston scored on its first two shots on goal. The Whalers outshot the Bruins 32–16 but Moog outplayed Sidorkiewicz and Boston advanced with a 3–1 victory at the Civic Center in Game 6.

"Our goaltending really struggled," Ley said. "Their goaltending was just a little bit better than ours."

The Whalers' fifth straight first-round exit did not go unpunished, as Ley was fired and replaced by Jimmy Roberts, the club's AHL coach. Roberts and Johnston were dealt an enormous blow from the start of the offseason, when Cullen and Verbeek each held out of training camp seeking raises.

Johnston enraged forward Todd Krygier by holding his rights, then publicly denigrating the former playoff standout. The GM finally dealt Krygier to the Washington Capitals on the season's eve, also trading stalwarts Dean Evason and Sylvain Côté, further disenfranchising the fan base and removing the club from its glory days.

Cullen ultimately signed a four-year contract, and the tinkering led to a 5-1-1 start, the best seven-game opening stretch in franchise history until 2019–20. But the moves didn't stop, as Johnston dealt Kevin Dineen to Philadelphia for center Murray Craven on November 13.

Dineen had met his wife Annie at a Whalers function and made his home in Connecticut, and his trade sapped Hartford of the final piece from the Emile Francis era. When news of his deal from Hartford broke, Dineen was in tears, telling the Associated Press "I'm disappointed to be leaving. I've grown as a person and a player here. There are a lot of good memories here. A lot of good guys."

"I think the first time has the biggest sting," Dineen said of being traded in 2019. "You feel like you're part of something and you're always going to be part of something but you could see they were slowly transitioning the team from what we were and moves were made, . . . but it doesn't lessen the sting at all."

Craven went on to score 24 goals for the Whalers, second-most on the team, but he wasn't Dineen, who was beloved in the Hartford area.

But even as the Whalers struggled with an identity crisis, they still were a shoo-in for the playoffs.

The Quebec Nordiques after all were in shambles. After using their first pick to take Eric Lindros, the big forward held out, saying he'd never play a game for the Nordiques, which ultimately would ring true. Quebec held Lindros's rights for the entire 1991–92 season, and the distraction doomed Quebec's campaign; the Nordiques finished fifth in the Adams Division for the fifth straight year.

While Lindros held out, Verbeek played in spite of his salary discrepancy—ultimately gaining an $820,000, one-year deal for 1992–93 from an independent arbitrator in February. The Whalers went 1-11-7 in a 19-game stretch that nearly sank their season, as both Peter Sidorkiewicz and Kay Whitmore, the supposed heir-apparent, struggled mightily in goal. Even with Cullen's team-leading 77 points, Hartford's offense finished with the third-worst goals scored (247).

Johnston surprised many when he acquired goalie Frank Pietrangelo from Pittsburgh and hung onto Verbeek—who had been the subject of trade rumors since the contract dispute.

Verbeek's contract dispute was just one of the many around the NHL in 1991–92, and it nearly ruined that season. With players craving a bigger piece of the ever-growing monetary pie, a 10-day strike—just two weeks before the start of the playoffs—postponed about 30 games and threatened the playoffs.

"As players we didn't have much leverage," Verbeek said. "The owners have leverage at the start of the season, and players have leverage at the start of the playoffs. As I look back at it, it was part of collective bargaining."

The two sides came to a two-year agreement, saving the playoffs, and the Whalers closed the season with their worst record since the 19-54-7 season in 1982–83. Still, their 65 points were good enough to be the Adams Division's number four seed for the fifth year in a row.

For the first time since 1989, Hartford would face off against the Montreal Canadiens, the Adams Division champion. Led by Patrick Roy, who claimed his third Vezina Trophy, the Canadiens finished with 93 points, nine better than the second-place Bruins.

The strike created a strange vibe around the NHL, but the playoff drama was still there. Every first-round series went at least six games, and six went the distance, including the Bruins' seven-game series win over the Buffalo Sabres in the other Adams semifinal.

The winner would face either Hartford or Montreal, and although the Habs finished 28 points better than the Whalers, they entered the series on an 0-5-3 stretch. The Canadiens were just 3-2-2 in seven head-to-head meetings, including one win in overtime at the Montreal Forum, making them eminently beatable.

But Montreal had won five straight postseason games against the Whalers and quickly enhanced that streak to seven with a pair of convincing victories in the series's first two games. Gilbert Dionne struck twice, and Roy shut the Whalers out, 2–0, in Game 1, then Denis Savard's four-assist game keyed Montreal's 5–2 win in Game 2.

The Whalers returned home searching for home-ice advantage. Yet, after middling through a bad season and trailing by two games already, they hardly received any support from fans in Hartford. Hartford sold 6,782 tickets for Game 3, and a record-low crowd of 5,602 attended the first playoff game at the Civic Center in 1992.

"I'm not sure why our crowds were so lean," said Whalers captain Pat Verbeek. "Maybe the people didn't think we had a chance."

Those in attendance watched Patrice Brisebois strike first for Montreal at 17:52 of the initial frame, and the prospect of another sweep was looking likely. But Hartford rallied to score five straight goals, including two from Craven, and Pietrangelo authored a tour-de-force performance by stopping 32 shots in the Whalers' 5–2 win.

Two nights later, the Whalers held serve. Although the Civic Center crowd still was well below capacity, it was nearly double that of Game 3, as the Whalers built a 2–0 lead and hung on for a 3–1 win.

Hartford claimed its first back-to-back home wins in four months, and Yvon Corriveau had a hand in all three goals, turning the best-of-seven series into a best-of-three.

Playing with renewed fervor, Hartford built a 3–1 advantage late into the second period of the pivotal Game 5. Pietrangelo was standing on his head, and Hartford seemed poised to build on that lead, and the series's tide appeared to be well with the Whalers.

But the Whalers faltered again, and it all started with two rings off the post. Instead of leading 5–1, Hartford was still only up two, and Kirk Muller's short-handed goal opened the floodgates. Brian Skrudland tallied just 36 seconds later, and the game was suddenly even.

Montreal unleashed a barrage of shots at Pietrangelo and finally cashed in. When the dust settled, the Canadiens scored four goals in 4:54, capped by Brisebois's with just five seconds in the frame. The Canadiens rolled to a 7–4, tide-turning win.

With the Whalers facing elimination, they again received little support from their home fans as less than 9,000 ventured to the Civic Center for their final first-round home game. Despite the meek turnout, Hartford gave its fans another thrilling experience.

Pietrangelo stopped 42 shots, and the teams traded early second-period goals and went to overtime even at 1. It was the sixth anniversary of Claude Lemieux's memorable Game 7 win over the Whalers.

But fate was with Hartford this time.

Corriveau's redirection 24 seconds into the extra session lifted the Whalers over the Canadiens, 2–1, in overtime. The series, which few had given the Whalers a chance to win, was just one game from being their second-ever playoff series victory.

The Whalers took to the road in their green sweaters and pants May 1, 1992, hoping to win their first playoff game at the Forum in more than four years.

The crowd was wired from the start, and Mathieu Schneider's power-play goal sent them into delirium and put Hartford in another Game 7 hole just 6:08 into the game.

After killing a penalty, the Canadiens went for the throat. Stéphan Lebeau took an errant pass from Adam Burt, passed to Gilbert Dionne, who stickhandled around Burt, and beat Pietrangelo for his third goal of the playoffs that made it 2–0.

The Forum went wild, roaring with its customary "Go Habs Go!" chant. With Montreal leading 2–0, and swarming for more, the Whalers' season was on the brink, but Pietrangelo stood tall. Still, the Canadiens went to their dressing room just 40 minutes from the Adams finals again.

But when Corriveau forced Schneider's giveaway, Andrew Cassels picked up the puck and flung a high wrist shot—Hartford's second shot of the second period—on his off-side that somehow eluded Roy, cutting Montreal's lead to 2–1 with about 30 minutes of regulation left.

Pietrangelo continued to keep the Canadiens at bay, and although Hartford failed on each of its four power plays, the tide began to swing. When Patrick Poulin and Bobby Holík occupied the Montreal defense, Holík found a wide-open Geoff Sanderson, who capitalized, tying the game at 15:36 of the second.

Sanderson's goal was his first of the series, and it sent the Montreal faithful into stunned silence. The Whalers had shown few signs of life in their awful season but were alive and breathing as the decisive game entered the third period.

With the score even, every rush became of utmost importance, and the third period offered breathtaking play. The Forum crowd built as the Canadiens surged toward the goal that would push Montreal ahead, then dejectedly groaned when Pietrangelo stopped the try—including Mike McPhee's breakaway with just a minute remaining in regulation that nearly slithered under the Whalers goalie but stayed out.

Roy was rarely tested but stood tall when Hartford did get chances. He also got some more help from his friendly goalpost in the third, as Cassels's shot, Hartford's best scoring chance of the frame, hit his shoulder, rang the crossbar, then sailed out of play.

It wasn't enough for either to break the tie. For the second time in their playoff histories, the Canadiens and Whalers headed to overtime in Game 7.

The Canadiens peppered Pietrangelo with shots in the extra session, and the Forum crowd smelled blood, but the diminutive netminder proved equal to the task. He got a glove on Brent Gilchrist's one-on-one chance early in overtime, then Pietrangelo somehow stopped Kirk Muller's chance at the side of the net.

With Pietrangelo standing on his head—he stopped 29 in a row between the third period and first overtime—and with only one shot needed to claim the series victory, the Whalers searched for the opportunity to counterattack. It nearly came when Sanderson baited Montreal into a giveaway in neutral ice, then set up Holík for a one-timer in the final minute of the first extra session, but Roy shut him down.

Double overtime would be needed to settle the final game, and the longer the game went, the more confident Hartford seemed to get.

But just as the Whalers warmed to the task, their season ended just as abruptly.

Whalers defenseman Todd Richards was pressured by Dionne and turned the puck over to Corson. Hanging out in the slot was Russ Courtnall, Montreal's 1989 hero who hadn't even had a shot in the series's first three games, was a healthy scratch in Game 5, and had not yet appeared on the scoresheet in the series.

Courtnall's play was coming under fire from the distressed locals—especially as his brother, Geoff, was posting a hat trick in the Vancouver Canucks' Game 7 win over the Winnipeg Jets in their Smythe Division semifinal.

Yet, at 5:26 of the second overtime in Game 7, Courtnall became an all too familiar thing: a hero in Montreal at the Whalers' expense.

Corson found Courtnall in the slot, and his first try was blocked by Randy Ladouceur as three Whalers tried to intercede. The puck fell back to Courtnall, who flung a shot that somehow sailed past Pietrangelo's right pad and hit the back of the net.

Longtime Whalers beat writer Jeff Jacobs still swears he saw the puck somehow go under the ice. But however it went in, the Forum exploded as Courtnall's teammates mobbed him, and Pietrangelo remained on one knee thoroughly dejected in his crease.

It would be the final playoff game in the Hartford Whalers' history.

Winning does not keep the wolves off a team's doorsteps, but it certainly helps.

Many clubs have moved or folded in the NHL's 100-plus years, but the last team to move after winning the Stanley Cup was the original Ottawa Senators, who left for St. Louis to become the Eagles in 1935 after winning 11 championships between 1903 and 1927. They even were revived as an expansion team in 1992.

The Whalers had reached the playoffs in six consecutive seasons, but their lack of series wins was keeping revenues out of owner Richard Gordon's pockets.

The Civic Center housed roughly 23,000 fans for three Whalers playoff contests, and their stance in Hartford was at a crossroads. A May 1992 *Hartford Courant* report revealed that revenues at the Hartford Civic Center were down 94 percent from the previous year, and according to the newspaper, had plummeted from $2.4 million at its high in 1987–88 to roughly $40,000 in 1990–91.

Gordon, caught up in the Colonial Realty Ponzi scheme, took a $4 million loan from Connecticut in 1992 to buy out Colonial Realty's share. Connecticut took control of the building, and the Whalers paid rent as a tenant.

As new revenue streams cropped up around the sports landscape—either via television or new arenas—the Whalers were not privy to money from concessions or parking at the Hartford Civic Center. Plus, their television deal—a 20-year, $20 million contract with SportsChannel New England that Howard Baldwin negotiated in 1982—went directly in Baldwin's pocket.

The Whalers had a season-ticket base of just 7,000 at the end of the 1992 season and were estimated to lose $5 million, according to the *Courant*'s reporting in the 1992–93 season. Gordon, called the deal "the worst in the league." The Whalers' lease with the Civic Center was up, and the 1992–93 season occurred without a deal in place.

The news surrounding the Whalers became about their future. Hartford had lost much of its vibrancy, as insurance companies—defrauded by Colonial and seeking greater profits and lower taxes—packed up and moved out to office complexes in the suburbs and even other parts of the country. Shopping malls also cropped up in the suburbs, which left the Civic Center Mall, adjacent to the Whalers' home, in shambles.

The state aimed to find new ways of gaining revenue, including renovations to the existing Foxwoods Casino in Ledyard. The renovations helped the gambling house's meteoric rise—and other casinos cropped up in the region—and Connecticut claimed 25 cents for every dollar earned.

Where the money went, so followed Gordon, as he kicked Ledyard's proverbial tires for a new arena, but to no avail. With a 76 percent ownership stake, no lease agreement, and the team hemorrhaging money, Gordon pleaded with the state and city for concessions to help generate revenue for the ailing franchise.

The Whalers were 23rd in attendance, out of 24 NHL teams, averaging just 10,144 in 1992–93, and NHL salaries had doubled in only two years. Gordon lost more than $50 million while owning the Whalers—even through two expansion terms—because of renovations he put into the Civic Center in an effort to keep money flowing in.

With disposable income drying up, and the team a veritable laughingstock on the ice, 15 Civic Center skyboxes were barren during the entire 1992–93 season, according to the *Hartford Courant*.

And when the Minnesota North Stars departed to Dallas, the proverbial wolves came to Gordon's door. Deep-pocketed owners lined up to buy the Whalers to move them out of Hartford, yet the owner did not put the team up for sale nor did he sell under those conditions, despite the state's conclusion that the Whalers' agreement was comparable to others in the National Hockey League—which wasn't inaccurate but would quickly change.

Hoping to keep the club in Connecticut, the sides came to an agreement on a 20-year lease with the provision that any potential sale of the Whalers could be matched by the state for 85 percent of the asking price. The state also agreed to wash out Gordon's debt in exchange for 100 percent of parking, luxury-box revenue, and a repayment of loans issued in the late 1980s.

The state also could buy the team for $45 million, should Gordon want to sell without a buyer in place.

Gordon had made swift changes to the on-ice product as well, firing Ed Johnston—who oversaw a roster overhaul that included the Ron Francis trade—and replacing him with Brian Burke.

The 36-year-old Burke was looking to get his budding front-office career off the ground and shape the franchise in an upward direction. Burke has since become one of the NHL's most charismatic personalities, but at the time the Providence, Rhode Island, native was leaving the Vancouver Canucks, where he'd been the director of hockey operations.

He has a gruff outward persona, particularly with the media, and likes his teams tough. But Burke has a big heart, particularly with his family, and has become one of the most beloved curmudgeons among people who know him best.

"I liked Burkey," said Whalers captain Pat Verbeek. "I thought he was smart. For me, he was a GM players would love to play for."

At his introductory press conference, Burke said all the right things, assuaging fears that the club's stance in the community was in peril.

"We intend to turn this around and stay for a long, long time," Burke told the *Hartford Courant*. "Our challenge is to rebuild what was once a winning hockey tradition in Hartford . . . to restore Hartford to the level where it was and take it to the next level."

Burke's first action was changing the team's color scheme from royal-blue, Kelly green, and white to navy, forest green, and white. The W remained on both home and road uniforms, with the patented negative space too, but a gray outline behind the logo gave the team a fiercer and newer-wave look.

"I thought it was a degradation because it took away the original's beautiful form," said Peter Good, the original logo's creator. "There was no need to complicate with outlines or a background color . . . but when any team starts losing, they think changing the logo will help, and it never does."

Burke fired Jimmy Roberts and replaced him with Paul Holmgren, the former head coach of the Philadelphia Flyers. Burke ousted short-lived mascot Wally the Whaler and even outlawed the team's iconic fight song "Brass Bonanza."

"I did because there were players who were embarrassed by it," Burke later told NHL.com. "An NHL team with a fight song? They were embarrassed by it."

Burke sought to make the team tougher as it was rebuilding, and the Whalers were one of the closest-knit teams—no small feat considering they finished with 58 points and missed the playoffs for the first time since 1985.

But the Brian Burke era in Hartford was defined by Gordon's cost-cutting and micromanaging. He instructed Burke to trade John Cullen, and the high-flying forward was offloaded to the Toronto Maple Leafs early in the season in a cost-saving measure—the Whalers received only a second-round draft pick.

Ironically if Gordon could've found a buyer sooner, Burke could've been the person who oversaw Hartford's turnaround. But as Gordon hung on, focused on turning the franchise's fortunes overnight so he could flip them for a heftier profit, Burke grew tired and bolted to take a front-office role within the NHL under commissioner Gary Bettman on September 1—less than five weeks before the Whalers' 1993–94 season opener.

"I had a falling out with the owner," Burke told Sportsnet in 2018. "He was about to fire me, and I called [Bettman] and said 'Are you still looking for someone at the league?' and that's how I made the shift over."

Burke also was worried about the franchise's stability in Hartford and was among the first to see the writing on the wall.

"He called me while I was on vacation," said Jeff Jacobs, the team's former beat reporter for the *Hartford Courant*. "He told me 'I want you to be the first to know: it's over.' It was out of nowhere, but it wasn't out of nowhere."

The Burke move highlighted the Whalers' dysfunction yet again, as Gordon trusted Burke to preside over Hartford's offseason moves and draft, which included selecting defenseman Chris Pronger with the second-overall pick—behind Alexandre Daigle, a notorious bust who famously said, "I'm glad I got drafted first because no one remembers No. 2."

Holmgren became coach and general manager, but the stress of handling both roles quickly became too much and he stepped down to focus on general managing in November. In March, Holmgren had been drinking at the Whalers practice rink at Avon Old Farms and veered off the road, hitting mailboxes and attracting police attention on the six-mile drive to his home in Simsbury.

When he finally made it home, police were there to meet him, and they arrested and booked Holmgren for DWI. Holmgren checked into the Betty Ford rehab clinic in California and has enjoyed a lengthy career in hockey, thanks largely to his sobriety, which has turned his life around.

"I remember talking to [Holmgren] in rehab," said Verbeek. "That particular point changed his life for sure. I guess you can look at it as a negative, but I like to look at that as a positive. I like Paul Holmgren a lot, and I think he's an incredible individual."

The Whalers were just 4-11-2 when 32-year-old assistant coach Pierre McGuire took over as interim coach. McGuire has a sharp hockey mind and came in with pedigree. He'd studied under legendary coach Scotty Bowman and was an assistant with the Stanley Cup champion Pittsburgh Penguins in 1992.

McGuire had the Whalers flying out of the gate. They went 13-11-1 in his first 25 games as coach, including a 7–3 stretch from December 18 to January 8, and were only three points out of a playoff spot after a 6–0 drubbing of the New York Islanders.

The Whalers were flying high as they took off for California for an important four-game road trip. But that's when a run of arrogance quickly led to their undoing.

McGuire, beat writer Jeff Jacobs, and radio broadcaster Chuck Kaiton went out for dinner at the Palm restaurant in Los Angeles, where they stumbled upon a charity function where celebrities waited on tables. Among the famous actors serving as guest waiters were Peri Gilpin, just starting as the character Roz Doyle on the *Cheers* spinoff *Frasier*, who served as the trio's server providing a lavish meal that included lobsters.

"And Pierre said 'stick with me, JJ, we're going places,'" Jacobs recalled. "And they had the worst record in the league after he said that."

Hartford did not win the rest of January, a span of nine games, and the locker room and media quickly flipped on the head coach.

"The media was critical to the point where it was unfair," McGuire recalled in 2012. "We were two years into a five-year rebuild, and they were expecting us to win the Stanley Cup."

Making matters worse, the UConn men's basketball team was enjoying another breakout season. It had been four years since the Huskies fell in the East regional final of the NCAA Tournament to Duke on Christian Laettner's buzzer-beater. After four straight uneven seasons, the Huskies rolled through the Big East and did not lose in January en route to a 16-2 Big East record.

McGuire grew resentful of UConn's coverage by the local media and tried to politic for his squad. But that also backfired.

"The Whalers don't get a fair shake from the TV people in this town," McGuire told the *Hartford Courant* in January 1994. "There should be a cameraman at practice in the morning of games. In every other city there is. In my opinion, they are very biased toward UConn athletics; almost to the point where it's slanted journalism."

The Whalers won only seven games between January 12 and March 30, and as the team struggled, more of the locker room checked out. It all came to a head in March when the Whalers were even defeated by the Buffalo Police Department.

Hartford had two days off between its game in Washington on March 22 and a Friday night contest in Buffalo. After a particularly tough practice in Buffalo on Wednesday, some players and coaches went out to Network—a bar and restaurant owned by then–Bills quarterback Jim Kelly that adjoined the downtown Main Place Mall.

The club, which opened the previous September, was shutting down at around 4:00 a.m., as is the customary last call in New York. But six of the Whalers, and two of their assistant coaches, were not ready to go. The nightclub's bouncers closed in and grew disgruntled while trying to get the players to leave.

"That was a tough night for all of us," Verbeek said. "We were having a few drinks with one another and having a little fun, and next thing you know the bouncers were telling us it was time to leave. And you turn around and it was a shoving match and then it was a wrestling match."

Drunk and indignant, the Whalers stayed, and the bouncers got hostile. They pushed the players out of the club into the shopping mall, and a brawl ensued. Police arrived on the scene and used pepper spray and beat the players with nightsticks, but the six Whalers and two coaches were arrested for trespassing—since the shopping mall was closed.

"The bouncers were aggressive; in my opinion they were wanting to fight," Verbeek said. "We didn't want to throw a punch, because if we get into this deal, we're in a bad way. The police showed up with a lot of intensity, and the bouncers kept pointing at us, and the bouncers had the home-field advantage, and they took us to jail."

Geoff Sanderson tried to run to escape the police, even hopping a six-foot fence to elude the officers. The Whalers organization was alerted at about 5:00 a.m., with assurances that the police would withhold player names so they could do damage control. But their info was leaked to a Buffalo radio station, which sent the media circus into action.

Making matters worse, rookie defenseman Chris Pronger was just 19 at the time, two years shy of the legal drinking age in the United States, and when cameras caught him moving from the courthouse to the street, he covered his head with a coat to keep his face from being seen.

"And [owner Richard] Gordon saw it and said 'oh my God, my first-round pick is looking like a drug dealer,'" Jacobs said.

Many of the Whalers later found out the club was forbidden territory for NFL teams, because of its penchant for trouble. Verbeek was one of four Whalers who were later sued after a bouncer broke his toe kicking them, and adding insult to injury, Gordon and the Whalers organization came down hard on those involved. Pronger was suspended for the remainder of the season, and the other five were suspended indefinitely.

"Everybody [in the organization] was worrying about the optics," Verbeek said. "At the end of the day, for me, from an organizational perspective, I didn't see everyone backing one another and standing up for one another, which is where I became angry."

NHLPA head Bob Goodenow had to intervene on the Whalers behalf, and within hours those suspensions had been overturned. Five of the six were in the lineup for Friday night's contest against the Sabres, and Pronger even scored one of Hartford's goals in its 6–3 loss—even though each assistant coach had his suspension upheld.

The overturned suspension started a rift between Gordon and Goodenow, who was also advocating on the players' behalf for higher salaries. Other NHL teams had also complained to the league about the suspensions, since the Whalers had games to play against teams angling for playoff spots.

The 1993–94 season was trying for the Whalers, dealing with the uncertainty surrounding Holmgren and miserable on-ice play. But the Whalers locker room was united in its disdain for McGuire—an anonymous poll conducted by the *Hartford Courant* found the players were near-unanimous in favor of his firing.

"I think it was a combination of trying too hard and probably being a little too motivated to climb the ladder too quickly," said Sean Burke, the team's goalie that season. "I know it rubbed me [the wrong way] a little bit at times."

The Whalers went 10-26-6 in their 42 games after McGuire's boastful proclamation in Los Angeles, and he was fired less than six weeks after the season, to the relief of many inside the Hartford locker room.

"It's unfortunate for Pierre, but as far as our team is concerned, this is the best thing that could have happened," Verbeek told the *Hartford Courant*. "There are times you can hate a coach, but you always have to respect him. That wasn't the case with practically our whole team."

The 1994 offseason was poised to be a key one for the Whalers, and it was even in hindsight. A throng of prospective buyers flew in with bids, and Gordon finally cut his losses, exercising the option to unload the team to Connecticut. The state spent $47.4 million on the deal, which was finalized on June 1, 1994—just 10 days after McGuire was ousted.

The state had no interest in maintaining the team, and they sold it to a three-man group of hockey men who vowed to turn the Whalers into winners.

Unfortunately as Peter Karmanos and Co. took charge, the NHL was changing, and not in a way that would benefit the Whalers.

Chapter 9

The Sun Belt Shift

August 9, 1988 was a day that changed hockey forever.

Wayne Gretzky was a marquee professional athlete in North America—even though he played in the relative anonymity of Edmonton, Alberta. He had been in the Canadian spotlight for decades following a stellar junior-hockey career in Ontario. Gretzky was heavily coveted by both the AHL and NHL, and only financial obligations kept him from perhaps spending his WHA and NHL career in Hartford.

"Jack Kelley went to talk to him and said 'hey, I can sign this guy,'" Howard Baldwin said. "I told him to hold off, because I thought it might cost us the NHL, and we may have been able to get him later."

Indianapolis Racers owner Nelson Skalbania signed Gretzky as a 17-year-old in 1978. When it became clear the Racers wouldn't be a part of the NHL merger, Skalbania, who also owned half of the Edmonton Oilers at the time, sold his share in Edmonton and Gretzky to Peter Pocklington for $700,000 just eight games into the 1978–79 season.

The Racers folded after 25 games, while Gretzky became "The Great One" in Edmonton. Gretzky not only set but also smashed numerous offensive records, posting 92 goals in 1981–82 and 215 points in 1985–86, marks that still stand and likely will never come close to being touched. As of 2020, his 894 NHL goals and 2,857 points are by far the most in league history—even though he came off as normal off the ice.

"He was very unassuming," said Blaine Stoughton, Gretzky's teammate with the Racers in 1978–79. "He was only seventeen, and I never even dreamt he'd be the player he'd end up being, but he's a real nice guy, a very humble guy."

The Oilers became the league standard too, winning four Stanley Cup titles in five seasons, including 1988 when they needed just 18 games—losing only two postseason games—to claim the championship, the fewest, as of 2021, of any team since the NHL went to best-of-seven in all four rounds in 1987.

Gretzky became the undeniable face of both the franchise and NHL, and his name became synonymous with hockey. In 1984, he appeared on the soap opera *The Young and the Restless*, as Wayne from the Edmonton operation of Newman Enterprises. He even appeared on the box of his own cereal called "Pro Stars," which later became its own cartoon in the United States.

Almost as quickly as Gretzky grew up in Edmonton, he seemed to grow out of the Alberta capital. The hockey culture in Edmonton can be a fishbowl, and Gretzky's future became the city's hot topic. Gretzky was dating American actress Janet Jones, whom he married on July 16, 1988 at a ceremony dubbed Canada's Royal Wedding that was broadcast across the nation.

But even as the Oilers were soaring, Pocklington's other entities were struggling. Los Angeles Kings owner Bruce McNall wanted to make a splash and initially asked Pocklington about a Gretzky trade in 1987, after Gretzky had led Edmonton to its third championship of the decade.

The Oilers owner didn't say no, and when McNall called a year later they made a deal.

Less than three weeks after the royal wedding, the Oilers sent Gretzky to Southern California with Marty McSorley and Mike Krushelnyski for Jimmy Carson, Martin Gélinas, two first-round draft picks, and $15 million.

The video of the ordinarily unflappable Gretzky sobbing at his going-away press conference is iconic, as are the images of signs and riots calling for Pocklington's head throughout Canada.

"We're all trying to do something that's good for Wayne, the Edmonton Oilers, the National Hockey League," Oilers general manager Glen Sather said at Gretzky's trade press conference.

At the time of the trade, the Kings were the only team in California and the NHL's southernmost franchise, geographically—with the Washington Capitals coming in as the second-most southern team.

But that didn't last for long. Jobs and people were moving out of the Northeast and Rust Belt to southern and western US markets. The NHL had to keep up.

"Gretzky's arrival triggered the expansion to non-traditional markets," said Helene Elliott, a longtime *Los Angeles Times* hockey columnist who was inducted into the Hockey Hall of Fame in 2005. "I think expansion would have happened anyway, because of population shifts in the United States . . . but the Gretzky trade hastened the process."

The rest is history. Gretzky took L.A. by storm— he made more than $717,000 in his penultimate season in Edmonton but got a base salary of $2 million in his first season with the Kings.

McNall was trying to keep up with the dynastic Lakers—with whom he shared the Great Western Forum in Inglewood—and Gretzky's arrival moved the Kings onto the marquee.

Movie stars like Tom Hanks, Sylvester Stallone, and Meg Ryan came to see Gretzky, and McNall made the VIPs feel right at home. John Candy, a Canadian actor who was fresh off box-office hits like *Uncle Buck* and *Planes, Trains and Automobiles*, even bought in as a Kings minority owner.

"I remember [McNall] walked into my office before a game against Toronto," said Barry Melrose, who coached Gretzky and the Kings from 1992 to 1995, "and I remember telling him 'don't worry, we'll win tonight. We've got this.' And Bruce said 'I know you do. I'm not worried about that. I've got 300 VIP tickets, and 500 calls from Hollywood stars who are trying to get in.'

"We had President Reagan come to all of our home games. It was an unbelievable time."

The Kings' attendance soared. Los Angeles averaged more than 15,000 fans per game from 1988 to 1995, and by then, expansion and migration south had taken off.

The Gretzky trade was a seminal moment in the National Hockey League's southward migration. But according to longtime hockey writer Stu Hackel, it was simply the tipping point of a grander plan at the time.

"The owners commissioned a study, right around the time of the Gretzky trade, called 'Vision For The Nineties,'" Hackel said. "It solely had to do with expanding the NHL and putting teams in non-traditional markets."

The plan was to expand the league from 21 to 30 teams by the turn of the century. The first domino of this "Vision" to fall post-Gretzky trade was in San Jose. Hockey had been in the Bay Area when Oakland got the California Golden Seals in expansion in 1967. The Golden Seals lasted just nine years before moving to Cleveland—at the suggestion of minority owners Gordon and George Gund—then ultimately merged with the Minnesota North Stars.

The Gunds wanted to bring hockey back to the Bay Area, but the NHL was leery of their commitment. Mere months after he left as managing general partner of the Whalers, Howard Baldwin swooped in and won the bid to put an expansion club in nearby San Jose in 1990.

To Baldwin, San Jose felt familiar.

"It reminded me of Hartford," Baldwin said. "The building was great, the mayor was great and there were no other sports there."

Baldwin founded the team and ultimately traded it to the Gunds for their share in the North Stars. The Sharks became the 22nd NHL team, and Baldwin's gut proved right about San Jose. Silicon Valley was just exploding with white-collar tech jobs that poured money into the region, and the Sharks have largely been a success story.

A year after the Sharks were founded, McNall convinced Disney CEO Michael Eisner to jump into the NHL, and he founded the Mighty Ducks of Anaheim.

The team was named for the now-iconic hockey trilogy *The Mighty Ducks*, and Anaheim initially preyed on the movie nostalgia, vibrant eggplant, teal, and jade color scheme, and a futuristic logo that became one of the most popular in the NHL.

The Mighty Ducks took Southern California on a run for the ages, reaching the Cup finals in 2003. Led by goalie Jean-Sébastien Giguère, the Mighty Ducks upset three better-seeded teams and pushed the heavily favored New Jersey Devils within a game of the championship. Giguère still earned the Conn Smythe Trophy that season, then backstopped Anaheim to the Cup four years later in 2007, earning bragging rights to the league and in the Los Angeles market.

But that didn't last for long. Five years later, the Kings overcame goal-scoring deficiencies and retook the Southern California market.

Coach Darryl Sutter, who replaced Terry Murray as coach in mid-December, helped the Kings sneak into the playoffs as the number eight seed in the Western Conference. Then behind Jonathan Quick, they rolled through the postseason, going 16-4 and winning the Cup with a six-game series win over New Jersey. Two years later, the Milford, Connecticut–born goalie claimed his second Stanley Cup in three seasons when Quick and the Kings stymied his favorite boyhood team, the New York Rangers.

The three California teams have been among the NHL's most powerful, particularly since 2010, and the sport has taken off at lower levels in California. More than 40 players born in California have reached the NHL, and in 2018, the Santa Margarita Catholic High School team, led by Hall of Fame forward Teemu Selänne's son Leevi, claimed the national championship in USA Hockey's top-tier high school tournament.

But Gretzky's influence wasn't just confined to California. With the league's blessing, the Kings took Gretzky for a preseason tour of the country each season. They played games in Miami, Tampa, Cleveland, Houston, Dallas, Phoenix, and even an outdoor game in Las Vegas against the New York Rangers in the Caesars Palace parking lot in 1991.

The demand for tickets to see Gretzky in Florida was so remarkable that a war was brewing to become the first group to plant the NHL flag in the Sunshine State.

In South Florida, Wayne Huizenga, the founder of Blockbuster Video, AutoNation, and Waste Management, was heading a group trying to make the Miami Ice an NHL team. Huizenga had become a household name in the region after purchasing a minority stake in the Miami Dolphins, and a controlling stake of Joe Robbie Stadium in Miami Gardens in 1990.

Huizenga was trying to add both hockey and baseball to his sports-holding portfolio and had been competing against two separate bids in the Tampa Bay region, which at the time was growing and also trying to get pro hockey and baseball teams. The area built a multi-purpose dome in St. Petersburg in 1990, which it used to lure a baseball team—first targeting the Chicago White Sox, Seattle Mariners, and San Francisco Giants before the Tampa Bay Devil Rays were founded in 1998.

A group headed by Hockey Hall of Famer Phil Esposito was attempting to ward off a team led by Peter Karmanos and Jim Rutherford in putting together a presentation for the NHL. Major League Baseball played hardball with Huizenga, telling him he couldn't found a team if he were the lead investor in a hockey project. With the prospect of losing 81 events at the stadium he owned to either Tampa Bay or Orlando, which was also aiming at an expansion baseball team, he backed out as the NHL team's frontman.

So John Henry, a minority investor in the project who had just set up an office in Boca Raton, became the face for hockey in Miami in 1990. Henry had relationships with important Florida politicians, including Jeb Bush, the son of President George H. W. Bush who eventually became governor of Florida.

Miami had already hosted a sold-out preseason game with Gretzky and the Kings and had a deposit list of 10,000 season-ticket holders. They'd negotiated favorable television and arena deals and had the support of Islanders owner John Pickett.

Yet when Henry was asked to make a presentation at the NHL's Board of Governors meeting on Long Island that spring, he balked at paying the full $50 million expansion fee. Henry wanted to pay $30 million in cash and the subsequent $20 million with future earnings.

The NHL, which in theory had a more firm offer from Esposito's group in Tampa Bay, chose their bid instead.

Esposito and his brother, fellow Hockey Hall of Famer Tony, somehow scratched out the full $50 million expansion fee and won controlling rights of the Lightning over both the Miami group and a rival group spearheaded by Karmanos and Rutherford. The group of Rutherford and Karmanos, like Henry's group, had the money but was willing to front only half of the expansion fee and spend the rest when the Tampa Bay hockey club began operation.

Posterity shows that Esposito's decision to push a club into Florida was a tremendous risk—that ultimately cost Esposito his marriage and nearly drove him to bankruptcy.

"What a gamble it was to be the first in Florida and the first in a southern market," former Lightning play-by-play announcer Rick Peckham said. "He had tremendous foresight and great perseverance."

The Esposito group was backed by Japanese golf magnate Takashi Okubo, and choosing that group is still one of the great controversies in NHL history, since rumors indicate the NHL never even met Okubo before choosing his bid.

But crowds came to the cavernous Thunderdome in St. Petersburg. The Espositos served as the first family of Tampa Bay hockey, and the arena set numerous attendance records—including for the franchise's first game there when 27,227 watched them lose to the Florida Panthers on October 9, 1993.

"It was a great potential market," Hackel said of Tampa. "But the arena was the big question."

The Lightning remained in St. Pete for just three seasons before settling in Tampa for the 1996–97 season. But before moving into what is now known as Amalie Arena, they played in front of a crowd of 28,183—still a record for the largest attendance at a Stanley Cup playoff game—when the Philadelphia Flyers defeated the Lightning 4–1.

The Lightning won the Stanley Cup in 2003–04, and have since become the NHL's model franchise under owner Jeff Vinik, who purchased the team in 2010.

Led by Vinik's deep pockets, and some shrewd maneuvering by longtime GM Steve Yzerman, Tampa Bay reached the Eastern Conference finals in 2011, 2015, 2016, and 2018, finished in the top-10 in home attendance every year from 2012 to 2019 according to ESPN, then tied the record for most regular-season wins (62) in 2018–19 and claimed another Stanley Cup championship in 2020.

"Mr. Vinik is an extraordinary man. He's done wonderful things, especially on the business side and in the community," said Pat Verbeek, who worked as an assistant general manager for the Lightning from 2010 to 2019. "I think the best thing is he gives us anything we need in the hockey ops side to be successful."

"[Vinik is] the best owner you could possibly have in this community," Peckham said in 2012. "He's put $40 million of his own money into a building he doesn't own to refurbish it."

And the Lightning's success has brought new opportunities for locals and led to a cavalcade of new hockey options in the region.

"High school hockey is televised on the local cable station down here," Peckham said. "Interest in hockey has really grown."

Huizenga reentered the picture a year later in 1993, with his Florida Marlins assured of MLB entry, winning a bid—along with Eisner's in Anaheim—to expand December 10, 1992.

The Panthers' existence has largely been considered a blight on the NHL, with just seven Stanley Cup playoff appearances as of 2021. Attendance in South Florida has waned, and the Panthers were already on the NHL's endangered species list by year three.

Their home arena in downtown Miami was neither big enough nor cushy enough to adequately house the Panthers. The building had been completed in 1988 to host the NBA's Heat and attract hockey, but it quickly became obsolete due to its lack of financial advantages—which became the norm across sports in the United States during the sports boom of the 1990s.

Plus who, other than transplanted northerners with preordained allegiances, ever heard of hockey in Miami?

"There was a belief that 1995–96 could be the Panthers' last in south Florida," said David Neal, the Panthers beat writer for the *Miami Herald* at the time. "There was not exactly a whole lot of talk about people buying season tickets and getting attached to them."

The offseason firing of head coach Roger Neilson soured the already-skeptical public on the Panthers and backlash led to a 12,087 crowd—more than 1,000 below capacity—at Florida's 1995 home opener when the Panthers beat Calgary 4–3 on October 8.

"The team made more moves in the offseason, and they transitioned toward younger players," Neal said. "The local populace wasn't excited about that. They didn't even sell out the home opener."

That night, team captain Scott Mellanby scored two goals, but it was after Florida's win that Mellanby created South Florida and NHL lore. A rat scurried across the Panthers locker room, and the sniper smacked the rodent with his stick, killing it against the locker room wall.

Panthers goaltender John Vanbiesbrouck dubbed Mellanby's achievement "the rat trick" and the now-famous Year of the Rat was born.

Fans latched onto the theme, lobbing rubber rodents on the ice after Panthers goals. The team also gained traction in the local community, mostly because the market's other clubs—the NFL's Dolphins and NBA's Heat—were unsuccessful.

The Dolphins lost eight of their final 13 games, including their swift playoff exit in the first round by the Buffalo Bills. The 1995–96 Heat toiled in mediocrity and were swept out of the playoffs by Michael Jordan and the eventual champion Chicago Bulls.

"Everyone else was having a down year," Neal said. "People around here said 'screw it, let's get behind these guys.' And they started to have fun that year."

The Panthers reached the playoffs as the number-five seed in the Eastern Conference but quickly polished off the fourth-seeded Bruins in five games in the first round of the playoffs. They followed with a 4–2 series win over the top-seeded Flyers before stunning Mario Lemieux, Jaromir Jagr, and the Pittsburgh Penguins in seven games in the Eastern Conference finals.

The first Stanley Cup finals game landed in Florida on June 8, 1996, and fans flooded the ice with rubber rodents after Ray Sheppard scored Florida's first goal in Game 3. Although the Panthers were swept by the Colorado Avalanche, thousands of new fans jumped on board and still fondly reminisce about the Panthers' Cinderella run to the finals.

After the year, Huizenga pushed for public money for a new arena, and local politicians gave it to him— albeit in the Fort Lauderdale suburb of Sunrise, about 30 miles north of Miami.

"The 95–96 season saved them in this market," Neal said. "At the start of the season, it would've been political suicide to promote a new arena in the Miami area. After the year, it became politically expedient to."

The Panthers have struggled to attract fans, so it's easy to forget they ranked fourth in the NHL in attendance in their first year at BB&T Center, 1998–99.

Fans checked out because of the arena's location and because the team won just seven postseason games in four playoff trips between 2000 and 2020. But because of the Florida Jr. Panthers program, an ancillary benefit of the team's existence, Florida natives like Shayne

Gostisbehere and Jakob Chychrun are among the brightest young NHL stars.

"If you want to say hockey has failed here, I'd say you're wrong," Neal said in 2011. "The NHL team has failed in South Florida, but youth leagues are flourishing and there are rinks here that would never have been here if not for the Panthers."

In 2018 the expansion Vegas Golden Knights took hockey fans and the sports world for a run for the ages, becoming the first team in 50 years to reach the Stanley Cup finals in their first year. Auston Matthews, who was born in California and grew up in Scottsdale, Arizona, became the first Sun Belt native selected first overall when the Toronto Maple Leafs chose him in 2016.

Not even hockey-mad Minnesota was immune from the Sun Belt trend. The North Stars had joined the National Hockey League in 1967 as part of The Next Six but toiled away in mediocrity despite two surprise runs to the Stanley Cup finals in 1981 and 1991.

After the 1990–91 season, owner Howard Baldwin sold his share to Norm Green, a Canadian businessman who was the catalyst for the Atlanta Flames' move to Calgary in the 1970s.

Green made his money building shopping malls in Calgary and had seen The Mall of America open next to the North Stars' home in Bloomington, Minnesota, in 1992 and had a vision for a walkway from the gigantic mall to the Met Center.

"If that had happened," Hackel said, "the North Stars never would have moved."

When Green and Bloomington could not agree on a price to finance the walkway, the owner shopped for a new building in downtown Minneapolis.

"He got a little carried away with himself at the end," Baldwin said of Green.

As salaries rose and new revenue streams cropped up in the NHL, the 15,000-seat Met Center just couldn't cut it. Plus the North Stars averaged fewer than 10,000 per game between 1989 and 1991. That improved to about 14,000 fans per game in 1992 and 1993 but was still only fifth-best in the six-team Norris Division.

On March 10, 1993—with his club solidly entrenched in the last Norris Division playoff spot—Green announced he'd move the club to Dallas. Minnesota ultimately missed the postseason, and the Dallas Stars were born.

The Stars were successful from the start, averaging more than 16,000 fans at Reunion Arena and making the playoffs in each of their first two seasons there. They even won a playoff series in their first year in Dallas.

Dallas had recognizable stars, including Mike Modano—the boyishly handsome captain and Livonia, Michigan, native who had a cameo in the original *Mighty Ducks* movie. He teamed up with Brett Hull when Dallas signed him to a three-year, $17 million deal before the 1998–99 season. Together the dynamic duo helped Dallas reach the Stanley Cup finals twice, and in 1999, Hull's controversial goal in triple overtime in Game 6 in Buffalo made the Stars the first Sun Belt team to win the Stanley Cup.

"I think we realized it was a special thing," said Pat Verbeek, who played for the Stars' Cup-winning team. "The group and the city were embracing one another at the same time. Rinks started to be put up in the Dallas area, and the city started to turn [toward hockey]."

The Stars have been back to the finals twice since winning the Cup, losing in 2000 and to the Lightning in the all–Sun Belt series in 2020. As of 2021, five active NHL players hailed from Texas, including perennial All-Star defenseman Seth Jones and his brother Caleb, the sons of former NBA forward Popeye Jones.

Dallas's success expedited the vision of the 1990s, which coupled with a devastating recession in Canada that killed the US-Canada exchange rate, led to a rash of departures from the North to non-traditional markets. Quebec City and Winnipeg, flagship-WHA markets, bolted for Denver and Phoenix, just a year apart.

"The motivation for the NHL was to expand so they could get in on more TV money," Neal said. "There wasn't a grand 'let's yank teams from Canada' plan. It just kind of happened."

The United States is still an extremely young and developing nation.

The country celebrated its 245th year of existence in 2021, but the nation's eastern cities have only truly developed by immigration in the past century. New York, Boston, Washington DC, Philadelphia, and others were natural landing spots when immigrants from Ireland, Italy, Germany, and other parts of Europe migrated west in the early 1900s.

Technology, particularly in transportation, made the country smaller, and as midwestern and western states began to lure business through tax breaks and cheaper labor, the country's populations and finances shifted.

And that is part two of the Wayne Gretzky trade's lasting impact: It was a symbolic start of nearly two decades of high-rolling, free-market NHL that also altered the finances of the league.

An unprecedented age of American economic prosperity, created by a tech bubble and an influx of cable-television money, built a booming sports marketplace. Television and licensing agreements turned sports into a multibillion-dollar enterprises. Player salaries skyrocketed and nearly every pro sports league was affected by labor stoppages, as players tried to gain a larger piece of the budding pie.

Corporate welfare became the norm, as businessmen leveraged jobs for infrastructure and tax breaks, and sports were no different. Team owners threatened to move to convince municipalities to build them new, publicly financed arenas and stadiums across North America. Old buildings were either renovated, bulldozed, or vacated as franchises moved to greener pastures.

Even the oldest, most established brands weren't immune. Six legendary NFL teams, the Cleveland Browns, St. Louis Cardinals, Baltimore Colts, Oakland Raiders, and Los Angeles Rams, left for greener pastures between 1982 and 1995.

New baseball parks in Baltimore and Cleveland helped make the Orioles and Indians wildly successful in the 1990s, and hockey teams also found new revenue streams, leading to a financial gap in the 1990s.

The NHL was more prone to relocating sick teams than the other three major North American leagues anyway. But if the Gretzky trade helped expedite the NHL Vision of the 90s, TV then the WHA and Eric Lindros saga were the modern catapults for player salaries.

Lindros was the top pick of the 1991 NHL Draft, selected by the Quebec Nordiques. Scouts drooled over Lindros's size, skill, and personality, but he balked at the prospect of signing in Quebec—even refusing to don the Nordiques jersey given to him by the team on that year's draft day.

Lindros held out the entire 1991–92 season and ultimately ended up with the Philadelphia Flyers via trade—which many believe expedited the Nordiques exit.

The NHL sought to keep up with previously unimaginable growth of the North American landscape around it. It had implemented Gary Bettman as the league's first commissioner in 1993, who entered his second season on the job seeking enhanced US TV money and cost certainty for the league and its member clubs.

"What Gary's done better than anything else is fix each one of these [sick NHL organizations] as they started to occur," said Peter Karmanos. "He's like a fireman."

As such, the owners locked out their players in hopes of curbing big-market spending by instituting a salary cap in 1994. Small-market clubs like the Whalers, Nordiques, and Edmonton Oilers sought the cap to keep finances in check, but NHLPA boss Bob Goodenow fought a cap every step of the way.

With the prospect of a canceled season fast approaching in January 1995, the NHL withdrew its hard-line effort for a salary cap, or even a luxury tax, and the players accepted controlled salaries for rookies.

The result created a boon for players, who could become unrestricted free agents at age 32, and big-market clubs like Detroit, Colorado, Philadelphia, and the New York Rangers threw hordes of money at free agents who were just entering their primes.

Revenues exploded thanks to the NHL's enormous expansion. The NHL added nine teams—San Jose, Florida, Ottawa, Tampa Bay, Anaheim, Nashville, Minnesota, Atlanta, and Columbus—between 1991 and 2001.

Ironically the Hartford Whalers were at the forefront of another financial boom. ESPN, based in the Hartford suburb of Bristol, Connecticut, got off the ground by broadcasting and showing Whalers highlights on their signature show *SportsCenter*. ESPN's meteoric rise made pro-sports live rights skyrocket—particularly in hockey with ESPN taking over in 1980 and broadcasting the NHL for 25 years.

SportsChannel America bought in for a $51 million deal, more than double what ESPN previously paid for national television rights, and stole exclusive league rights from the worldwide leader and put more money into owners' pockets. Upstart Fox ponied up $155 million to outbid CBS to become the national-TV home in the United States in 1994.

Regional television deals became lucrative as well, as teams saw their own brands grow. Networks like Madison Square Garden (MSG) network in New York, New England Sports Network (NESN) in Boston, Empire Sports Network in Buffalo, PASS Sports in Detroit, and Home Team Sports in the Baltimore/Washington area funneled money back into teams' pockets.

With the advent of cable and satellite television—plus NHL Center Ice and NHL Gamecenter coming around the corner—every hockey fan could watch any team at any time. Transplanted fans didn't have to visit the local arena to see their favorite team, and legacy clubs became more popular than ever at the expense of smaller-market teams.

In 1994 New York cashed in with a lineup of All-Stars that helped the Rangers win their first Stanley Cup in 54 years. Brian Leetch may have won the Conn Smythe Trophy as playoff MVP, but four other future Hall of Famers were on the team, including captain Mark Messier. Only Leetch and fellow defenseman Sergei Zubov were homegrown, as Messier, forward Glenn Anderson, and defenseman Kevin Lowe were each acquired through trades.

The Rangers continued to spend more in the late 1990s, acquiring Gretzky, Lindros, and countless other superstars, but it did not net them any more titles. And while New York became a punchline thanks to seven straight playoff-empty seasons, the high-spending Colorado Avalanche were the NHL's Indians, selling out 487 consecutive games over an 11-year span en route to six conference-finals trips in seven seasons and a pair of Stanley Cup championships.

Colorado had lost an NHL franchise in the early 1980s and clearly wanted to prove that was a fluke. Buoyed by ticket sales, the return in the Lindros trade, and several years of high drafting in Quebec, the Avalanche sported an All-Star-laden lineup throughout the late 1990s and early 2000s.

Only Joe Sakic and Peter Forsberg were holdovers from Quebec, as Patrick Roy, Claude Lemieux, Sandis Ozolinsh, and Jari Kurri were each acquired via free agency or trade. The excitable market quickly became a dream television market, satisfying the largest city in the Mountain Time Zone.

The Avalanche developed a huge rivalry with the Detroit Red Wings—which gripped the league. After a prolonged era of mediocrity in the 1980s, the Red Wings became a dynasty, reaching the Stanley Cup finals three times in four years between 1995 and 1998 and winning the Cup twice. Detroit built its club through shrewd trades and with a seemingly limitless budget, thanks to a lucrative local-TV deal and the city's status as "Hockeytown USA."

The Red Wings were forward-thinking, becoming the first NHL team to truly scout Europe. They convinced Sergei Fedorov, Vyacheslav Kozlov, and Vladimir Konstantinov to defect from Russia when the Iron Curtain broke. The Wings then added Igor Larionov and Viacheslav Fetisov by trade, making the famous "Russian Five."

Scouting was important, but Detroit also had the means to retain many of their talented homegrown players. Without any deterrent—there was no salary cap in place—the Wings flexed their muscle, particularly in goal, first acquiring Mike Vernon from the Calgary Flames before adding Hall of Famers Dominik Hašek and Curtis Joseph to shore up the position behind a roster of superstars.

The Philadelphia Flyers enjoyed a huge era of success aided by free agency, and the Lindros trade, and reached the Eastern Conference finals three times in six years, including a run to the Cup finals in 1997. The Toronto Maple Leafs attracted free agents to the league's largest market, making the conference finals four times in 10 seasons, including back-to-back years in 1993 and 1994—only Gretzky's Kings thwarted a dream Montreal vs. Toronto Cup finals in 1993.

As player salaries rose, NHL teams also searched for new revenue streams, which is where an influx of new arenas cropped up. Boston

Garden, Maple Leaf Gardens, and the Montreal Forum were all replaced in the late 1990s, and markets that had lost teams—like San Jose, Minnesota, Colorado, and Atlanta—attracted new teams with state-of-the-art arenas and cushy lease agreements

While the haves enjoyed the spoils, the have-nots hit an era of despair. Small markets suffered cruel punishment, with the era serving as purgatory for hockey-obsessed places like Pittsburgh and Buffalo. After successful playoff runs through the 1990s, the Penguins and Sabres both went bankrupt and narrowly dodged moving to Kansas City.

Only a Mario Lemieux compromise kept the Pens in Pittsburgh. The former superstar had been forced into retirement in 1997 by non-Hodgkin lymphoma but the team still owed him $32 million. Instead of suing the club, Lemieux agreed to accept $20 million as equity to buy a majority share in the franchise in 1998.

Lemieux's appearance led to a new television deal, and that led to further financial stability. Plus, he singlehandedly sold tickets by returning to the ice in 2000 and helping Pittsburgh reach the Eastern Conference finals in 2001. Lemieux remained as a player/owner until 2006—helping mentor budding superstar Sidney Crosby—before re-retiring back to the owner's box after the 2005–06 season.

Tom Golisano, the deep-pocketed creator of Paychex and a former New York gubernatorial candidate, saved the Sabres by buying into Buffalo's hockey club in 2002. Such a move, coupled with the salary cap created after the 2003–04 season, paved the way for Buffalo's mid-2000s period of success.

Other robust hockey markets endured less dramatic, but still trying, periods of mediocrity. The Boston Bruins and Chicago Blackhawks were mired in a seemingly endless period of futility, as their penny-pinching owners pocketed revenues and let their fan bases go stale.

After Messier led the Edmonton Oilers to the Cup in 1990, Edmonton watched superstars Coffey, Messier, Kurri, Anderson, MacTavish, Lowe, Grant Fuhr, and Esa Tikkanen bolt for greener pastures—as the Oilers became a feeder program for the rest of the NHL.

Others, like Quebec City, Hartford, Winnipeg, and Minnesota suffered the worst fate, losing their beloved hockey teams altogether.

The only true outlier to the trend was in New Jersey. Under the shrewd management of Lou Lamoriello, the Devils won three Stanley Cup championships and reached the Cup finals four times in nine years despite a league-average payroll. New Jersey's payroll was about $31 million when it won the Cup in 2000—less than that of Montreal, Chicago, Vancouver, Anaheim, and the Rangers who all missed the playoffs that season—and that payroll was more than $10 million less than the Flyers and Stars, two teams it eliminated in the postseason.

Still New Jersey wasn't fully immune from the Sun Belt trend. In 1995 they were strongly considering a move to Nashville, Tennessee, and only the Devils' run to the Stanley Cup that season forced the state and then-owner John MacMullen to agree on a new arena lease at their home in East Rutherford.

Between 1996 and 2020, 17 teams either played for or won the Stanley Cup from a market that didn't exist before 1991. And of those just 10—Tampa Bay (3), Anaheim (2), San Jose, Nashville, Florida, Ottawa, and Las Vegas—were expansion teams. That means seven such clubs relocated from northern cities then went on to win hockey's ultimate prize.

So when the Whalers' financial troubles finally became too much, it's no surprise a Sun Belt market would come calling.

Chapter 10

The End in Hartford

Peter Karmanos gets credit as the villain who moved the Whalers out of Hartford, but he's something of a misunderstood character.

The son of Greek immigrants Peter Sr. and Faye, Karmanos fell in love with hockey while watching the Detroit Red Wings as a kid growing up in suburban Detroit, and that led to a lifelong career of service to hockey.

Karmanos is in both the United States Hockey Hall of Fame and Hockey Hall of Fame in Toronto, largely due to his founding of the Compuware youth program, which revolutionized youth hockey in the US and attracted future NHLers like Alfie Turcotte, Pat LaFontaine, and Kevin Hatcher. He later became the first American owner in Ontario Hockey League history when he purchased the Windsor Spitfires in 1984.

"His deep, true passion has always been the game," said Paul Maurice, who coached under Karmanos first in Windsor before taking over as Whalers head coach in 1995. "It's absolutely never been a money-making proposition in his mind. When you look at his history of all the players and people that he developed through all of those minor programs with Compuware that still goes on today, there's an awful lot of guys who became NHL players through his program."

Maurice saw a unique side of Karmanos—a loyal and generous boss who stuck by him for almost a decade when he was the youngest head coach in the history of North American professional sports, then again when Carolina rehired him in 2008.

"For me, personally, Mr. Karmanos has always been the bearer of opportunity," Maurice said. "He truly treated the people around him as family. That's been my experience."

Karmanos, Jim Rutherford, and Tom Thewes had designs on owning an NHL team, and after falling short on the Tampa Bay expansion bid, then failing to get off the ground in their inquiries into purchasing the St. Louis Blues and Minnesota North Stars, they finally achieved their goal of purchasing an NHL team when Karmanos bought the Whalers for $47 million from governor Lowell P. Weicker in 1994.

"It was available, and the price was right," Karmanos said in 2019.

There is no loyalty toward Karmanos in Hartford, and the feeling is mutual. Many believe Karmanos bought the Whalers simply to move them closer to his midwestern roots—either Columbus or Minnesota.

But he initially saw promise in Hartford as a market—being the only professional act in an affluent section of the pro-sports-mad Northeast. Many desperate fans clung to belief in Karmanos's group. For starters, Karmanos said all the right things, proclaiming he "knew hockey" and promised to keep the Whalers in Hartford for at least four years.

Rutherford was perceived as a modern version of Emile Francis—a small-statured former professional goalie turned franchise savior.

Things were looking up. A slew of new clubs and hot spots cropped up near the Hartford Civic Center, which also hosted the NHL Draft in 1994. The entire league headed to Hartford to see firsthand what the city had to offer.

Karmanos first raised ticket prices, hoping to recoup some revenue in the vastly expanding NHL marketplace. Then he put together a plan to make Hartford successful both on and off the ice.

"We had to build a state-of-the-art arena and provide a real entertainment experience," Karmanos said. "Simultaneous to that, we also had to build a team, because the best marketing in all of sports is winning."

With financial security in place, there was excitement surrounding the organization as the 1994–95 season drew near. Yet, in the one step forward, two steps back world of the Hartford Whalers, more disaster struck. In an effort to deter rapid revenue growth, the NHL owners locked out their players for more than 100 days in the fall and winter of 1994, and the news around the NHL was alarming.

"We had a brief players strike earlier in the decade, but this one seemed to be more bleak," former longtime NHL commentator Mike

Emrick said. "We were hearing that some of the teams at that time lost less money by not playing."

And as the NHL didn't play, the Whalers slipped out of Hartford's conscience. The UConn men's basketball team won more games than the Whalers in 1993–94, then started hot again in 1994–95. The Huskies won 28 games that season and reached the regional final before falling to eventual-champion UCLA, and Ray Allen, Donyell Marshall, and Kevin Ollie became stars across the state.

Geno Auriemma's women's basketball program also leapt onto the national stage, capturing the state's imagination along the way.

Behind superstars Jen Rizzotti and Rebecca Lobo, the Huskies went 35-0 in 1994–95 and won the National Championship—the first major championship in the state's history. UConn's run, and its ensuing dynasty, led to lifelong women's basketball fans. It also was aided by the Huskies' budding relationship with Connecticut Public Television—which aired the majority of UConn's games for the first time that season—that raised the program's players to stars within the state.

Even when the hockey season was saved early in January, the state was swept up in the women's team's win streak. Connecticut took great pride in housing a major sports champion for the first time and seemed to forget that the Whalers were still there.

The only people in Hartford genuinely excited about the lockout ending, aside from the Whalers themselves, were the local business owners. The four-month work stoppage cost the city a reported $14 million.

Still, after three straight seasons averaging less than 11,000 fans per game, Whalers attendance improved by about 1,400 per game in 1994–95.

The Whalers won just three of their first 14 games, but after rallying to beat the Canadiens in overtime in front of a sellout crowd at the Civic Center, they sat in the Eastern Conference's penultimate playoff spot on April 14 with just nine games remaining.

"That was the loudest I ever heard the building," said Whalers fan Michael Glasson, who also called it his most memorable game in 10 years of attending games at the Civic Center.

EASTERN CONFERENCE PLAYOFF STANDINGS
April 15, 1995 (top eight get in)

	W	L	T	Points
Quebec	27	9	4	58
Philadelphia	22	13	4	48
Pittsburgh	25	11	2	52
New Jersey	19	14	7	45
Boston	19	16	3	41
Washington	17	15	7	41
HARTFORD	17	17	5	39
Buffalo	16	16	6	38
NY Rangers	17	19	3	37
Montreal	15	19	5	35

A playoff run could have put the Whalers back on the marquee in Connecticut after two straight years out of the postseason. Hartford was just two points out of the number-five spot—which the Stanley Cup champion New Jersey Devils ended up occupying.

The Whalers fell to the Devils on April 16 on a goal from Scott Stevens with just 1:03 remaining. That, coupled with Sabres and Rangers wins, created a tie between New York and Hartford for the eighth playoff spot.

Hartford had reason to push the Rangers into its rearview mirror. On March 23, Rutherford made his first major move as Whalers GM, dealing struggling captain Pat Verbeek to New York for Glenn Featherstone and two draft picks—including the Blueshirts' first-rounder in June. The worse New York finished, the better the pick would have been for Hartford.

"I went to an Original Six team, which was a completely different thing after playing in Hartford and starting my career in New Jersey," Verbeek said. "I went in and played on a line with Mark Messier and Adam Graves, and at different times I played with Luc Robitaille and Ray Ferraro."

The Whalers won in Buffalo on April 18, pushing them into a tie with Washington for the number six spot in the East. Goalie Sean Burke was standing on his head on a nightly basis for the Whalers, as he stopped 32 shots in Hartford's win, then made 37 saves two nights later in New York—despite playing with Lyme disease.

But the Whalers wilted under the heat, winning just one of their final seven and missing the playoffs for the third straight year.

"We had a tough time in those games where everybody's playing their best hockey," Burke said. "We competed hard; we were there every night; but unfortunately you end up getting beat for the most part by better teams."

The Bruins went on to claim the East's number four seed, with the Devils, Capitals, Sabres, and Rangers rounding out the eight spots.

FINAL EASTERN CONFERENCE PLAYOFF STANDINGS (top eight get in)

	W	L	T	Points
Quebec	30	13	5	65
Philadelphia	28	16	4	60
Pittsburgh	29	16	3	61
Boston	27	18	3	57
New Jersey	22	18	8	52
Washington	22	18	8	52
Buffalo	22	19	7	51
NY Rangers	22	23	3	47
Florida	20	22	6	46
HARTFORD	19	24	5	43

The Whalers finished in a tie for 10th with the Canadiens, who also posted 43 points. The Rangers then stunned the Nordiques in the first round before falling to Philadelphia in the second round, and Quebec ultimately left for Colorado at season's end.

Few teams were safe from the threat of moving that offseason. Even the Devils were rumored to relocate to Nashville, until their Stanley Cup run ultimately quashed any prospect of a move—the state renegotiated its lease with owner John MacMullen shortly after the team's championship party.

The near-playoff run excited Hartford, and many of their games down the stretch were either sellouts or near-capacity crowds. But when all was said and done, the organization lost more than $11 million during the lockout-shortened campaign—despite icing a payroll of just $15.6 million in the 1994–95 season.

With a new financial structure in place, salaries took off—Rangers captain Mark Messier made $6.29 million during the 1995–96 season alone, and he still trailed Wayne Gretzky's $6.54 million deal that year.

Hoping to further generate buzz and improve his team, Jim Rutherford acquired All-Star forward Brendan Shanahan from the St. Louis Blues for defenseman Chris Pronger.

Pronger endured a difficult two-season tenure in Hartford, where he was arrested and suspended for his role in the Buffalo brawl during his rookie year before enduring a tumultuous second season, scoring only five goals and 14 points in 43 games.

The number two overall pick from the 1993 draft was still unable to drink legally in the United States, but his career was about to take off in St. Louis under the tutelage of former Whalers great Joel Quenneville, who took over as coach in 1996.

"He had some growing pains [in Hartford]," said Glen Wesley, Pronger's teammate with the Whalers during the 1994–95 season. "Things probably didn't go as well as he'd want it to, and he'd admit it. A great guy, a great leader. He obviously grew on and off the ice and matured into a great player."

Pronger's booming slap shot made St. Louis's power play one of the league's best, and he was named captain in 1997. Pronger was paired with fellow future Hall of Fame defenseman Al MacInnis, and the Blues consistently had one of the NHL's best defenses.

"He learned pretty quickly that he could handle himself and he could play a certain way and be intimidating," Whalers goalie Sean Burke said. "But he was young, and it was going to take time, and his years in Hartford were very much just developing years. So like a lot of our team, he was trying to find themselves in the game, and it was coming, but it wasn't going to come in that short period."

The Blues made the playoffs in each of Pronger's nine seasons in St. Louis, highlighted by their Presidents' Trophy campaign in 1999–2000 when he won the Norris Trophy and Hart Trophy, as league MVP. He was inducted into the Hall of Fame in 2015, even though he was still under contract with the Arizona Coyotes at the time.

"I think by the time I played with him in '99 he was very comfortable with his game," said Brad Shaw, a former Whalers defenseman who played with Pronger in St. Louis. "He knew exactly how to impact a game offensively, defensively, physically. Leadership-wise, he was a phenomenal guy in the locker room. He was a shift-by-shift example of how to compete."

Shanahan had been in St. Louis for four seasons after the Blues signed him in 1991, but he became a casualty of coach Mike Keenan's penchant for tinkering.

Shanahan had slept with line-mate Craig Janney's wife, whom he later married. The affair created a rift in the St. Louis dressing room, and it was easy for Keenan to decide between Shanahan and Brett Hull when ownership directed him to offload one of their two highly paid wings.

Shanahan was a bona fide superstar at the time and at 26 years old was just entering his prime. The second overall pick of the New Jersey Devils in the 1987 draft landed in St. Louis when he signed a four-year contract in 1991.

Shanahan scored 156 goals in a Blues jersey, highlighted by consecutive 50-goal seasons in 1992–93 and 1993–94. In 1993–94, he scored 52 goals and posted 104 points, then scored 20 goals and his 41 points—despite the 48-game season—trailing only Hull's 50.

"I was hugely excited when the team brought in Brendan Shanahan," said Whalers fan Michael Glasson. "I thought that was a move that would really help the team."

But Shanahan had doubts about Hartford, most notably the fact he couldn't get a straight answer about the team's future. Shanahan had directed his agent Rick Curran to find a trade that would get him playing for a contender.

Instead, he wound up in Hartford.

"I was approaching the midpoint of my career, and what I thought would be the back-nine," Shanahan said in 2018. "I wanted to have the opportunity to win and play in pressure-packed environments."

Shanahan already had friends in the Whalers organization. Goalie Sean Burke had lived with Shanahan during their tenure in New Jersey and was the best man in Burke's wedding. He also knew general manager Jim Rutherford from his days with the Windsor Spitfires.

"I was excited as everybody else was when we got [Shanahan]," Burke said in 2019. "Every player wants to see a commitment from the organization that we're trying to get better and trying to win, and those kinds of moves, even though they always come at a price, it just shows a commitment to try and build a winning team."

Shanahan trusted Rutherford but wanted assurances that he could stay in central Connecticut for the foreseeable future.

"I had lunch at his house, and I said 'my biggest issue was if I could lay down roots [in Hartford]. Even if you can't tell the public, can you tell me are we staying or are we going?'" Shanahan said. "And he said it hadn't been worked out and there was a lot of uncertainty, and I told him 'if you don't know then why did you trade for me?'

"And he said, let's give it a year and see whether we can get this figured out with the state and if we can stay in Hartford."

St. Louis retained a large chunk of Shanahan's lofty salary and took on Pronger. Coach Paul Holmgren wanted to make Shanahan the team captain, which the ninth-year forward balked at initially but ultimately accepted. Hartford named him captain September 18, 1995.

With the stalwart forward leading the way, the Whalers became a chic pick to make the playoffs. Shanahan had six assists in their first five games of 1995–96, making the press look good by starting the season 4-0-1.

But Shanahan tore two tendons in his wrist in the Whalers' first game, a 2–0 win against the New York Rangers, and the injury nagged him the rest of the season. After their unbeaten season start, Hartford lost five of six, and were outscored 25–4 in the process. Rutherford fired Paul Holmgren as head coach November 6, after a 6–1 drubbing to the Philadelphia Flyers, and replaced him with Paul Maurice.

Maurice played junior hockey as a defenseman for the Windsor Spitfires, rising to team captain in spite of an injury that cost him significant vision in his right eye at 17. The Philadelphia Flyers still used their 12th-round selection on him in the 1985 NHL Draft.

"When he was a rookie he got a puck in the eye," Peter Karmanos recalled in 2019. "He was good enough to be the last person drafted in the last round of the draft."

The Spitfires needed to free up a roster spot when goalie Pat Jablonski returned from the St. Louis Blues, and general manager Jim Rutherford met with Maurice and offered him an assistant coach position in 1988, as a 21-year-old. Karmanos was moved by Maurice's decision to quit and move behind the bench.

"He'd been there for a few years and was captain of the team, and we had the opportunity to add an overage player that we thought would take us to the next level, and Paul, even though he knew what it meant, said 'I'll drop out,'" Karmanos recalled. "I looked at him and said wow. The team is No. 1, and that's putting your money where your mouth is really, and we made him the coach because all the players looked up to him and respected him."

Maurice remained with Karmanos-owned teams through 2003, then returned to coach the Carolina Hurricanes in 2008. But when he started as Whalers coach, he was just 28 years old—the youngest coach in the history of the four North American professional sports at the time.

"When I came in there was never any talk of me replacing [Holmgren]," Maurice said. "I was uncomfortable with the idea of going there as an assistant. I was twenty-eight years old. I was awful young to even be an assistant in the National Hockey League let alone a head coach."

Maurice became the team's third head coach in three seasons—and its sixth since Tex Evans was fired midseason in 1987–88. He put up a good front despite his age, but he was in awe of his role behind the bench in the NHL.

"I think the biggest 'Oh my God, how young I am' moment came my first day," Maurice said. "I had the realization that [Whalers forward] Brad McCrimmon in his first year of pro, I was in grade seven. That kind of slapped me in the face."

Maurice was tasked with getting the most from Hartford's roster—no small chore, especially when Shanahan missed eight games with the wrist injury in November. Hartford bottomed out with an eight-game winless drought to close the calendar year.

"Once I could get a cortisone shot and taped it up every game, I could find the back of the net. But I couldn't fight. I had like two fights all season and I was in excruciating pain both times," Shanahan said. "We had a really tough team. It was not like I was unsupported, but I liked to do that on my own. It was like I was going into a gun fight and was hoping the other guy didn't have any bullets.

"The injury was frustrating because I couldn't do as much as I'd hoped."

Shanahan still finished atop the team with 44 goals and 78 points, and the Whalers turned things around when January arrived. Buoyed by the line of Shanahan, center Jeff O'Neill, and right wing Nelson Emerson, the Whalers pulled even for the final playoff spot on February 13.

But the Whalers won just four of their final 14 games, missing the playoffs yet again. Late in the season, after one of their excruciating losses, Rutherford addressed the team to commend its effort and growth—much to Shanahan's dismay.

The perception is that Shanahan hated his time in Hartford, but he disputes that. The team was a close-knit group, and his teammates liked him too—he's still friends with O'Neill and Emerson and spent a night in teammate Brad McCrimmon's hot tub drinking and bonding after the team's Halloween party in 1995 before hoofing it to the rink to get on the ice in time for practice.

"I sort of got into the team," Shanahan said. "People have this misconception that I didn't like living in Hartford, but I've been a New Englander for a long time. Simsbury is the nicest town I've ever lived in. I liked the team. I liked the guys who were working for the team."

Shanahan made it clear he was interested in consistency with a Stanley Cup contender. He felt the Whalers were on their way to respectability but wanted to be certain it was going to be in Hartford.

His wrist healed, and Shanahan represented Canada at the 1996 World Cup of Hockey, earning a silver medal in the first NHL-sanctioned international tournament. When the tournament ended, Shanahan met with Jim Rutherford at Swiss Chalet in Toronto and asked if the situation in Hartford was solved. When Rutherford said no, Shanahan asked to be moved.

"I enjoyed the pressure and passion of those [World Cup] games," Shanahan said. "And he said 'you're not coming back, are you?' And I asked him if the situation had changed, and it hadn't."

Rutherford's only demand was Shanahan go public with his trade demand, which made Whalers fans irate. The home crowd booed its captain every time he touched the puck in Hartford's 1–0 win against the Phoenix Coyotes on October 5, 1996.

But Whalers fans briefly saw a glimmer of hope after giving Shanahan a hero's ovation after he scored a short-handed goal in Hartford's 7–3 win against the Pittsburgh Penguins three nights later. But that quickly gave way after Shanahan's public postgame comments.

"I remember being asked if [the ovation] changed anything," Shanahan said, "and I said I appreciated the response, but it doesn't."

Rutherford could have traded Shanahan to the Capitals, Flyers, or Detroit Red Wings, and Washington actually offered Hartford the best deal. But Rutherford respected Shanahan's willingness to give Hartford a shot, and rewarded him for it by trading him to the Red Wings, where he became the missing piece to three Stanley Cup championship teams.

"That's the part I appreciate about Jimmy," Shanahan said. "He asked me to give an honest effort, and saw that I'd worked hard and knew I was hurt, and he worked hard and worked with me to get a deal done with Detroit."

The Whalers dealt Shanahan on October 9, just one day after his goal against Pittsburgh, for defenseman Paul Coffey, forward Keith Primeau, and a first-round pick in the 1997 draft. It was the very start of Hartford's final season hosting NHL play.

Ironically the Shanahan trade laid the foundation for championship teams, both for Detroit and ultimately the Whalers organization after it moved. But some feel his departure from Hartford served as a seminal moment in the Whalers' downfall.

"It was a situation of coming to a team that was regarded by some as second rate," said John Forslund, the team's television play-by-play broadcaster. "He could've embraced [Hartford], but I understand why he didn't. When a player of that profile says no, it is a stigma you can't shake."

But Shanahan swears that if Karmanos, Rutherford, and Whalers management could have come to a deal with the state, things could've been different. "If [Rutherford] had told me 'we've worked out an agreement with the state, and we're staying' I probably would've stayed," Shanahan said. "He didn't know if we were going; he didn't know when we were going, and he didn't know where we were going. I was entering my tenth year in the league, and if he had said it's Hartford [as the final location] I probably would've bought a house and stayed as captain."

Hearing Shanahan's opinion of Hartford, some 25 years later, stunned Whalers fans and even writers and broadcasters who were around the team. It even shocked the team's owner Peter Karmanos.

"We couldn't give him any assurances," Karmanos said in 2019 upon hearing Shanahan's perspective. "You can't make him promises you can't keep."

The trade blindsided some in the locker room, as they thought the first Shanahan trade was the start of a grander plan to build a winner in Hartford. Coffey wanted nothing to do with Hartford, and spent just 20 games in a Whalers uniform before demanding a trade—he was dealt to the Flyers just 66 days after Hartford acquired him.

The Whalers still tried to spin things positively for 1996–97. Rutherford acquired Kevin Dineen on December 28, 1995 and named him captain after the Shanahan deal. After six seasons of virtually nonexistent game coverage outside of SportsChannel New England, the Hartford WB affiliate, WBNE or Channel 59, upped their number of Whalers game broadcasts to 20 on network television, the most since 1990.

The Whalers again averaged fewer than 12,000 fans per game in 1995–96, which prompted Connecticut politicians to join Jim Rutherford in a ticket-selling initiative, with the goal of saving the Whalers in Hartford.

The team did its part too, posting a respectable 10-7-4 record in the first quarter—including a 7-4-1 record at the Civic Center. The fans started to come: Hartford averaged 13,400 fans per game over the first quarter of the season.

But financially, the Whalers were on life support, which prompted an emergency meeting at Governor John Rowland's mansion with Karmanos and NHL commissioner Gary Bettman on January 9.

"We met at the governor's mansion, and [Bettman] said [to Rowland] 'do not say if we don't get an arena, the team has to move,'" Karmanos recalled. "We had at least an hour-and-a-half conversation with them and said 'don't say that.'

"First fucking question, someone says 'If [the Whalers] don't get an arena, will the team have to move?' And the governor says 'yes, the team will have to move if we don't get an arena.'"

Karmanos perceived the slight as Rowland kicking the team out. He stopped fighting for Hartford and began calculating the Whalers' exit from Connecticut.

His first choice was Columbus, Ohio—a midwestern market where he could be closer to home. Columbus didn't have an arena at the time, but Karmanos eyed an old airport hangar to play in while a publicly funded arena was erected in the city's southern end near the Scioto River. He was so confident he had a deal he told the players he was "99 percent sure" they would be playing there in 1997–98 during a meeting in the season's waning days.

But the people of Columbus voted down using public money to build an arena in a referendum in May 1997. Ultimately, four Ohio natives ponied up $100 million for an expansion team—and Nationwide Insurance offered $150 million to build the arena that bears its name and has hosted the Columbus Blue Jackets since 2000.

St. Paul, Minnesota, was Karmanos's second option, though he had some reservations about that market too. He also was stymied when the NHL announced an expansion team, named the Wild, would return to the Twin Cities on June 25, 1997.

Karmanos had discussions with dozens of potential markets, including San Diego, but Columbus and St. Paul were the only two he visited aside from Raleigh, North Carolina.

While Karmanos calculated his exit, fans and the players were none the wiser. Karmanos had promised four years in Hartford, and in year three the Whalers were winning and occupied a playoff spot at the season's official halfway point.

EASTERN CONFERENCE PLAYOFF STANDINGS
January 8, 1997 (top eight get in)

	W	L	T	Points
Philadelphia	26	12	4	56
Pittsburgh	22	15	4	48
Florida	21	10	9	51
NY Rangers	22	16	6	50
Buffalo	21	15	5	47
New Jersey	21	15	3	45
HARTFORD	17	16	7	41
Montreal	16	18	8	40
Washington	17	20	4	38

With the team flourishing on the ice, and the owner drowning in a sea of lost money, Rowland searched for $150 million for a new 20,000-seat arena in the northeast section of Hartford that would serve both UConn and the Whalers—on the site of what is now a minor-league baseball stadium.

There is a perception among Whalers fans and Connecticut residents that Rowland didn't appreciate the Whalers and was focused on luring the Patriots from Foxborough, Massachusetts, to the Connecticut capital. They feel his complacency about the Whalers doomed the team, which Karmanos also believes.

"We tried to get the people involved with the state to understand the financial situation we were in," Karmanos said on the Carolina Hurricanes 10th anniversary documentary. "Unfortunately the governor of the state at that time had a different agenda, so he sent us packing, so to speak."

Even some former Whalers players believe that.

"I know the governor at the time was basically for-move, would be my impression that I had at the time," said Dineen. "I remember being at a benefit, and he went up and was speaking and was joking about it and so on.

"I think it takes the emotional side of it, but he wasn't looking at that. He was looking at it strictly from the business side, and for the state. Unfortunately he gave away the only major-league franchise they've had."

That opinion is misguided though, according to Rowland's camp.

"There's nothing further from the truth," said Brendan Fox, who served as Rowland's deputy chief of staff during his first term before becoming his chief counsel. "Governor Rowland understood the importance of the Whalers and the presence of the Whalers in downtown Hartford and what that meant from an economic development perspective.

"For anyone to suggest that the governor did not care about the Whalers and was focused solely on the Patriots and allowed the Whalers to leave in order to enhance the opportunity for the Patriots is wrong. They're wrong."

Rowland was offering Karmanos an arena, plus relinquishing two years worth of rent as back-pay for money the owner lost. According to the *Hartford Courant*, Rowland guaranteed the Whalers $50 million per year in revenue in exchange for a $2.5 million annual rent payment.

"Governor Rowland committed every reasonable resource to keep the Hartford Whalers right where they were in Hartford," Fox said.

Further complicating things, the state legislature was looking for a revenue-neutral deal so Connecticut would collect as much money as it shelled out for an arena or concessions they provided Karmanos.

Karmanos wanted to play in the new arena rent-free, like so many other NHL and pro-sports teams ended up doing, and wanted the state to cover revenue losses in the $20–40 million range for three years while the arena was being built. But the governor held a hard line on both.

"In my opinion we offered them everything they asked for," Fox said. "I did have a sense that the bar continued to move as we negotiated the transaction. Every time we said, 'yes, we will do that' we had another demand put on the table."

Karmanos recalled things happening differently.

"Out of our whole organization, I was the one who wanted to stay in Hartford," Karmanos said. "I tried to deal with that governor, and people don't want to hear it but I couldn't figure out what was going on.

"I wanted to build an arena right downtown, but I was naive. You can't have a special tax on the tickets. We're having a hard time selling tickets now. I'm not going to guarantee this and that. I can't do that.

"He was trying to construct the deal that made no sense. Who has built a revenue-neutral arena ever? . . . You can make anything revenue-neutral if you take it out enough years and then figure out what new sources of revenue. They didn't talk about revenue-neutral back then, by the way."

Even though it cost him a $20.5 million exit payment and without a destination for the 1997–98 season, Karmanos announced March 26 that the team would leave at the end of the 1997 season—a day after old nemesis Patrick Roy stopped 46 shots for the Colorado Avalanche in their 4–0 win in front of a near-capacity crowd at the Civic Center that put Hartford on the outside of the playoffs.

"I am very pleased and honored I could go out there and give the Hartford fans the very best game I could," Roy told the *Hartford Courant* after the game. "I have so many great memories going against the Whalers. . . . Over the years, we had some great battles."

After 25 years of mismanagement, moderate highs, and embarrassing lows, the Whalers were about to be history. The players knew, but team employees were kept in the dark, with many finding out when the Hartford-area NBC affiliate broke the story on the 11:00 p.m. news.

The bad blood between Whalers fans and the owner that moved them clearly lingers today. Karmanos, for better or worse, has not shied from the vitriol. He has been openly hostile to the market and doesn't care how he's perceived by fans in Hartford.

"If you look at the last year's attendance, it shows the average attendance was about 13,700 or so," said Jeff Jacobs, sports columnist for the *Hartford Courant* at the time. "But the state had struck a deal that they would get the revenue for the luxury boxes, and [Karmanos] refused to count them in the attendance. They averaged more than 14,000 per game that season.

"For the rest of time, it will say that [the Whalers average attendance] was 13,700 for the last year, and I'll never forget it because it was such a petty thing to do, and it's stamped there for eternity."

The *Courant* named Karmanos "1b" on its list of 10 villains in the newspaper on March 27—with former owner Richard Gordon occupying the 1a spot for putting Karmanos in the financial mess they were in in the first place.

Ultimately there is ample blame to go around, including for Rowland.

"We were $3 million apart when this whole deal fell apart, and the unfortunate thing about the $3 million is that money was coming in anyway because that's the money the visiting players pay in state income tax," said Tom Ritter, the state speaker of the house at the time. "The governor didn't want to count that money because he had campaigned on eliminating the income tax, and was running for his second term, and if he included that money as revenue coming in then it would look like he's breaking his promise to eliminate the income tax."

Karmanos had told the team about Columbus, but the deal wasn't finalized so he did not reveal where he was going. He'd only say he was moving the team from Hartford—adding insult to the city's already-wounded psyche.

While Karmanos was orchestrating the team's departure, Maurice was fixated on keeping the team focused on the ice. Each subsequent home game had a funeral-like atmosphere—as fans returned to get one final glimpse of the Whalers. But Hartford picked up its play, winning four of its next six to creep back into the final playoff spot in the Eastern Conference.

"If there was a year that I think it affected us negatively, it was that year," said Sean Burke, the Whalers goalie that season. "It seemed like the writing was on the wall now for sure."

Two years earlier, the New Jersey Devils appeared destined for Nashville before winning their first Stanley Cup. Despite its on-ice success, New Jersey was a market similar to Hartford—one that struggled amid its big-market neighbors.

Perhaps if Hartford got into the playoffs and ran to the championship, the NHL would have been forced to intervene, and Karmanos could either hang on in Hartford or perhaps a newly interested majority owner could swoop in, buy the team, and keep it in Hartford.

EASTERN CONFERENCE PLAYOFF STANDINGS
April 7, 1997 (top eight get in)

	W	L	T	Points
New Jersey	44	21	13	101
Buffalo	39	28	12	90
Philadelphia	44	23	12	100
Florida	33	28	19	85
NY Rangers	37	33	10	84
Pittsburgh	37	33	8	82
Montreal	30	35	14	74
HARTFORD	31	37	11	73
Ottawa	28	36	15	71

The Whalers fell behind 3–0 in Ottawa on April 7 but rallied with three third-period goals, two from Andrew Cassels, tying the game at four. Randy Cunneyworth's power-play goal at 12:49 of the frame lifted the Senators to the all-important win, pulling the clubs even with two games left.

Needing to win their final two games, and needing help after the Senators topped the Detroit Red Wings two nights later, Sami Kapanen's first-period goal on Long Island pushed the Whalers ahead in the crucial contest. But Hartford wilted under a barrage of goals, with two shorthanded and three more on breakaways.

After a 6–4 loss to the Islanders, coupled with the Senators' 1–0 win in their season finale over the Buffalo Sabres, Hartford's swan song at the Civic Center would go down as a meaningless game.

Don't tell the fans of Hartford that though. Despite the fact they averaged the third-worst attendance in the NHL in 1996–97 and had not won a playoff series in more than 10 years, the Whalers played in front of a sellout with 14,660 cramming the Hartford Civic Center on April 13, 1997.

"I remember driving into downtown [Hartford] from Springfield, Massachusetts at six or seven in the morning," said Forslund. "And it was a nice day, with some clouds rolling in, and as I got closer to Hartford there were these dark storm clouds that just hung over the city."

Forslund opened by calling it "the meaningless game with tremendous meaning," and color commentator Bill Gardner donned his original Whalers sweater for the game's entirety.

"I was devastated, probably more than the fans knew," Forslund said. "I was shook up, but the problem for me was not a lot of people knew it or wanted to talk about it with me.

"I had grown up in Springfield, and was a Bruins fan because they were first. But I loved that team, and I loved that market. I never told anyone because no one has asked me, because obviously the go-to guy was Chuck [Kaiton], and deservedly so. But the perception about me was 'he's going to be OK because he's Karmanos's guy' and that I was only loyal to the people that were giving me a paycheck."

In a cruel and ironic twist, the Whalers hosted the Tampa Bay Lightning in their final home game—the team Karmanos fell short of owning in expansion, and whose existence opened the door for the Whalers to bolt to another Sun Belt city.

"It was really weird," goalie Sean Burke said. "We were playing Tampa, and I think there was an excitement with the team that we were moving, so you knew now at least there was an answer.

"But I had built a lot of relationships there and good friends there. Both my oldest children were born there, and it just didn't seem real."

The Whalers stepped onto the Hartford Civic Center rink to the tune of "Brass Bonanza"—their legendary former theme song. It was a moment that harkened fans back to a brighter time in Whalers history, one that was full of optimism and potential.

The Whalers gave Hartford that boost. There were many, specifically those in and around Hartford, who were emotional at the end. For some, the ache has not subsided.

"I cried, literally cried," said Joanne Cortesa, a former season-ticket holder and member of the Whalers booster club since 1986. "I wore a black armband to the game on my jersey."

A major-league franchise in central Connecticut may seem ridiculous to those in more traditional markets, but having the NHL was a source of self-esteem to that region. Unfortunately the people took it for granted until it was too late.

"I kind of had some ill will with the City of Hartford because it felt like it was unsupported," said Dave Schneider, a Bridgeport native, Whalers season-ticket holder, and the lead singer of the band The Zambonis. "I wrote this song [in 1999] called 'Bob Marley and the Hartford Whalers,' and it's literally about that. You know, like support your local hockey team . . . because I feel they weren't supported."

I remember hockey games
Played right here in my state
That's where all the people came for their local hockey team
Those days are still around, unfortunately not in my state
Support it can't be found
It's in the press, and now we're all depressed.
Bob Marley and the Hartford Whalers are not around
Bob Marley and the Hartford Whalers have left town.

Schneider spent most of the final game in the arena's gift shop scooping up Whalers merchandise before leaving heartbroken. While much of the SportsChannel pregame show was dedicated to heartbroken Whalers fans like Schneider, Cortesa, or booster club members, they also played a role in the organization's demise. *Hartford Courant* columnist Stan Simpson lambasted the fans, citing their inability to come through with season tickets and calling the market "fickle."

"I felt really really bad for the fans that always came and lived and died every word Chuck Kaiton called," Jacobs said. "Part of me was cold by people who hadn't come to games, acting like they lived and died with the team. It was really weird."

Jacobs, who adopted the Nutmeg State as his home when he took the job as the *Hartford Courant*'s Whalers beat writer in 1984, dubs Connecticut "169 petty fiefdoms"—accounting for each state's municipality that chooses to look out for itself. As the Whalers' ship sank, those who could have offered a life raft chose not to—particularly those in New Haven County.

"The people from Avon, Simsbury and Farmington bought tickets like they were motherfucking Canadians," Jacobs said. "The support from those towns was enormous. But the ferocity of that support was not wide enough. In my mind, there was always a level of resentment from New Haven County that they were the Hartford Whalers. Maybe if they were the Connecticut Whalers, they could have existed."

Painted at center-ice was "To Our Whalers, Thanks for the Memories," and the years 1975 and 1997 in black ink, referencing the Whalers lifespan in Hartford. The SportsChannel telecast paid homage to Whalers history, airing a graphic of the Whalers' all-time lines and defense pairings, according to Kaiton, who had called every NHL game in their history.

Hartford came out flying in front of its home fans, and Glen Wesley broke the ice at 2:30 of the first period. Tears were shed when Kevin Dineen struck 24 seconds into the third period, breaking a 1–1 tie and delivering the knockout punch on Hartford's send-off victory.

"He was John Wayne," Jacobs said. "He was the last man standing."

The Whalers' third-round pick in 1982, who had returned to Hartford during the 1995–96 season and whose dad Bill helped Hartford's run of success in the 1980s as the director of amateur scouting, scored his 235th goal for Hartford. It was both the final goal in Whalers history and the game-winner in their last NHL game.

"That was certainly an emotional day in that city," Dineen said. "I think you see a window closing, and it's an emotional moment."

Forslund offered a subdued version of his signature "hey, hey whatta you say" call, for good reason.

"I went to a very sedated call of that second goal," said Forslund. "I was not going to be excited. There wasn't this wave of positive emotion."

Dineen's goal put almost the perfect ribbon on Hartford's 2–1 win, even though he twice missed the chance at an empty net in the third period, including when the horn and goal light mistakenly went off with 13 seconds remaining.

Despite two decades of missed opportunities, failed rebuilds, and false starts in the NHL, the Whalers sent their heartbroken fans out with a win. They saluted the sellout crowd by raising their sticks at center ice—long before the practice became universal in the NHL—and tossed equipment and pucks into the stands as "Brass Bonanza" blared from the Civic Center's speakers.

The emotion reached a fever pitch when, after several minutes of a raucous standing ovation, Dineen took the microphone.

"It's been my pleasure to be associated with you, the fans," Dineen said. "For your support and enthusiasm you've shown in this building, there's none other. For all the players that have loved Hartford and are sitting on this bench, we want to say thank you, and God bless and thank you very much."

That improvised moment also stood out for Dineen looking back more than 22 years later.

"You feel responsibility, but it's pretty hard to put into words how to express that gratitude for the support they've given," Dineen said in 2019. "Again, a real emotional night. At the end of it was certainly a

FINAL 1997 EASTERN CONFERENCE PLAYOFF STANDINGS (top eight get in)

	W	L	T	Points
New Jersey	45	23	14	104
Buffalo	40	30	12	92
Philadelphia	45	24	13	103
Florida	35	28	19	89
NY Rangers	38	34	10	86
Pittsburgh	38	36	8	84
Ottawa	31	36	15	77
Montreal	31	36	15	77
HARTFORD	32	39	11	75
Washington	33	40	9	75
Tampa Bay	32	40	10	74

little draining. That was not any fun for anybody . . . but at least we got to address them and show our appreciation for the fans."

That the Canadiens ultimately finished as the East's number eight seed only stings further today. Montreal, which dispatched Hartford in three of its seven playoff defeats including the 1986 Adams Division finals and in double overtime in its last playoff berth in 1992, was just two points better than the Whalers after the 1997 season.

The franchise was headed south, where the organization's proverbial winds changed forever.

Chapter 11

The Hurricanes

The histories of the Hartford Whalers and Carolina Hurricanes are eerily similar, outside of a couple of puck bounces.

To an outsider, that statement might seem preposterous. The cities are separated by more than 600 miles—with thousands more in philosophical differences. Second, despite the fact the Whalers and Hurricanes were both run by the same people, Carolina has enjoyed multiple deep playoff runs—four trips to the conference finals or better as of 2019—whereas Hartford claimed just one playoff-series win in the NHL.

Yet, when you dig a little deeper, you realize how alike the organizations are.

When Howard Baldwin moved the Whalers to Hartford, they were the city's first professional sports organization, giving the small market known mostly for insurance and the University of Connecticut a professional identity.

When Peter Karmanos announced the Whalers were relocating to Raleigh, North Carolina, May 6, 1997, he gave the college-basketball haven and tobacco hub a pro-sports identity it had not previously known.

"They're running different but parallel lines in the hockey universe," Paul Maurice, the Hurricanes first coach, said of Hartford and Raleigh. "Neither one of them is a traditional market in either size or geographic location. They were both incredibly passionate and truly loved their team, and both cities were constantly fighting naysayers about whether it could work."

The Whalers' NHL story began in basketball-mad Springfield, Massachusetts, while their arena in Connecticut's capital was made suitable for NHL hockey. The Hurricanes' story began in basketball-mad Greensboro, North Carolina, while their future home in North Carolina's capital—about 75 miles east—was finished.

Raleigh, along with neighboring Durham, Cary, and Chapel Hill, make up North Carolina's "Research Triangle." The name comes partly from the sterling academic reputation of area universities including Duke, UNC–Chapel Hill, and North Carolina State. Since 1959, the region has also been home to Research Triangle Park. The Triangle region houses more than 200 companies, mostly in the tech sector, and it serves as a boon to the North Carolina economy—with more than 50,000 workers employed there as of 2016.

Raleigh is mostly made up of transplants, but locals love their regional sports rivalries—most notably in college basketball where UNC–Chapel Hill and Duke, and North Carolina State and UNC, have fueled tensions for years.

The Whalers spent 18 years in the National Hockey League but made the playoffs seven times. But in the Hurricanes' first 22 NHL seasons, they made the playoffs only seven times—with dramatically different results.

Karmanos's decision to migrate south was one that left people confused and bitter. Old-time hockey fans resented southern migration, and the Whalers' departure, which came shortly after the Quebec Nordiques departed for Colorado and Winnipeg Jets moved to Phoenix, signaled a shifting landscape in the NHL that cloaked many markets in doubt.

But the move mostly left people confused, including those in North Carolina. Despite hockey's Sun Belt shift, moving the Whalers to Raleigh to become the Carolina Hurricanes seemed like the team went from Hartford to Hartford, only without the backing of the richest state and its longstanding hockey passion.

Consider Raleigh's demographics at the time. North Carolina's capital was the state's second-largest city in 1997 but had only approximately 256,000 people, and Wake and Durham Counties—which house Raleigh and the Triangle—housed fewer than a million residents, making it one of the NHL's smallest markets.

Few in North Carolina demanded an NHL team, and they didn't know what to make of hockey in general.

"There was a lot of surprise," said Steve Politi, who covered the team's inaugural season for the *Raleigh News & Observer*. "It was a bit of a shock for it to actually happen. There wasn't a lot of people in North Carolina saying 'We need NHL hockey.'"

But there had been clamoring for a new arena in Raleigh for NC State basketball, and that's where it became an inviting locale. The Wolfpack's previous home, Reynolds Coliseum, was worn out, and the state green-lighted a new arena to open in 1998.

Karmanos traveled to Raleigh to review plans after city officials called him about the Whalers. After the move, he pushed for the players, front office, and staff to move to Raleigh and become part of the community. They practiced at Raleigh IcePlex, and staffers bought houses, enrolled their children in schools, and drummed up excitement in the Triangle.

But the Hurricanes needed a place to play in the interim. The Greensboro Coliseum was about the only appropriately sized place, and the building managers knew it, but Karmanos and minority owner and general manager Jim Rutherford had to try and get a better deal—taking the media 83 miles south to rural Fayetteville, North Carolina, where an 8,500-seat venue was close to being finished.

"The move was premature; there wasn't even a lease agreement on a building," said Dave Droschak, who covered the team for their website and later the Associated Press. "I remember touring the Fayetteville Arena with Jim Rutherford with hard hats on, saying 'there's no way an NHL team will play in Fayetteville, North Carolina.'"

Karmanos lost more than $100 million in the Hurricanes' two years in Greensboro, but it beat being in Hartford, for him at least.

"Greensboro looked ideal," he said. "It had an 18- or 19,000-seat arena. It was reasonable to play in."

Greensboro has mostly been known for its college-basketball history. The Greensboro Coliseum hosted the NCAA Final Four in 1974 and as of 2021, has hosted the ACC men's basketball tournament 26 times since 1967. It's still regularly a site for early-round NCAA tournament games.

Greensboro is 76 miles northwest of Raleigh—a straight shot down scenic Interstate 40. That might seem like a short ride for a weekend trip to the ACC Tournament or NCAA Tournament games, but expecting fans to make that trip 41 nights per year for hockey was lunacy.

"They didn't understand the distance; they didn't understand the traffic," said Luke DeCock, a *Raleigh News & Observer* sports columnist and former Hurricanes beat writer. "These were two separate markets. People from the Triangle would only go to Greensboro for the ACC Tournament, and [Karmanos] didn't understand the disconnect."

Karmanos admitted more than 20 years later that shoehorning the team into Greensboro—instead of putting money in to renovate and play at Dorton Arena, the seven-season home of the ECHL's Raleigh IceCaps—was a mistake.

"We really should have put $20 or $30 million into the building on the fairgrounds in Raleigh in retrospect," Karmanos said. "We could've made it fit and had a good, solid fan base versus in Greensboro that were interlopers.

"The difference between the Triangle and the Triad—Greensboro, Winston-Salem and High Point—is like sixty years. That's the old, old south. The Triangle is the new south."

The organization desperately attempted to get fans to the sprawling Greensboro Coliseum for hockey. They raffled off a car every game the first season—which inspired visiting media to buy tickets in the hopes they might luck into a new ride. They had former NASCAR driver Richard Petty drive the Zamboni, as the ice resurfacing machine was a novelty to people in North Carolina.

"I remember a great big security guard who was in charge of standing watch outside our locker room," said Stu Grimson, a forward for the Hurricanes their inaugural season, "and he proudly announced in his thick, good ole' boy accent 'Stu, you guys are in for a great game tonight. The ice will be perfect. I sat here and watched that Zamboozi go around the ice four times this afternoon!'"

Because of the hasty move, there was little-to-no marketing plan other than car giveaways, and sometimes the results indicated that. Hockey fans in Greensboro had spent seven seasons paying ECHL prices to watch the Greensboro Monarchs, which left them resentful when they started having to pay full freight when the NHL came to town. They sold 3,000 season tickets and averaged 9,106 in the 20,000-plus seat arena that first season—though fans in attendance were actually far fewer.

"People used to call it 'Green Acres,'" Droschak said. "Because the seats were green, and there were just acres and acres of empty seats. They drew about 4,000 or 5,000 fans per night."

Everything, from their home arena to their name and mascot, seemed hastily cobbled together. Karmanos chose the name Hurricanes, despite two such natural disasters that caused billions of dollars in damages in North Carolina the year prior. Their pig mascot was problematic because of a 25-million-gallon hog-waste lagoon that had collapsed in coastal North Carolina in 1995 that polluted the New River, which runs from Jacksonville to the Atlantic Ocean.

Then there was Stormy the Pig's unveiling. They planned to introduce the mascot by having him pop out of a Zamboni, with dry ice creating smoke to add dramatic effect. But when the Zamboni opened, 32-year-old Phil Madren's legs began convulsing, as the dry ice sapped oxygen inside, sending him into a seizure. Fortunately for Karmanos, Madren didn't sue them, only wishing for his job back.

Plus, the on-ice product wasn't any better. The team in Carolina was similar to the one that had missed the playoffs the previous five seasons in Hartford. Rutherford cobbled together a roster of tenacious players, as violence can sell hockey in nontraditional markets.

But with everything going against them, having a good salesman was beneficial, which helped because coach Paul Maurice was as good as they came.

"He was a telegenic guy," Politi said. "He knew not to discuss the neutral-zone trap. He kept it basic."

At the time, Maurice was a fresh-faced, 30-year-old from Sault Saint Marie, Ontario, who coached the club for 152 games in Hartford then stuck with the team when it moved south.

"You were selling in an unusual market," Maurice said. "It taught me the responsibility of the head coach to be open to the fans in terms of media access and how I answer questions and how I deal with reporters."

Maurice realized he had a hard sell and made sure not to talk down to fans or even the media, who may not have known the ins and outs of the sport.

"There were some pretty ridiculous questions that he was asked in the early years," Droschak said. "And he answered all of them. Good questions, bad questions. He made time for everyone."

"He was a great coach for that moment in time," Grimson said. "The fact that he was so approachable endeared our team to that area, in my opinion."

Maurice has enjoyed a lengthy coaching career and is one of the most thoughtful and informative interviews in the NHL, and he credits that largely to his time in Greensboro.

"I think that had a real big impact on me for the next twenty-five years," Maurice said. "Still in my press conferences and dealing with the media, I still feel that responsibility to sell the game and explain the game and educate the game."

Maurice tried to make the most of a bad situation, but it was a mess. The team held its morning skates in Raleigh then each player schlepped to Greensboro—with many checking into a hotel for every home game.

"You had the choice of checking into a hotel, having a pregame meal and nap and play the game and driving home, or else you could go home, eat, take your nap and get up early and drive to Greensboro to play the game," said Ron Francis, who signed with the Hurricanes in 1998. "It's an hour-and-15-minute ride. There wasn't the [Interstate]-540 highway at the time, so you had to take some back roads through Raleigh. It was not the most convenient [environment] for a player."

"It was a crazy time for the players," Grimson said. "Every game was like a road game."

The facilities at the Coliseum were no better. Cramped dressing rooms, built for basketball, led to terrifying moments for players and reporters. Maurice even had to kick construction workers out of the home locker room just minutes before their home opener against the Pittsburgh Penguins.

"The locker rooms were puny," Droschak said. "One night I stepped on Stu Grimson's foot, and I thought he would kick my ass."

Plus the crowd support was nonexistent. The Hurricanes averaged fewer than 10,000 fans per game in 1997–98 and only 8,188 per game in 1998–99—despite the fact Carolina won its division that season.

"There are a thousand memories of 'this is not normal. This is different,'" Maurice said.

They realized they had to bide their time in Greensboro and build a winning team in hopes of generating interest in Raleigh. They quickly did, drawing on the past to also tie the organization together. They signed Francis to a four-year contract the first offseason, then won the Southeast Division in their second season in Greensboro—the first of their three playoff appearances in a four-year stretch.

"I think at the time he was overpaid, because you had to overpay to get a guy like that," said John Forslund, who has been a commentator on television and radio since the team's days in Hartford. "So Karmanos and Rutherford went out and did that, and instant credibility. All of a sudden it was 'Alright, Ron Francis wants to play for the Carolina Hurricanes.'"

"We changed when Ron Francis joined our team," Maurice said. "That was the change in our franchise."

Francis had twice won the Cup in Pittsburgh, and the perception people had of him in Hartford had completely shifted by the time he signed in Carolina. But the longtime Whalers captain rejoined the team, in part, thanks to a familiar face from his Hartford days.

"There was certainly one market I could have gotten more money to go play in, but I felt this was the best place for me to be and raise my family," Francis said. "Kevin Dineen was here at the time, and I kind of asked him some questions about the market and stuff, and I thought it was a pretty cool and unique challenge to sell our game, which I firmly believe in, to a new market and certainly one in the South."

Carolina players quickly gravitated to the 35-year-old center, who became a father figure in the dressing room, since he was five years older than Maurice.

"Ronnie was a great leader on and off the ice," said Bates Battaglia, a forward for the Hurricanes from 1997 to 2003. "He was more like a coach than a player. Everyone in the room learned from him."

The team moved into the RBC Center in Raleigh in 1998, and Rutherford's shrewd moves set the Hurricanes up. On January 23, 2000, Rutherford traded captain Keith Primeau, a notable piece of the Brendan Shanahan trade who had been holding out, to Philadelphia for a package that included Rod Brind'Amour.

"I remember sitting in Philadelphia with [Flyers general manager] Bobby Clarke and [owner Ed] Snider saying 'Why do you want Primeau?'" Peter Karmanos said. "I'm the owner saying in good conscience, I'm telling you this guy is holding a gun to our head."

Francis was named captain again, joining Dineen as the only people to wear the C in both Hartford and Carolina.

"Primeau had put himself ahead of the team a little bit, and they didn't like that," Forslund said. "So they went out and got a guy who is about as team-first as anybody I ever covered, and then he comes here and he's subordinate in leadership to Francis, and you know, it's still Ronnie's team."

The Hurricanes unofficially arrived in Raleigh in 2001. After falling behind 3–0 in their series against the New Jersey Devils, Carolina rallied to win Game 4 in overtime, then stole Game 5 in New Jersey. Despite a 5–1 loss in Game 6, the team earned a standing ovation in the third period in Raleigh, and many feel that series cemented the Hurricanes'place in Raleigh for good.

"In that year we learned what playoffs were all about," said Maurice.

But the magical spring of 2002, then their run to the Stanley Cup four years later, are what secured the Hurricanes' status in the Triangle.

The Hartford Whalers' dreams of hoisting the Stanley Cup were largely sabotaged by shoddy playoff goaltending.

But the Carolina Hurricanes' postseason experiences have been hallmarked by unlikely success from their most important position.

Carolina made four trips to the Eastern Conference finals in four postseason appearances between 2002–19 and got significant contributions from two goalies in three of those four trips.

Carolina's first run to the Stanley Cup finals, in 2001–02, started the trend and was as improbable as it was magical. Few thought Carolina was a contender entering the season—and Maurice barely survived the season. Rumors were swirling as the Hurricanes entered their December 8 game in Florida on a four-game losing streak where they'd been outscored 19–7.

With three days off between their 4–2 loss to the Buffalo Sabres in Raleigh and their next game against the Panthers, Maurice was concerned he wouldn't be employed when the team headed south.

"All I kept telling the assistant coaches was 'We've just got to get on the plane.'" Maurice said. "That's our only hope that we get on the plane."

"They underachieved. They just weren't playing well," Forslund said. "In those years the only place you got any information was *Hockey Night in Canada*. So on the hot stove, which was during the second intermission, one of the reporters said, 'Paul Maurice, if they lose this game, is getting fired.' They had a source in Florida that was telling them all that stuff."

After Carolina fell behind two goals, Maurice could feel the walls closing in.

"I remember very clearly getting down 2–0 to Florida, and thinking 'I'm done. I'm getting fired,'" Maurice said.

But the Hurricanes rallied, led by Sami Kapanen's five-on-three power-play goal midway through the third period that helped flip the script in their 3–2 win. Carolina used that win as a springboard for an 8-1-1-2 stretch to close the calendar year.

"That saved me," Maurice said, "but I remember. I don't know if shaky ground is remotely accurate, but I was on extremely borrowed time."

The Hurricanes finished with 91 points and won the Southeast Division for the second time in three seasons, earning a date with the New Jersey Devils for the second straight year.

Carolina may have opened at home, but it was the underdog. The Devils were the NHL's model franchise and outclassed the Hurricanes the year prior en route to the Stanley Cup finals. New Jersey hadn't trailed at any point in the series' first three games, and Carolina had more players injured by bone-crushing body checks from Devils captain Scott Stevens (two) than goals scored through Games 1 through 3 (one).

"The Devils were the appropriate first round team, because here they come again, and they were the model," Forslund said. "They were the team that was still in the now, and still the team that everybody thought would win."

For the second straight year, tailgaters flooded the scene at RBC Center for Carolina's playoff opener. Carolina's arena is adjacent to the Carter-Finley Stadium, home of North Carolina State football and where tailgaters flood the parking lot Saturdays in the fall.

Though some have tried, no NHL team tailgates quite like Carolina in the postseason. Fans set up at least four hours before puck-drop and invite friends, family, or even opposing fans and curious onlookers to their tent for a beer or drink, hot dog, or some dip and hospitality.

"I grew up in New England, so I thought that tailgating means you drive to the parking lot, open up the cars and have your beer and go watch the game," said Forslund. "Tailgating in the South is a community. Tailgating in the South is about your family.

"It also means that's your spot. . . . When they're season-ticket holders they get a spot with their number. So that's like their place, and it gets pretty elaborate. Then the people go from car to car, and they get to know each other."

The energy spilled over in the arena for the first two games. There were no crushing hits this time, but Carolina goalie Artūrs Irbe stopped 64 of 66 shots through two games, helping his team go to New Jersey with a 2–0 edge after Bates Battaglia's overtime goal in Game 2.

"Scoring that OT winner was probably one of the most important goals of my career," Battaglia said. "I'll never forget that one."

The two-game advantage was the franchise's first since 1987, when the Whalers won the Adams Division but bowed out to the Quebec Nordiques in the Adams Division semifinals. Still, some inside the organization feared a similar collapse and were skeptical Carolina could pull out the series—even with the series lead.

"After Game 2, Jimmy Rutherford says we should put [backup goalie] Kevin Weekes in for Game 3," Maurice said. "At that point, I think the man's lost his mind."

The Hurricanes goalie turned Whalers-like, as Irbe stopped just nine of 12 shots before Maurice pulled him for Weekes in their 4–0 loss in Game 3. Two nights later, New Jersey won again and Irbe got pulled again, evening the series at 2.

Weekes came out of relief and played well, stopping 35 of 37 shots in Games 3 and 4, and Maurice went with him for the pivotal Game 5. The move was unconventional, but the players trusted Maurice's decision to start the untested goalie.

"When Weekes went in, we were all behind it," Battaglia said. "We all pulled on the same rope from beginning to end."

The teams took the ice tied at one for the third period, and Weekes battled New Jersey goalie Martin Brodeur shot for shot, including the Carolina goalie's sprawling glove save on forward John Madden—which Carolina fans refer to simply as "The Save."

"He makes the save on John Madden he never, ever should've made," Maurice said. "I shouldn't take that away from him. No goalie should make that save."

"That save was one of the greatest highlights in the history of the team," Forslund said.

But Patrik Eliáš scored with just 8:14 left, and it appeared the Devils would again take full control of the series. But Holík, the former Whaler and dominant shutdown center, was penalized for charging with just 1:50 remaining. Only seconds into the power play, Whalers holdover Jeff O'Neill beat Brodeur and tied the score at 2 with less than 90 seconds left. Josef Vašíček won it at 8:16 of overtime, lifting the Hurricanes to a 3–2 win and a 3–2 series lead.

The Hurricanes returned to New Jersey hoping to close the series at the Continental Airlines Arena—which had become their house of horrors. The Hurricanes were just 1-4 in the Garden State in two playoff years, managing only one goal in their two losses earlier in the series.

Yet the suddenly scalding Weekes could do no wrong. He stopped all 32 shots he faced in Carolina's shocking 1–0 win. Weekes' stunning shutout in Game 6, coupled fittingly with Ron Francis's second-period goal that became the game-winner, lifted the Hurricanes to the franchise's first playoff series win in 16 years and its first seven-game series win that set up a date with the Montreal Canadiens.

Montreal had posted only an 87-point season, but goalie José Théodore reminded many of Patrick Roy in 1986 and ultimately won both the Vezina and Hart Trophies that season.

"José Théodore was having an MVP season, never mind the Vezina Trophy," Forslund said. "So how are you going to get through this guy?"

The Hurricanes won Game 1 2–0, behind Weekes' second straight playoff shutout, but Théodore became an even scarier proposition after he stopped 78 of 80 shots in Games 2 and 3, boosting Montreal to a 2–1 series lead.

Things looked especially bleak when the Canadiens built a 3–0 lead after two periods in Game 4. Maurice pulled the suddenly struggling Weekes, after he stoppepd just seven of nine shots, and the raucous Molson Centre crowd was anticipating a 3–1 series lead and another playoff win over their former Adams Division rivals.

But the series' momentum flipped innocuously. Montreal coach Michel Therrien was hit with an abuse-of-officials penalty early in the third and Sean Hill struck for a five-on-three goal that cut Montreal's lead to 3–1 and built belief on the Hurricanes bench.

"There's always a little doubt when you're behind," Battaglia said, "but once we got one goal we knew there would be more coming."

Battaglia struck about nine minutes later, and with Irbe on the bench, Erik Cole scored his fourth goal of the series with just 41 seconds in regulation. Niclas Wallin capped the comeback win, which has since been dubbed the Miracle at Molson, at 3:14 of overtime, knotting the series at two.

"It was where our team was," Maurice said. "We were rolling. We were playing well, and we threw everything at them and the kitchen sink."

Therrien is still trying to live down the stunning comeback in Montreal, but Maurice remembers how close he came to being the goat.

"I never played my fourth line, and I ran the entire third period, and I don't think they touched the ice," Maurice said. "I get in overtime, and in my head I'm thinking 'I've got to get my fourth line on the ice.' I got an offensive-zone faceoff, and I've got my third line out, and I'm hoping [Therrien] leaves his third line so I know his fourth line is coming off, and he changes and puts his fourth line on the ice.

"So I am absolutely motherfucking myself on the bench. I'm so mad, because I'm going to put my fourth line out, and [Montreal's top line] is coming out and I am absolutely giving it to myself because I think I've lost the hockey game.

"We won the faceoff back and Nic Wallin bounces it five times and in, and Mike Therrien gets killed for having his fourth line on the ice for a defensive-zone faceoff. That's the beauty of hockey."

The rally started a flood of goals—Carolina scored 17 in the final seven-plus periods of the series and chased Théodore with five goals on 13 shots in the series-clinching 8–2 win in Montreal in Game 6.

The Hurricanes had won more playoff series games than in the franchise's previous 22 years. And they weren't done yet. Irbe allowed just four goals in four games, building a 3–1 series advantage against the Maple Leafs in the Eastern Conference finals—a series pundits thought Toronto would dominate.

Toronto staved off elimination with a 1–0 win in Game 5, then appeared to cheat death again on Mats Sundin's goal with 21.8 seconds remaining that tied Game 6.

The Hurricanes still had not won a win-or-go-home game in their NHL existence—and were a goal-against from Game 7. But after an intermission to curb their nerves, Martin Gélinas redirected Vašíček's pass past Curtis Joseph to send Carolina to the Stanley Cup finals—Carolina's third OT victory of the series and their sixth in seven trips to extra time during the playoffs.

"There were a lot of big goals that year in the playoffs," Battaglia said. "It was almost like we wanted to go to OT because we knew we would be the ones to score."

The Hurricanes' shocking run put them on the NHL's biggest stage for the first time, where they'd meet another Original Six foe—the Detroit Red Wings.

The 2002 Red Wings are widely deemed the greatest group of talent ever assembled. They were coached by Hall of Famer Scotty Bowman. Hall of Fame forwards Brett Hull and Luc Robitaille joined mainstays and future fellow Hall of Famers Nick Lidström, Chris Chelios, Steve Yzerman, Brendan Shanahan, and Igor Larionov for a practically unbeatable roster. Then Detroit acquired Dominik Hašek, arguably the greatest goalie ever, in a trade from the Buffalo Sabres on July 1, 2001.

Detroit finished with 116 points and reached the Cup finals with a 12-6 record in the Western Conference playoffs. Few gave Carolina a chance. Even though they were both favorites and more experienced, the Red Wings weren't going to take the Hurricanes lightly.

"It didn't surprise me," Shanahan said when asked about meeting Karmanos, Rutherford, and many of his former Whalers teammates in the championship round. "I had said all along that Jimmy was going to find a way to build a winner."

But things got interesting when the Hurricanes shocked the mighty Wings, again in overtime fittingly on a goal from Ron Francis 58 seconds into the extra session for a 3–2 win that gave Carolina a 1–0 lead in the best-of-seven series.

"It was special, especially at the time because it gave us a lead in the series," Francis recalled in 2019.

The Red Wings seethed at the loss, with Hašek throwing his equipment after the stunning defeat. Detroit jumped out quickly in Game 2 but found itself tied at 1 through 40 minutes, staring at a potential 2–0 hole. But the Red Wings responded with two late third-period goals and claimed a 3–1 win.

Carolina had done what it set out to do: steal a game in Joe Louis Arena. But the Hurricanes proved they were capable of running with the Wings in Game 3—their first home Cup finals game, which fans and attendees still talk about.

"The fans were amazing," Battaglia said. "The tailgating, the fan support around town was great. It was all anyone was talking about."

The raucous crowd stood behind the team all night, and the Hurricanes took the lead in the third period on Jeff O'Neill's goal at 7:34.

Carolina was mere minutes from having arguably the greatest team ever on the ropes, and the home crowd could sense it.

But that's when Hull turned the series on a dime. His redirection on Lidström's shot from the point, with Hašek on the bench, tied the score with just 1:14 in regulation, sending the clubs to overtime.

"I ran into Brett Hull at Kid Rock's wedding years later," Karmanos said, "and he said 'It was lucky,' and I said 'I knew it!'

"He said if you guys had won that game, our sticks were already really heavy."

Game 3 of the 2002 Cup finals became the longest game in Whalers/Hurricanes history, and the third-longest game in Stanley Cup finals history. But when Igor Larionov scored with 5:13 left in the third overtime it lifted Detroit to the second of its four straight wins that would bring the Stanley Cup to the Motor City for the third time in six seasons.

"That's how close that series was," Shanahan said. "That tying goal changed our fortunes. If we don't tie it up, we're down 2–1 and still in Carolina for Game 4."

Detroit's 3–1 victory in Game 5 was the last game of Bowman's incredible coaching career, and he donned skates and carried the Cup like a player as the crowd roared in approval. Many point to his coaching, and Detroit's dominant roster, when referencing the 2002 Cup finals.

"I don't like to look back and wonder what could have been different," Battaglia said. "We played hard, and Detroit had a pretty damn good team that year too. Three-quarters of the team was Hall of Famers."

But the Hurricanes were a game opponent, one whose final payroll ($33 million) was more than half of Detroit's NHL-leading budget of $66.6 million that season. One could simply say the Wings talent overwhelmed Carolina.

"We were 1–1 going back to Raleigh and up a goal late and they scored kind of a weird, fluky goal to tie it and beat us in triple overtime," Francis said. "I think if we win that game, I still think to this day that we had a strong chance of pulling maybe [one of] the greatest upsets ever."

But Carolina wasn't going to be the underdog much longer.

The Carolina Hurricanes' championship run in 2006 was probably the most serendipitous in NHL history.

After falling to the Red Wings in 2002, then two straight seasons outside of the playoffs, the Hurricanes became the beneficiaries of a mountain of available talent after a season-long lockout canceled the 2004–05 season and created a hard salary cap of $39 million.

"We didn't have any choice," said Peter Karmanos, Carolina's majority owner at the time, referencing the season-long lockout. "If you go back and look at the financial shape and attendance dropping and teams going bankrupt, we didn't have any choice.

"I think everybody benefited."

The NHL enacted a slew of new rule changes designed at curtailing the aptly named "dead-puck era" of the late 1990s and early 2000s. The league cracked down on obstructing penalties, calling infractions more tightly especially in 2005–06, and it led to a faster pace and higher-scoring games.

"It was a slow game," Karmanos said. "I'd been complaining to [NHL commissioner] Gary [Bettman] for years that I won't even take clients to the games anymore. It was boring. You had these stupid fights—these staged fights bullshit—and when we came back out for the 2005–06 season, it was like night and day. It was exciting, and it still is."

The Hurricanes were in a particularly positive position coming out of the lockout. Carolina's low pre-lockout payroll of $36 million enabled general manager Jim Rutherford to bring in talented free agent forwards like Cory Stillman and Ray Whitney as other teams were shedding payroll to get under the cap. Peter Laviolette was Carolina's coach, and his run-and-gun style fit perfectly in the new post-lockout NHL.

"We knew we had a very good team on paper," said defenseman Glen Wesley. "When you have a good team on paper you obviously have to prove it, and I think everybody bought in and we believed in the style and what we had to adapt to and it just kind of snowballed from the start of the season.

"There was a lot of character in that locker room, and I think that's why we were so successful on the ice."

Carolina even caught a break in terms of the lockout's timing. The canceled season enabled Eric Staal, the number two pick in the 2003 draft, to play a full season for Carolina's minor-league affiliate in Lowell, Massachusetts.

Staal had struggled in his rookie season, posting just 11 goals and 31 points in 81 games. But he led the Hurricanes with 100 points, and they breezed to 112 points and the Southeast Division crown and a first-round date with the Montreal Canadiens.

The Canadiens had an uneven season in which they fired coach Claude Julien on January 16 and replaced him with general manager Bob Gainey. But they took off under Gainey and carried that into the playoffs where they bombarded goalie Martin Gerber in Game 1, scoring six times on just 21 shots in a 6–1 win at RBC Center before building a 3–0 lead in Game 2 behind three first-period goals.

The franchise's best season was at a crossroads when Laviolette replaced Martin Gerber with rookie Cam Ward—the Hurricanes' Kay Whitmore-like goalie of the future.

Gerber had struggled in the season's second half—and had difficulty acclimating to the heavy workload of being an NHL starting goalie. He was the starting goalie for Switzerland in the Torino Olympics—guiding his home country to a sixth-place finish, its best finish in the Olympics since 1952.

But the Hurricanes scuffled after the Olympic break, and so did Gerber. He won just 10 of 19 starts after the break and posted a .905 save percentage in 20 appearances in that stretch.

"Gerber, like the team in March, wasn't as good as he was earlier," said John Forslund, the Hurricanes television play-by-play announcer from 1997–2020. "Gerber was one of the best goalies in the league all year, went to the Olympics, brought Switzerland to a new level, then came back and just wasn't the same."

Ward had won 14 regular-season games. But he had just turned 22 years old in February and was a rookie who had never experienced the pressure of the Stanley Cup playoffs. The players had faith in Ward, but there still was uncertainty in Carolina's locker room.

•

"You never know until you put a young goaltender in an important game and an important situation that he's never been in before," Wesley said. "Everybody trusted what [Ward] did. He had a great regular season, and even though he was the backup that was one of those things that we bought into as a group."

With Gerber struggling, battling both the Canadiens and illness, Laviolette didn't have much choice.

"Gerber had the flu and was losing weight and just wasn't right the first two games against Montreal," Forslund said. "The way Ward had played all year, Laviolette was ready to make a move anyway."

The move ignited the Hurricanes, and they roared back for four straight goals. Even though they lost 6–5 in overtime and fell behind 2–0 in the series, Carolina found continuity in goal in Ward.

Unlike the young and inexperienced Whalers goalies in the postseason, the moment somehow never got too big for Ward, specifically during his Cinderella run in 2006. He stopped 105 of a possible 110 shots (.954) over the next four games, four straight Carolina wins, and the Hurricanes moved on.

That unbeaten run reached seven straight after Carolina took the first three of its second-round series against the New Jersey Devils. The Devils themselves entered the series rolling, with 15 straight wins—11 in a row to close the season and four straight in their first-round series sweep of the New York Rangers. But after Carolina rolled 6–0 in Game 1, it found itself on the right side of a rule change in Game 2.

When Scott Gomez redirected Zach Parise's slap shot past Ward with just 20.7 seconds remaining in the third period, it stunned the home crowd in Raleigh and it looked as if the teams would go to New Jersey even.

But Devils center John Madden won the ensuing center-ice draw so cleanly that the puck sailed all the way into the Devils defensive zone.

Ordinarily, Devils goalie Martin Brodeur would field the puck and sink the remaining time by pitching it into neutral ice. But the NHL had enacted a trapezoid behind the net—aimed at goalies like Brodeur who were adept puck handlers—and made it a penalty for goalies to play the puck outside the restricted area.

"I think the series swung on a rule change," said Mike Emrick, who called the series for OLN. "The Devils were in control with seconds left. John Madden won the faceoff from center ice all the way into the defensive corner. Marty Brodeur could not play the puck because of the rule."

The relentless Hurricanes swarmed as New Jersey furiously tried to clear the puck and deflect shots away from Brodeur. But Staal redirected Justin Williams's centering feed past the helpless New Jersey netminder, tying the score at 2 with just three seconds left.

The fans roared as each side went to its dressing room, realizing they'd get bonus hockey instead of a series-evening loss. For the second time in as many playoff runs, Niclas Wallin was the hero in overtime, giving Carolina a dramatic 3–2 victory just 3:09 into the extra session.

"The series wasn't officially over," Emrick said, "but the road forked with that event." The teams split in New Jersey, and although the Devils took a 1–0 lead just 57 seconds into Game 5, it only delayed the inevitable. The Hurricanes were the more powerful team, and when Staal scored his third goal of the series into the empty net, sealing the 4–1 series-clinching win, he double-pumped his fists, realizing his club was just four wins from the Stanley Cup finals.

The Hurricanes prepared for the terrifying Buffalo Sabres, who had been among the NHL's best all season. Like Carolina, Buffalo won 52 regular-season games and eight of its first 11 playoff games. Rookie Ryan Miller backed the Sabres with a .921 playoff save percentage entering the conference finals.

Miller outplayed Ward in the first three conference-finals games, and Buffalo built a 2–1 series advantage. Ward was pulled after allowing four goals on 26 shots in the Sabres' 4–3 win in Game 3, and Laviolette, sensing Ward was running out of steam, went back to Gerber for the all-important Game 4 in Buffalo.

Gerber rewarded his coach by stopping all 22 shots in Carolina's 4–0 win that evened the series at two.

"The team loved Marty Gerber," Forslund said. "He was a great teammate, and often overlooked, and I make sure to point that out when I talk about that team, because if ever they get together and there's a reunion, hopefully he can come back and be a part of it because he was a huge part of that team."

Gerber was pulled in Game 5, but Ward reentered the series refreshed, even though Carolina trailed 3–1 in the pivotal game in Raleigh. Ward stopped all 15 shots he faced, and the Hurricanes attacked the injury-ravaged Sabres defense, who by series' end had lost regular blue liners Henrik Tallinder, Teppo Numminen, Jay McKee, and Dmitri Kalinin.

"[The Sabres were] good," said Kyle Hanlin, the Hurricanes public relations director at the time. "They kept getting decimated by defensive injuries. By the time the series was over, they were down to their ninth and tenth defenseman."

Carolina scored three straight, including Stillman's power-play goal at 8:46 of overtime, and went back to Buffalo ahead 3–2 in the series.

"That was good for Ward," Forslund said of Gerber's challenge. "That was a little bit of a wake-up call for Ward. He was flying high, and he was really young, and then that kind of brought him back down to earth and gave Marty a chance to make a contribution to the team."

The Sabres forced Game 7 with an overtime win in Buffalo, then built a 2–1 advantage entering the third period in Game 7. But Carolina would not be denied, tying the game early in the third before benefiting again from a new NHL rule for the 2005–06 season.

In previous years a goalie would be assessed an automatic two-minute penalty for shooting the puck straight out of play from the defensive zone. But after the lockout, the NHL expanded that rule to penalize skaters who did so as well.

"I think it was a great change to the rule," Hurricanes defenseman Glen Wesley said. "A lot of defensemen did it on purpose to stop play and get a break, and I think that was one of the good changes the NHL did."

With Game 7 tied midway through the third, Sabres defenseman Brian Campbell was hemmed in his own zone and accidentally shot the puck out of play on his backhand and was whistled for a delay-of-game penalty. Brind'Amour scored on the ensuing power play for the game-winner that pushed Carolina back to the Cup finals for the second time in four seasons.

"Stupidest thing ever," Miller told the *Buffalo News* after the game. "I don't see how that [rule] should ever decide a game. Two guys forechecking a player, [Campbell] goes to make a quick play in the bad ice in springtime, and it goes out of play. You're telling me that's a rule?"

Buffalo's loss was Carolina's gain, and the Hurricanes quickly turned their focus to the upstart Edmonton Oilers in the Stanley Cup finals.

"We had a few breaks in there," Karmanos said. "The guys get mad at me, but I said we got every break you could get."

The Oilers, a former WHA rival of the Hartford Whalers, came out of nowhere with a stunning playoff run that had gripped Edmonton. They'd stunned the Presidents' Trophy–winning Detroit Red Wings before dispatching the heavily favored San Jose Sharks and Mighty Ducks of Anaheim.

The Oilers were nearly doomed in the regular season by inconsistent defense and goaltending but entered the Cup finals with a 12-5 record, largely due to defenseman Chris Pronger and goalie Dwayne Roloson.

The 36-year-old goalie played every minute of every game, entering the finals with a .931 save percentage, and Pronger, the former Whalers defenseman deep in the prime of his Hall of Fame career, led the Oilers with 17 points in their first 17 playoff games and entered the finals as a legitimate Conn Smythe Trophy candidate.

The tailgaters arrived early for Game 1 and were treated to a wild affair. Edmonton, unfazed by the crowd and focused on bringing the Cup back to the Canadian city of champions, scored the first three goals—including Pronger's penalty-shot goal that was the first such tally in Stanley Cup finals history.

"We didn't play the way that we should've for the first two periods," Wesley said in 2020. "We probably got caught up in the moment of playing in front of your home fans and not playing the right way.

"We were embarrassed by the way we had played the first two periods."

True to form, Carolina didn't quit, scoring the next four goals including Justin Williams's short-handed tally that gave the Hurricanes a 4–3 lead with 9:58 left. Still, when Aleš Hemský tied the score less than four minutes later, it appeared the teams were destined for overtime.

But Roloson was injured when Oilers defenseman Marc-André Bergeron pushed Hurricanes forward Andrew Ladd into him in the third period. Edmonton backup Ty Conklin entered the crease with just 5:36 remaining for the first playoff action of his NHL career.

Conklin stopped the first two shots against, and the teams remained tied in the final minute of regulation. But trouble began when defenseman Mike Commodore flipped a seemingly innocuous clearing attempt behind the Edmonton goal with 36 seconds left. Conklin came out to play it and tried to move the puck on his backhand to defenseman Jason Smith, but Smith mishandled the pass, and Brind'Amour stole the puck and stashed it into the empty net.

The arena went bonkers, and Carolina's 5–4 win is considered one of the craziest games in Cup finals history. Conklin's gaffe, which became one of the worst in playoff hockey history, came in his only postseason game that spring. But it was huge, particularly since the Hurricanes won two of the subsequent three games and returned to Raleigh with a 3–1 advantage, poised to clinch the Stanley Cup on home ice.

The crowd could sense it even if the Hurricanes weren't quite ready for their moment.

"I knew before Game 5, there was something different in the room," Hanlin said. "You could tell they were not winning that game."

Game 5 again started wildly, with Edmonton taking the lead just 16 seconds in. A pair of power-play goals from Staal and Whitney gave the Hurricanes a 2–1 advantage, but Edmonton struck twice again and took a 3–2 lead into the locker room after one.

Staal tied the score with Carolina's third power-play goal on its seventh man-advantage of the game midway through the second period. The Hurricanes man-advantage was firing at 24 percent for the finals, scoring eight power-play goals through regulation of Game 5. So when Oilers defenseman Steve Staios took a tripping penalty in overtime of Game 5, the Hurricanes fans could practically taste the Champagne.

But Stillman was affected by Ethan Moreau's forecheck, and Fernando Pisani intercepted his soft pass and rifled a shot past Ward for a stunning short-handed goal at 3:31 of extra time that put the celebration on ice—the first short-handed, overtime goal in the history of the Stanley Cup finals.

"It was gut-wrenching," Wesley said. "I think Cory Stillman obviously if you look back at it wouldn't have thrown a seam pass coming out of his own end. . . . You had to feel for him. He probably didn't sleep well that night."

"The parade was being planned, and there were a lot of things getting out of the team's control," Forslund said. "Cory Stillman gave the puck away, and unfortunately in that fifth game Stillman was on his way to the Conn Smythe."

The Hurricanes traveled across the continent back to Edmonton for Game 6, and the team's friends and close family took a chartered plane for the potential road Cup celebration.

"When he scored that goal, I said 'shit, we have to go back to Edmonton,'" Hanlin said.

Carolina also received a boost when forward Erik Cole returned to the lineup for the potential clincher. Cole had nearly been paralyzed with a broken neck after he was driven headfirst into the boards during a regular-season game against the Pittsburgh Penguins in March.

Cole, who still finished fifth on the team with 59 points in 60 regular-season games before the injury, had flown to Edmonton by way of Denver—Hurricanes forward Mark Recchi arranged a meeting with a specialist in the Colorado capital for Cole prior to Game 6.

Cole ducked into the Carolina locker room less than two hours before puck drop and played. But it didn't matter, because Jussi Markkanen and the Oilers took their game to another level in Game 6. The Oilers' 31-year-old goalie, who replaced Conklin after Roloson's injury, needed to stop just 16 shots in Edmonton's 4–0 win that forced a Game 7 in Raleigh.

"Then they go to Edmonton in Game 6 and get waxed," Forslund said. "Totally dominated, and Erik Cole's return and the fact they were going to get him back, and he played that game, and it was a mess."

"Probably the best thing to happen to us was we got smoked in Game 6," Wesley said. "It kind of lit a fire under us knowing how bad we'd played."

While family members took one more flight home to Raleigh, the team holed up in the Hotel MacDonald for an extra night to regroup.

On a June night in the Canadian Rockies, the sun stayed out past 11 p.m. Mountain Time, and rowdy and excitable fans tried to rattle the already-shaken team by honking horns and causing a ruckus.

But freshly rested and back at home, Carolina refocused. Laviolette stressed the importance of family during a pregame address to the players, and the Hurricanes were comfortable despite the do-or-die game with the Cup on the line.

"To be home you couldn't have written the script better for us," Wesley said. "That day I just felt great. I felt comfortable with it being game seven. I wasn't nervous by any means."

The fans brought a palpable energy to Game 7, which is the lasting memory for many of the 2006 Cup finals. Some fans were in the parking lot 12 hours before the opening faceoff. The sellout crowd netted Karmanos an extra $2 million in gate receipts, and the vast majority of fans didn't sit down from the moment Holly Wilbur finished each national anthem through the Stanley Cup celebration.

"I think [being at home] was comforting," Brind'Amour told the *News & Observer* in 2020. "I do remember a big lump in my chest for game five and game six. In game seven, it was gone because you just knew there was no tomorrow. This is it. The weight was off our shoulders. We were home, in front of our home crowd, and it gave us that little edge we needed."

The players were calm. The crowd was excited. But Carolina's boss was a wreck.

"I remember pacing the whole day," Karmanos said. "For whatever reason, I never doubted we were going to win. I was a nervous wreck, but I still thought we were going to win."

It was a scene that fans in Hartford never got to witness, even if some Whalers fans made the 600-some-odd-mile trek from Connecticut for the championship game.

The relentless Hurricanes fed off the home crowd's fervor and struck first on Aaron Ward's goal less than 90 seconds in that sent the building into further hysteria.

Carolina nearly made it 2–0 with four seconds left in the first when Craig Adams's backhand try eluded Markkanen, but Staios pulled the puck from over the line and out. The Hurricanes were irate by the no-goal call, and the fact they were not given a penalty shot when Staios gloved the puck in the crease, but they refocused during the intermission.

"We knew that the goal had gone in," Wesley said. "We could've lost our minds as a group. Pete got us into the locker room, and there was nothing we could do about it and we had to move forward and play the way we were capable of playing."

František Kaberle's power-play goal did give Carolina a 2–0 lead in the second, and although there were tense moments—specifically when Pisani struck for his 14th goal of the playoffs that cut the lead to 2–1 early in the third—Carolina wouldn't be denied. Ward stood tall, making 22 saves, including his full-extension pad stop on Pisani that would've tied the game with 3:41 remaining in regulation.

It was Justin Williams, a 24-year-old forward from Coburg, Ontario—just establishing himself as Mr. Game 7—who sealed the game with an empty-net goal with 1:01 left. Eric Staal moved the puck to him, then began leaping in the air in celebration as Williams carried the puck toward the vacant cage before stashing it in and sealing the first title in the franchise's 26-year NHL history—and first since the New England Whalers won the WHA championship in 1973.

"When Justin Williams scored the empty-net goal, that's when [the nerves] all went away," Karmanos said.

The win vindicated both Karmanos for moving the team in the first place, and Rutherford for building a championship team. But back in Hartford, Carolina's win added insult to injury, even if Chuck Kaiton and John Forslund—broadcasting on radio that night—had kept those people in mind.

"There was a strong tie back to Hartford and the people that had supported the team," Forslund said. "I felt that we were both announcing to those people too. There was a part of us that were not just entrenched in this market here but also with a tie back there."

The people in Connecticut, especially those who aren't Hurricanes fans, still wonder what could've been.

"I think there's a sense of unfinished business," said Ryan Shannon, a Darien, Connecticut, native who won the Stanley Cup with the Anaheim

Ducks the next year. "People feel a strong sense of resentment, and sort of like 'hey man, we got the short end of the stick,' especially when Carolina goes down and wins the Stanley Cup."

Even Glen Wesley, a member of the 2006 championship team, shared those sentiments. "There was definitely some thoughts of what could have been in Hartford," he said.

The win helped cement Carolina's place in hockey history—and probably is the reason the Hurricanes still exist today. Meanwhile, Hartford's seems more tenuous every day.

Chapter 12

The Future

Whether Hartford should have another chance at an NHL team depends on your biases.

In 2012, Howard Baldwin, a Whalers founder and managing general partner from 1972 to 1988, proudly announced the team had the 11th highest merchandise sales of any NHL franchise—a remarkable feat considering the Whalers aren't an active NHL franchise and haven't been in 15 years.

The Whalers boast the highest sales of any defunct NHL team and have for years. Fans can't seem to get enough Whalers.

Some saw Carolina's Whalers Nights as the team returning to the ice, but that largely was the Hurricanes capitalizing on the Whalers momentum boost brand-wise in the early 2010s, fueled by a sudden boom of merchandise sales.

Some, like Peter Karmanos, don't want to hear it. But there is a case to be made for NHL hockey in Hartford.

Hartford may be Connecticut's third-largest city population-wise, behind Bridgeport and New Haven. But the Nutmeg State always ranks in the top two in terms of statewide wealth, and there still is robust corporate support for a major-league team—with 46 major corporations having a presence.

"This is the richest state in the USA," said Rich Coppola, the sports director for Fox Connecticut from 1989 to 2019. "The businesses should be able to get behind a team."

Hartford is still central enough to the rest of the state, geographically, and it borders hockey-mad New Haven County and Hampden County in Massachusetts, home of Springfield and an almost 700,000-person metro area. The region, dubbed the New England Knowledge Corridor, is the 20th largest market in the United States, and is smaller than only Toronto and Montreal among hockey markets in Canada.

"Buffalo, Raleigh, Nashville are all smaller markets than Hartford-New Haven," said Jason Mandell, a former Connecticut resident, and Whalers fan. "It's the largest sports market without a major professional team."

But all that doesn't add up to a major-league team in the state, and there are several reasons why.

Some fans were heartbroken by the Whalers' departure, but others had their sights set on bigger fish. Governor John Rowland and New England Patriots owner Robert Kraft excited the populace when they unveiled a proposal to build the NFL team a new stadium in Hartford in the fall of 1998.

But Kraft walked away from the deal, choosing to stay in Foxborough, Massachusetts, after the state offered him a new stadium. Many Connecticut residents have since realized they were being used as leverage against Massachusetts, but lawmakers and others who had gotten their hopes up were heartbroken after the Patriots deal fell through.

That slight, on the heels of the Whalers departure and the Colonial Realty Ponzi scheme, damaged the region's psyche. Even Karmanos noticed the difference late in his tenure there calling Hartford "negative."

"The market lost its self-esteem," Baldwin said. "And the people here have stopped believing."

Baldwin sought to capitalize on the Whalers' brand boost by returning to Hartford to run the American Hockey League team there in 2010. He set up his own NHL-caliber office in Hartford out of one of the biggest buildings in the city of Hartford, 280 Trumbull Street, a 350-foot high, 28-floor skyscraper.

Their headquarters sat on the 21st floor, across the street from the XL Center. Old pictures of ex-Whalers and magazine ads adorned the walls of the office, harkening employees back to a bygone era.

Baldwin tried to get the corporate community involved—the same way it had been in the 1980s—but it ignored his requests, failing to see the value of investing in an AHL team. He got creative by rolling out a plan for a renovated XL Center, which included $105 million of public money. The state legislature, trying to handle a $1.2 billion budget deficit during the Great Recession, balked.

"The trouble with Hartford is it has this can't-do attitude," Baldwin said in 2013. "They don't think of ways they can do things, they find ways not to do them. They've settled for this level of mediocrity and the people and this market deserve better than that."

Connecticut might be the wealthiest state, but UConn controls it athletically. The state university enjoys splitting its games on campus at Gampel Pavilion, and the revenue it gets from playing men's and women's basketball games at XL Center, and it hasn't advocated for renovations or used its muscle to push for a new arena in Hartford—even after it received $92 million in state money for Rentschler Field, the stadium in East Hartford where the Huskies football team has played since 2003.

"I was sure that if UConn had gone out of its way to work with the Whalers, they could've pulled something off," Hearst Connecticut Media Group sports columnist Jeff Jacobs said. "The pettiness that engulfs this state sickens me. Now we're still arguing [more than 20] years later about a new arena."

If Baldwin saw hope in the early 2010s, it's because a fellow former World Hockey Association market executed his plan. The Winnipeg Jets' move from Manitoba to Phoenix left the province heartbroken, but not despondent. They rallied around the International Hockey League's Manitoba Moose in 1996, when area business mogul Mark Chipman purchased the Minnesota-based team and moved it to Winnipeg, jumping at the opportunity to be a hockey market again.

The IHL went under, but the AHL noticed the fan support in Winnipeg. Chipman founded True North Sports & Entertainment, which then built the MTS Centre, a sparkling 15,000-seat arena that became the league's best.

Seeing that True North was doing everything in its power to make Winnipeg appear viable to the NHL, the locals did their part by pushing the Moose's attendance to number two in the AHL the last four years of their existence.

"The people in Winnipeg got behind it," Baldwin said.

Then when the Atlanta Thrashers became financially sick, True North bought the team and moved it to Winnipeg. The club re-took the "Jets" name and played its first regular season game back in Manitoba against the Montreal Canadiens in front of a sold-out, raucous crowd of 15,004 on October 9, 2011.

Four seasons later, led by former Whalers coach Paul Maurice, the Jets reached the playoffs for the first time. Three years after that, Winnipeg advanced all the way to the Western Conference finals in 2018.

Winnipeg's re-entry proves that the NHL is willing to give markets a second chance. Besides Winnipeg, the NHL expanded, left, then returned to Atlanta, Colorado, Minnesota, and the Bay Area. And Baldwin believes if Hartford's populace and ownership had the foresight, the Thrashers' departure could have been for a different destination.

"If the city had responded sooner," he said in 2011, "that could have been Hartford."

In the mid-2010s, Carolina was an NHL market rife for potential relocation. The Hurricanes struggled through an identity crisis after missing the playoffs nine straight seasons between 2010 and 2018 and finished in the bottom five in NHL attendance five straight seasons—including three straight seasons with the worst attendance—from 2015 to 2019.

But Carolina enjoyed a brand boost after Tom Dundon purchased a majority stake in the team from Karmanos in 2018—even after Dundon replaced franchise legend Ron Francis as general manager with Don Waddell.

Dundon leaned into Whalers history and embraced nontraditional marketing. It started with Justin Williams, who helped start postgame Storm Surges after home wins, with the players participating in elaborate crowd-inspiring celebrations. When former legendary hockey commentator Don Cherry called them a "bunch of jerks" on *Hockey Night in Canada* in February 2019, the Hurricanes leaned in by referring to themselves as such, even printing shirts with the phrase.

Coached by Rod Brind'Amour, and buoyed by a competitive team and the fun marketing that included the Whalers Nights, Carolina ran to the Eastern Conference finals before getting swept by the Boston Bruins. Crowds flooded PNC Arena in 2019–20 as the Hurricanes again embraced the Bunch of Jerks and Storm Surge celebrations and averaged about 16,800 fans per game until the COVID-19 pandemic halted play leaguewide March 12.

People in Hartford may have targeted Carolina as a sick team, but the Hurricanes are likely staying put for the foreseeable future—especially after the Hurricanes were rewarded with an outdoor game at Carter-Finley Stadium as part of the 2021 Stadium Series before it was postponed due to coronavirus.

Plus Hartford has to prove to the NHL it deserves a team.

Like Winnipeg, Hartford had its chance to embrace minor-league hockey after the Whalers left.

Fans in Connecticut initially committed to the AHL's Hartford Wolf Pack, averaging more than 7,000 fans in three of the first four seasons after the Whalers left. The Wolf Pack also delivered Connecticut's first professional championship when they won the Calder Cup in 2000.

But as the years went on, they had a hard time dealing with the minor league's slower pace. It wasn't just in Hartford either, as the Bridgeport Sound Tigers—a minor-league affiliate of the New York Islanders—struggled in Fairfield County too.

"I think there's a hockey market that is unserved," said Ryan Shannon, a Darien native and former NHL player. "Connecticut people want something that is their own. They don't want to support players that are just trying to make the Islanders."

Plus old-school Whalers fans have a hard time bringing themselves to cheer for the Rangers affiliate.

"There are a bunch of us that just don't like the Rangers," said Joanne Cortesa, the Whalers Booster Club president. "We supported the team and overlooked the fact that they're a Rangers farm team. That was the only way I'd be able to root for them, but I don't like the way they treat [the booster club]."

At this point, Hartford's pro hockey forces can't even find middle ground. The still-functioning Whalers Booster Club and Wolf Pack fans have struggled to coexist.

"They wouldn't let the Whalers Booster Club on the concourse," Cortesa said. "Wolf Pack people do not like the Whalers. They don't like 'Brass Bonanza.' They hate it. They literally hate it."

The booster club put their support behind Baldwin when he returned in 2010, with his mission of bringing the NHL back to Hartford. He was initially hired by the New York Rangers as the Hartford Wolf Pack's director of marketing, but he rose to the organization's chairman and chief executive officer within 90 days of returning.

At Baldwin's re-introductory press conference on June 2, he announced formation of the Whalers Sports & Entertainment marketing group, which facilitated the 2010 Summer Fan Fest and Reunion where former Whalers returned to sign autographs and pose for pictures. Later that year, hoping to capitalize on the suddenly hot brand, Baldwin rebranded the Wolf Pack as the Connecticut Whale.

"He thinks big," said Sean Pendergast, a Whalers fan from Simsbury, Connecticut, and radio personality in Houston.

On November 27, the Connecticut Whale took the ice against the Bridgeport Sound Tigers at the XL Center, with the Whale taking a 3–2, shootout win. It was a moment that harkened back to the Whalers' opening game at the Hartford Civic Center, 35 years earlier, when the New England Whalers beat the San Diego Mariners 4–3 in overtime.

Baldwin also sought a signature event as part of his return, and on the heels of the AHL's first outdoor game in Syracuse in 2010, Baldwin announced Hockey Fest, a two-week celebration of hockey, featuring high school, college, and pro teams from Connecticut at Rentschler Field.

But even Hockey Fest was marred by the typical trappings of hockey in Hartford. Each high school team was required to pay $7,000 to play outdoors, with all money going to the Whale.

The event's marquee event was the Whale's game against the Providence Bruins on February 19, 2011, which set a league record with 21,600 tickets sold. But inclement weather kept many home, and only 15,234 people showed up.

Plus there were unforeseen costs that weren't accounted for.

"They budgeted $20,000 for snow removal, and it ended up costing $200,000," said former Connecticut Whale staff writer Bruce Berlet.

The rebrand produced only slight improvement attendance-wise, which left the Whale front office unnerved—particularly Baldwin's son, Howard Baldwin Jr., whom the elder assigned as the organization's president and chief operating officer.

The Whale thought they had a marketing coup when they hosted former Bruins great Raymond Bourque to watch his two sons, Chris and Ryan, play against each other for the first time professionally when the Whale hosted the Hershey Bears on December 1, 2011. But the date aligned with the first round of the Connecticut Interscholastic Athletic Conference's state football playoffs, and only 1,917 showed up to see the Whale's 4–2 win over the Bears.

Baldwin Jr. was beside himself. He issued a statement to the Whalers Sports and Entertainment fan base, declaring "together we need to eliminate lulls like the crowd of less than 2,000 that attended Tuesday night's Whale game." Baldwin also sought a press conference to take the fan base to task, but was talked out of it by cooler heads.

"He wanted to lay into the fans," Berlet said. "It would have been a disaster."

Baldwin Jr.'s handling of things set the organization backward. But in the end, the Whale were doomed by the same problem as the Whalers: an ambivalent fan base and a shoddy lease agreement that created too much debt to crawl out from.

The Connecticut Whale finished the 2011–12 season 22nd in attendance in the 30-team AHL, averaging only 4,573 fans per game at the XL Center. With paltry attendance and a lease almost three times the AHL average, Baldwin announced to then–*Hartford Courant* sports columnist Jeff Jacobs that costs had become too much to bear.

"We not only have the highest expense level, we have the lowest revenue opportunity," Baldwin told Jacobs in his March 13, 2012 column. "By the way, it's my fault for agreeing to it, start with that. My head and heart weren't functioning right, because I care so much to try to bring this thing back."

Baldwin was the Whalers' managing general partner, operating the day-to-day with the backing of the corporate community. Without support from them in 2012, it was no shock that he came up short financially.

"Howard doesn't have any money," Berlet said. "He's a wheeler and dealer who likes to get people to back him."

Just three-and-a-half months after Jacobs's dire column was released, on June 26, Madison Square Garden announced that the Rangers and Whalers Sports and Entertainment would part ways when the parties' contractual agreement expired after the 2012–13 season.

But Baldwin did not even get a ceremonious exit. On July 9, 2012, sports and entertainment company AEG declared it would take over the Connecticut Whale's business operations, effective immediately.

"We want to assure fans that AEG will continue to work tirelessly so that professional hockey has a future in Hartford," XL Center senior vice president and general manager Chuck Steedman announced via a press release. "We are unequivocally dedicated to the ticket holders, community partners and sponsors that support the Connecticut Whale."

Despite his unceremonious departure, Baldwin still loves the city.

"My heart is still in Hartford," he said in November 2013. "The city is a train wreck right now, but I loved the experience I had there."

At the start of the 2013–14 AHL season, the Whale changed their nickname back to the Hartford Wolf Pack. With the Whale's failure, the odds of an NHL team in Hartford seem longer than ever. When NHL expansion came knocking in 2016, Hartford had no seat at the table as Las Vegas jumped in as the 31st team. Two years later, Seattle became the 32nd team—and named Ron Francis as its first general manager in 2019—a nice round number that likely negates further expansion.

And even if the NHL were to grow to 36 or even 40, places like Quebec City, Kansas City, Houston, and Portland, Oregon, likely are better-positioned suitors—with reasonable arenas and deep-pocketed owners—for hockey.

"You need a multimillionaire owner willing to invest, a suitable NHL building with luxury suites," said longtime hockey writer Stu Hackel.

Hartford's stalled momentum certainly wasn't all Baldwin's fault though. In the end, Connecticut's indifference dooms the state's chances of bringing a team back. Fans in Canada—whether it's Winnipeg or Montreal, which is striving to get the MLB's Expos back—put forth their best efforts to show their market's viability, even for minor leagues. Yet, others in Connecticut don't care enough to alter the status quo. They're fine sporting the Whalers logo while rooting for teams in other states—like the Red Sox, Giants, Yankees, and Patriots.

"Hockey in Hartford since the Whalers left hasn't been the same, because the AHL doesn't replace the NHL for a lot of people," said Michael Glasson, a former Whalers fan who worked for the Whale. "The players in the AHL want to jump to the NHL. It's a developmental league, so you don't have the same drive to win and excitement."

Plus, as US markets evolve, people are tending to move out of Connecticut. The wealthiest state with the oldest money is proving too lavish for young people. The state's population is growing only marginally—Connecticut's population has grown by just 300,000 since 1986, while states like California, Arizona, Texas, Florida, and Nevada have watched their populations explode by double in size or more.

And while it seems dire, some still try to make NHL hockey in Connecticut work. Cortesa leads about 200 people in the Whalers Booster Club, and even though the market has been lukewarm on hockey since Baldwin's departure, Hartford underwent a resurgence in the late 2010s and into the 2020s.

As urban spaces have exploded with millennials, Hartford has seen a population spike. Insurance companies The Hartford, Travelers, and Aetna eschewed their suburban campuses and moved back into offices in the city.

Connecticut also wisely invested in its state capital. The state opened a commuter train line in June 2018 that connects New Haven, Hartford, and Springfield, Massachusetts. A one-way ride from New Haven to Hartford is $8 and takes roughly 55 minutes, which has led those who work in either Hartford or New Haven to live in the other—also prompting a slew of new real estate development in the capital. And though

COVID-19 may have pushed people out of New York and Boston, Hartford's development boomed even through the pandemic.

Perhaps more importantly, the state commissioned a study to assess how to entice an NHL team to Hartford and discovered the XL Center needs about $250 million in upgrades. Connecticut governor Ned Lamont committed $100 million in public money to XL Center upgrades—earmarking $55 million for 2020 and 2021 in the budget he rolled out in February 2020 in addition to the $45 million the Dan Malloy administration committed previously.

That money, which Baldwin had sought about 10 years earlier, will go toward making the XL Center lower bowl state-of-the-art, with premium seating and suites, and widening the existing concourse in hopes of luring more concerts and enticing high-end clients to events.

Those upgrades have already begun. The region's hope is that a billionaire sports fanatic will take notice and consider relocating a new pro team to the Connecticut capital.

"Once the improvements are done, [Connecticut] hands him the keys to the building and ownership of it—all building revenue streams go to him," said Peter DeMallie, chairman of the New England Knowledge Corridor Partnership and a Whalers Booster Club member. "For $150 million, a team owner can take title to a state-of-the-art and profitable NHL arena, and own the twentieth-largest market in the USA—the same size as Denver and St. Louis—[which is] a wealthy market rich with large corporations."

The Bruins are also willing to cede Springfield, Massachusetts, as part of its marketing region, which they refused to do when the Whalers first existed. The market, which has roughly 700,000 people and is less than 50 miles from Hartford, would be Whalers Country—albeit in a territory of longstanding Bruins supporters.

As word of that has come out, NHL teams have scouted the market's viability, and NHL commissioner Gary Bettman even returned to Connecticut to assess Hartford. Between that and the Whalers' astonishing merchandise sales, all hope is not entirely lost for the NHL returning to Connecticut down the road. A little hope goes a long way, but the Whalers continue to hang in purgatory for the foreseeable future.

Whether hockey returns to Hartford, the Whalers survive in their merchandise and alumni, many of whom rave about their time in central Connecticut. Whenever former Whalers players get together, there is no shortage of stories, memories, and laughs to be had.

It's through those stories and "Brass Bonanza" that the Whalers continue to live on.

Notes on Research and Sources

The Hartford Whalers are remembered fondly by many, most notably the ex-players who are always willing to talk about their tenures in Connecticut.

That fact is what made this book possible. I tried to talk with as many former Whalers players as possible, and the final count was 25. Dave Babych, Sean Burke, Kevin Dineen, Jordy Douglas, Ken Holland, Ray Ferraro, Ron Francis, Mark Howe, Jody Hull, Grant Jennings, André Lacroix, Paul Lawless, Rick Ley, Mike Liut, Larry Pleau, Brian Propp, Joel Quenneville, Mike Rogers, Ulf Samuelsson, Brendan Shanahan, Brad Shaw, Blaine Stoughton, Dave Tippett, Pat Verbeek, and Glen Wesley.

This story features anecdotes and quotes from three of the four Whalers founders, two owners, and two other coaches who didn't play for the team: Howard Baldwin, John Coburn, Peter Karmanos, Paul Maurice, Pierre McGuire, and Godfrey Wood. It also includes tales from George Ducharme, the former Whalers marketing director, and Dan LaTorraca and Mike Forman, who work in marketing for the Carolina Hurricanes.

I covered sports in Connecticut for five years as sports editor of the *Fairfield Citizen*, then began covering the NHL in 2013. Fortunately, I've made some friends in hockey—both through book writing and covering the sport. The following were immensely helpful with this project: Michael Arace, Bruce Berlet, Owen Canfield, Rich Coppola, Terry Crisp, Luke DeCock, Dave Droschek, Helene Elliott, Mike Emrick, Stan Fischler, John Forslund, Stu Hackel, Jeff Jacobs, Chuck Kaiton, Barry Melrose, David Neal, Rick Peckham, and Steve Politi.

This story also would not be possible without getting fans' perspectives, and I conducted interviews with Mark Anderson, Joanne Cortesa, Peter DeMallie, Matthew Greene, Michael Glasson, Sean Pendergast, Jason Mandell, Ross Mandell, and Dave Schneider.

These people also were instrumental sources: Bates Battaglia, Tom Cross, Brendan Fox, Peter Good, Stu Grimson, Kyle Hanlin, Dan Murphy, Tom Ritter, and Ryan Shannon.

Many of the hockey numbers and figures from the book were verified by Hockey-reference.com and NHL.com, which features a box score for every NHL game in league history. World Hockey Association figures came from the website WHAHockey.com. Attendance figures are from HockeyDB.com. Most power-play facts and per-period shot facts were found from Flyershistory.com and BigMouthSports.com and verified by the above websites.

Archival research came from video clips posted to YouTube and also from the *New Haven Register* and *Hartford Courant*, and are cited where referenced. Some details about the WHA merger were from an article by Vice Sports, and some details of Howard Baldwin's life were from his book *Slim and None: My Wild Ride from the WHA to the NHL and All the Way to Hollywood*. Other facts and anecdotes came from *15 Years of Whalers Hockey*, a book commissioned by team writer Jack Lautier in 1987.

Acknowledgments

When I started the process with this book, I was just a 23-year-old kid with an idea. I had never seen the Whalers play in person and had never even covered a pro hockey game.

But the hockey community is made up of spectacular people, and I'm forever grateful for their help with this life-changing endeavor.

My former Sacred Heart University *Spectrum* newspaper colleague Brad Holland connected me with his dad, then–Detroit Red Wings GM Ken Holland. If you notice, Ken is not quoted in the book, but he's the first person I spoke with and who connected me with Mark Howe.

I'm grateful for every former player who spoke for this project but also for the NHL public relations people who set up each interview. Thanks to Rich Nairn of the Arizona Coyotes, Brian Breseman of the Tampa Bay Lightning, Adam Rogowin of the Chicago Blackhawks, Mike Sundheim of the Carolina Hurricanes, Rich Jankowski of the St. Louis Blues, Todd Sharrock of the Columbus Blue Jackets, Todd Beam of the Detroit Red Wings, Scott Brown of the Winnipeg Jets, Katie Townsend of the Seattle Kraken, and Steve Keogh of the Toronto Maple Leafs. I can't forget Kyle Hanlin, formerly of the Hurricanes too.

I'm grateful for Diane Murphy and Jordan Miller of Blue Sky Sports & Entertainment, who helped me coordinate with Gerry Cheevers for the exceptional foreword.

I appreciate Howard Baldwin, who gave me substantial access to his operation in 2011, and Peter Karmanos for welcoming me to Michigan for a meeting in 2019. I'm thankful for John Coburn and Godfrey Wood, who founded the team with Baldwin and also made time to speak with me.

I'm so ecstatic Mike Emrick agreed to assist in this, since he was both my idol and entry point to hockey, as broadcaster for the New Jersey Devils. Mike is a world-class human, who also inquired about the book's progress whenever we'd meet at a rink or speak via phone or email.

I'm so appreciative for John Forslund, Rick Peckham, Chuck Kaiton, Jeff Jacobs, Stu Hackel, Pierre McGuire, Stan Fischler, Bruce Berlet, Helene Elliott, and the other media members who may not even remember helping me tell this story. I revered each before this process but can now call many colleagues and friends.

I'd be remiss if I didn't also thank Doug Bonjour, Jim Doody, Luke Fox, Naila-Jean Meyers, Allan Kreda, Cristina Ledra, Tal Pinchevsky, Cat Silverman, and the other writers/editors who made me better. This will always be my first book, and they all helped immensely. Thanks also to Tim Parry who chipped in many of the photos featured.

My family and friends rode the roller coaster of this story, including my wife Krystle, sister Meghan, brother-in-law Dave, and my parents Tom and Geri. I'm also grateful for my daughter Eleanor and son Harris, who brighten each one of my days.

Thanks to close friends Bobby Aanonsen, Tim Butler, Peter Cunha, Brian Fitzsimmons, Kelsie Heneghan, Corey Hersch, Lindsay and Jason Perry, Bart and Jocelyn Piekarski, Joe Raja, and all the other friends who helped me mentally through this process.

I'd like to thank the Hartford Whalers Booster Club for essentially adopting me as one of their own. Special thanks to Joanne Cortesa, Peter DeMallie, Mark Anderson, and Matt Greene.

Lastly, I'd like to thank Ken Samelson, Niels Aaboe, Rick Rinehart, and the people at both Rowman & Littlefield and Globe Pequot Press. I always knew this story was worthy of being published, but I appreciate each for taking a chance on me and helping me become a first-time book author.

I'm grateful for every person who has read this far and has followed my career. This book has been a dream come true, and it couldn't have been possible without you all.

Index